The Atlas of
LOST TREASURES

The Atlas of LOST TREASURES

Rediscover ancient wonders from around the world

JOEL LEVY

A GODSFIELD BOOK

An Hachette Livre UK Company
www.hachettelivre.co.uk

First published in Great Britain in 2008 by
Godsfield Press, a division of
Octopus Publishing Group Ltd
2–4 Heron Quays,
London E14 4JP
www.octopusbooks.co.uk

Distributed in the United States and Canada by
Sterling Publishing Co., Inc.
387 Park Avenue South, New York, NY 10016-8810

ISBN 978-1-84181-336-3

A CIP catalogue record for this book
is available from the British Library

Printed and bound in China

2 4 6 8 10 9 7 5 3 1

CONTENTS

Introduction

Gold is almost synonymous with treasure, perhaps because both conjure up similar associations: beauty, extreme value, rarity. Treasure fascinates because it combines these characteristics; it stirs the materialistic, acquisitive impulse we all have, but treasure also delights the senses and excites the imagination. It inspires a potent combination of greed, romance, adventure and excitement, springing from sources that are as diverse as bedtime stories, schoolroom history, big-budget films, folklore and dreams of striking it rich.

Treasure becomes even more fascinating when it has an interesting back-story, which is where this book comes in. In these pages you will find treasures that span a wide range of definitions, locations and time periods: mighty treasures on an imperial scale, and personal treasures that speak of families and friendship; treasures that are valuable because of what they are made of, and those that are valuable because of what they mean; treasures that were destroyed; and even treasures that never existed. Above all, you will find treasures that have been lost. Some have been rediscovered, sometimes as the result of obsessional quests, sometimes by pure chance; others remain resolutely missing, resisting the most determined and intensive efforts to track them down.

This atlas tells the stories of these treasures, explaining what they are or were, who made the objects or owned them, what happened to them and where they might be found today. It also tries to tell the stories behind the treasures; to show why they are important to historians and archeologists, what they mean in context, what they can tell us about people and cultures far distant from our own, but close to us because of the

things we share – not least, our fascination with treasure.

WHAT COUNTS AS TREASURE?
Many archeologists dislike the term 'treasure'. The idea of 'treasure', they argue, is responsible for the threats and problems that increasingly assail our archeological heritage, from 'nighthawking' (see page 11) to black marketeering. But the lure of treasure is not to be denied. To the world beyond the university department, treasure is the most alluring and important aspect of archeology, the ultimate prize for those who delve beneath the earth or sea. And in this conception, treasure usually implies a fairly narrow definition – gold, silver and precious stones.

TREASURE IN LAW
This is not too far removed from the legal definition of treasure. England, whose legal system informs the practices of many nations around the world, has a long-established legal tradition concerning treasure, known as Treasure Trove, which dates back to at least the 12th century CE. One of the oldest laws in British history, Treasure Trove decreed that

any gold or silver that was found in England, and for which an owner could not be traced, belonged to the Crown. Tradition and regional considerations qualified this, but essentially the law defined treasure as gold and silver without traceable owners. Primarily this law was intended to cover incidents where someone stumbled across a buried cache of loot, stashed in the past for safekeeping, but (for whatever reason) never recovered.

In 1996 the law of Treasure Trove was updated, but the new definition remained fairly narrow, essentially referring to objects of more than 10 per cent gold or silver that are over 300 years old.

BROADER DEFINITIONS
Is this a broad enough definition of treasure? It fails to satisfy on many counts, as the definition of treasure can be variable and highly personal. For individuals, anything with sentimental value might be a treasure; to historians or archeologists, the most valuable treasures are often those made of commonplace materials and with everyday functions, as these reveal precious information about the least-known aspects of life in the past. The British Museum, for instance, considers that one of the most precious treasures ever discovered in Britain is the collection of Roman letters known as the Vindolanda tablets – although these are nothing more than slivers of wood inscribed with carbon ink, concerning mundane domestic and commercial matters, they are priceless to historians.

In this book there are several examples of what might be called treasures of the history of science, such as the Antikythera Mechanism (see page 102), which is nothing more than corroded brass and wood, and the Phaistos Disc (see page 104), which is just clay. Although of no material value, these are indisputably treasures because of what they mean for the history of science and technology. And what of the artefacts retrieved from the wreck of the *Titanic* (see page 142)? Although (as yet) few precious jewels or bullion have been recovered, for many people the more poignant and

Left *Howard Carter (kneeling) and companions open KV-62, the tomb of Tutankhamun, in 1922, the prelude to arguably the greatest treasure discovery of all time. The tomb had lain undisturbed since the second millennium* BCE.

Right Bamiyan Valley, Afghanistan. The empty niche bears mute testimony to one of the greatest acts of cultural vandalism in the modern era, when in 2001 the Taliban destroyed the giant Buddha that had stood there since the 6th century CE.

'The Buddhas of Bamiyan hardly conform to the normal definition of treasure, but they were national treasures of Afghanistan.'

personal items that salvors have found, such as a battered top hat or a pack of playing cards, might be considered treasure. Similarly, the toothpick/ear-cleaning implements that make up part of the Hoxne Hoard (see page 22) might rate as more valuable to some people than the thousands of silver coins found alongside them, because of their personal, human significance.

At the other end of the scale, some artefacts or items might be considered treasures because of their significance on the scale of nations or cultures. For instance, the Lewis Chessmen (see page 112), a set of wonderfully expressive carved chess pieces dating back to the 12th century CE, are considered by many to be Scotland's greatest national treasure (despite the fact that they were made in Norway and possibly originally destined for a customer in Ireland). The Buddhas of Bamiyan (see page 116), colossal statues that were destroyed by the Taliban in 2001, hardly conform to the normal definition of treasure, but they were national treasures of Afghanistan and artistic/cultural treasures of the whole world. In this atlas we have cast the net wide to encompass many of these different aspects of treasure.

LOSERS

An obvious question regarding lost treasure is how it came to be lost in the first place. There are six main ways in which treasure came to be lost.

1 Accidental loss

People lose things all the time, but it is arguable how often they lose treasure. By its very nature, it is usually looked after with special care. Nonetheless, people do misplace precious items, particularly jewellery – as shown by the number of rings misplaced each year. There have been many instances of jewellery/ornaments (such as brooches and buckles) that have been found after apparently being dropped at some time in the past. For instance, the Raglan ring, a large golden signet ring found in Monmouthshire in Britain, dating to the 15th century, was discovered in a field. How did it come to be there? Perhaps it was lost by its owner while out hunting. Probably the most spectacular example of misplaced treasure, if it really existed, would be the royal treasure of King John (see page 78), which he supposedly lost while crossing a tidal estuary.

For archeologists, items that have been accidentally lost can be treasure, even if they are not gold or silver, since everyday items are more likely to be misplaced in this way. In fact the richest hunting ground for archeological treasure is often the rubbish heap or midden. However, the most common and widespread form of accidental loss, at least as far as treasure is concerned, is the shipwreck, where loot is lost at sea. Huge quantities of gold and silver are thought to lie at the bottom of the world's oceans (see pages 126–147).

2 Theft/looting

There are obvious incentives to steal treasure, and many of the examples in this atlas disappeared from the historical record after they were pinched – but not by simple thieves. In most cases the theft was an act of looting during war. Often such looting was actually the primary motivation for war. Such acts date back to ancient times, but the worst looters have been modern criminals, in particular the Nazis and the Soviets during the Second World War (see the Amber Room on page 122 and the Stechovice Treasure on page 54).

3 Burial for safekeeping

Until relatively recently there were no banks, and the alternatives, such as depositing valuables at a monastery, were fraught with their own difficulties. Burying caches of wealth made good sense. Obviously the intention of the buriers was to retrieve their loot at some future date, but the same reasons that might have prompted the act – invasion and war, for instance – may also account for their failure to return (see the Oxus Treasure on page 16 and the Hoxne Hoard on page 22).

4 Burial as grave goods

Many religious systems, past and present, include the belief that, just as the spirits of the dead cross over to the next world, so the spirits (or spirit-essence) of inanimate objects can also cross over. Hence the prevalence of grave goods. The higher the status and wealth of the person being buried, the more treasure might accompany them. Attempting to retrieve this treasure often pits archeologists against tomb-raiders – the latter are interested only in the value of the finds, whereas to the former the context of the finds is a vital aspect of their value.

5 Burial as offering

Deliberate ritual deposition of objects was – and is – a common feature of many belief systems. The more valuable the object being buried, the more potent an offering it made. But archeologists urge caution in the interpretation of such finds, since it is hard to assert the motivations of people in the past.

6 Treasure never existed

One definition of 'lost' is 'cannot be found', and this certainly applies to treasures that never existed in the first place – or, rather, existed only in myth or folklore. Thanks to the runaway success of what is sometimes known as fringe or speculative history, including the *Da Vinci Code* school of history, this type of treasure is now the best known, most popular and most widely sought.

'If you do find any loot, you should disturb the site as little as possible, remove nothing and report the find to the authorities.'

FINDERS

Treasure hunting sounds glamorous and romantic, but in academic circles it is a dirty word (or phrase). Archeology is a relatively young science; its roots were in the 18th century, and only in the 19th century was there a general appreciation that removal of treasure from its context, without careful and proper excavation and analysis, undermined its value. Even as late as the 1870s some archeologists, such as Heinrich Schliemann, the discoverer of Troy, were little better than tomb-raiders (though Schliemann had his defenders). Today, however, a fierce debate rages between those who resent interference and regulation on the one hand, and those who accuse treasure hunters of being looters, grave-robbers, desecrators, profiteers and

criminals. This debate takes in large-scale professional operations – like the salvors who hold the rights to the wreck of the *Titanic* and who have been engaged in years of courtroom battles over what they can and can't do with those rights – and hobbyists, who accuse archeologists and governments of being elitist and criminalizing harmless amateurs.

There is evidence in favour of both sides of the argument. In Britain, for instance, some 95 per cent of treasure finds reported each year are the work of amateurs (mostly metal detectorists). Professional wreck salvors argue that without their expertise and massive investment (hunting for treasure galleons can cost hundreds of millions of dollars), lost wrecks and their cargoes would simply never be located or recovered. On the

other hand, there is evidence that looting is actually a growing problem. In Britain, for example, the British Museum and English Heritage have raised the alarm about 'nighthawkers' (metal detectorists who illegally search protected historical sites and remove material without permission, to sell for personal gain) looting the nation's heritage. In Iraq, Afghanistan and other parts of the world the problem is far worse, with the plundering of heritage on an industrial scale and even threats to collections in national museums (see page 96, for example). To the reader whose interest in treasure is more than academic, the most important message is that if you do find any loot, you should disturb the site as little as possible, remove nothing and report the find to the authorities. In most countries of the world, if your hunt was conducted legally, you should be fairly rewarded, while also enormously enhancing its value to posterity and helping to guarantee that everyone can share in the excitement of treasure lost and rediscovered.

Opposite *A squid guards the remains of a clock on the wreck of the* SS Republic, *one of the richest shipwrecks ever to have been explored.*

Above *A reconstruction of the Amber Room, a magnificent chamber from the palace of Catherine the Great at Tsarskoye Selo lined with priceless amber panels, which vanished during the Second World War.*

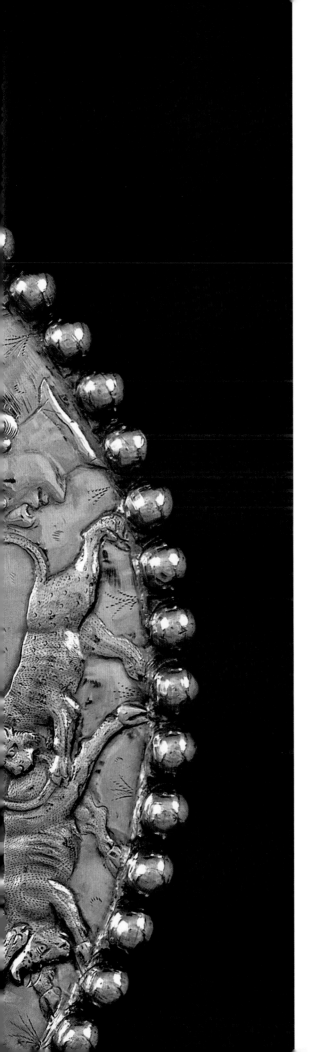

PART 1

HOARDS AND BURIED LOOT

In an archeological sense, treasure can mean anything from ancient shopping lists to Roman toothpicks. But for the general public one image applies above all – a chest overflowing with precious gems and golden doubloons, dug out of the ground or rescued from a hidden cavern. This image is based on reality; for most of human history there were no banks or safe-deposit boxes and hiding wealth was one of the best ways to safeguard it, especially in unsettled times. Valuable objects were also buried or hidden for other reasons. Ritual deposition was a common feature of many religions and belief systems, with offerings being made to secure good fortune and the indulgence of the gods. In particular it was believed – and still is in many parts of the world today – that goods buried with the dead could be helpful to them in the afterlife. For archeologists this ancient habit of burying treasure is good news, because it preserves what might otherwise be lost. For treasure hunters it is even better news, for it offers the possibility of stumbling across a treasure trove. This section tells the stories of several troves that were buried or otherwise hidden, but subsequently found, and of others that are yet to be discovered.

KAZAKHSTAN

UZBEKISTAN

TURKMENISTAN

TAJIKISTAN

Tillia Tepe

IRAN

AFGHANISTAN

The Bactrian Hoard and the Golden Mound

One of the greatest finds in the archeology of Central Asia, the Bactrian Hoard has survived the perils of invasion, looting, fanatical enmity and greed. This collection of beautiful and sometimes moving pieces is a vital part of the heritage of Afghanistan, bearing testament to the rich mix of influences on its culture and to the artistry of its ancient inhabitants.

The Bactrian Hoard, also known as the Bactrian Gold, is the name given to a collection of more than 20,000 mainly golden ornaments discovered in 1978 in a burial complex known as Tillia Tepe, the Golden Mound, in northern Afghanistan in a region that in ancient times was the kingdom of Bactria. The ornaments adorned the clothes and bodies of five women and one man, assumed to be ancient royalty from the opulence of their grave goods. The presence of coins in the tombs helped to date the burials – the youngest was a Roman coin (or replica) of the emperor Tiberius (ruled 14–47 CE), fixing the burials in the 1st century CE. Apart from the quality and quantity of the treasure discovered in the Golden Mound, its most remarkable aspect is the sheer range of cultural influences represented, from Classical Greek and Persian motifs to Indian and Chinese designs.

THE VAULTS OF KABUL

The Hoard was excavated and taken to Kabul, but not long afterwards the Soviets invaded Afghanistan and it was thought prudent to store it in the vaults of the central bank in the

presidential compound. Although it was displayed once to foreign diplomats a few years later, the treasure was feared lost in the chaos of the 1990s, when it disappeared from view. In fact it had simply been hidden in chests in the heavily fortified vault, the keys to which were guarded by loyal bankers determined to preserve the Hoard from harm.

Even when the Taliban came to power in the late 1990s and interrogated and then severely beat the chief steward, he valiantly refused to give them the codes for the locks, which were strong enough to resist all attempts to force them. Had the Taliban succeeded, they would undoubtedly have destroyed the figurative pieces and probably melted down the gold. The Hoard also survived the looting that emptied the National Museum of around 80 per cent of its treasures, and was finally revealed, intact, to the world in 2003.

In 2004 the entire collection was photographed and catalogued, and in 2006 elements of the Hoard went on show in France, the first stop in a short international tour intended to raise money for a suitable

showcase museum in Kabul. Except for a few months after their initial discovery, however, the people of Afghanistan have never been able to see their nation's heritage, and there is little prospect that they will be able to do so in the near future.

PRINCESSES OF THE GOLDEN MOUND

The bulk of the Hoard consists of golden ornaments that would have been worn on the person or sewn onto the clothes of the prince and princesses who were buried at Tillia Tepe. Their identities and even their ethnicity are unknown. The range of cultural influences of the Hoard suggests that they were Saka Scythians, nomadic peoples who roamed the plains of Central Asia, but who traded with China, India, Persia and beyond, along the early Silk Road. Alternatively they might have been members of a royal dynasty of the Yuezhi, an Indo-European people in the area who went on to found an empire that spanned the area of modern-day Afghanistan, Pakistan and northern India.

Many of the pieces show the Hellenic influences brought to the region by

> '*The most remarkable aspect of the treasure discovered in the Golden Mound is the sheer range of cultural influences represented, from Classical Greek and Persian motifs to Indian and Chinese designs.*'

Alexander the Great (ruled 336–323 BCE) in the 4th century BCE and maintained by his successors, with Greco-Indian kingdoms surviving in India for centuries. They include remarkably fine carvings of Eros, intaglio rings with profiles of Athena, representations of Aphrodite and Hellenistic dolphins (a rare sight in Bactria). There are also bronze mirrors from China, ivory from India, coins from Parthia, Roman Gaul and Buddhist India, and golden pendants of an ibex in Achaemenid style (see page 18) and of kings contending with dragons and horsemen leaping over fantastical creatures, which show the sort of syncretic influences associated with Scythian nomads. This extraordinary level of syncretism (the fusion of two different belief systems) is perhaps best demonstrated by an Indian coin showing a man wearing apparently Hellenistic garb, but pushing a wheel (a Buddhist symbol), inscribed with the legend 'The one who pushed the Wheel of Law'. It is thought to be an early representation of Buddha, possibly based on ancient Greek archetypes of Dionysus that were brought to the region by Alexander.

A clue to the geopolitical affiliations of the buried potentates comes from a coin that was found in the hand of one of the female corpses; a gold copy of a Parthian coin showing the Parthian king Gotarzes I (early 1st century BCE), which is stamped with the depiction of another head, probably a local chieftain. The added stamp, however, has been carefully positioned so as not to deface the portrait of the Parthian king, suggesting that whoever made the coin knew where his loyalties lay, and wished to avoid offending his powerful neighbours.

Left This extraordinary crown is one of the most striking of all the treasures exhumed from Tillia Tepe. It is made from gold, and decorated with semi-precious stones and flowers cut from thin gold sheet. The crown is collapsible – perhaps reflecting the nomadic nature of its former owners?

The Oxus Treasure

Bandits on the Silk Road; an act of gallantry by an intrepid British officer at the uttermost limits of the empire; an amazing treasure of incalculable value – not the ingredients of a fictional thriller, but the true story of the Oxus Treasure, a hoard of priceless and exquisite gold and silver artefacts that bears testimony to the vanished glory of the first world empire.

In 1880 British officer Captain F.C. Burton, a political agent and player in the Great Game – the international intrigue between the Great Powers competing for control of Central Asia – took pity on the plight of a party of three Muslim merchants of Bokhara travelling through the perilous passes between Kabul and Peshawar. The merchants had been robbed by bandits, but Burton could not have guessed at the value of their merchandise.

With typical British derring-do, Burton intercepted the bandits and managed to recover about three-quarters of the precious cargo, an amazing haul of gold and silver artefacts of breathtaking workmanship and priceless historical worth. The grateful merchants gave Burton the chance to purchase an item and the extraordinary antlered armlet (a bracelet for the arm) that he snapped up is now among the most famous of the Oxus Treasure pieces.

The merchants disposed of the rest of their loot in the bazaars of Rawalpindi, but many of the items were hunted down by British officer-collectors and eventually the treasures passed into the collection of the British Museum, where most of them reside today.

THE THRONE OF KAVAD

The 170 pieces of the Oxus Treasure are thought to have been discovered on the banks of the Oxus River (or Amu Darya), a Central Asian river that flows into the Aral Sea, in a region known in ancient times as Bactria. They were dug out of the sand on the north bank of the river near a ferry crossing, a site since identified as a low hill known as Takht-i-Kobad – the Throne of Kavad. It is thought they may have been stashed here after being moved from the temple of the goddess Anahita at Bactra (also known as the Oxus Sanctuary), the largest temple in the region, possibly to preserve them from being plundered in a raid in the 2nd century BCE.

ORIGINS OF THE TREASURE

What is of greater significance to historians, however, is how they came to be at the temple in the first place. The Treasure is made up of artefacts from the Persian Achaemenid Empire, which ruled a vast area stretching from Egypt and the Levant to the borders of

Above *Griffin-headed gold amulet at the British Museum; the companion piece to that bought by Captain Burton after rescuing the Oxus Treasure from bandits in 1880.*

THINGS OF BEAUTY

The pieces that make up the Treasure are gold and silver artefacts, some of extremely sophisticated design and execution, with patterns and styles that demonstrate the range of influences that made Achaemenid culture unique. To their own Persian aesthetic, the Achaemenids added the ancient traditions of Babylon and Assyria and a touch of Greek style, together with artistic influences from the nomadic steppe peoples of Central Asia. Less remarkable elements of the Treasure include coins, finger rings, seals, cups and other vessels. The highlights include:

• **Dedicatory plaques:** small, rectangular embossed plaques or lozenges. There are more than 50 of them in the Treasure, making up the bulk of it, and they vary in length from less than 3 cm (about 1 in) to almost 20 cm (8 in). The most common design is of a human figure, similar to ones found in reliefs at the Persian capital of Persepolis. For instance, a particularly finely wrought plaque shows a man in the costume of a Mede (the Medes were neighbours and early conquests of the Persians, whose traditions of administration and courtly life formed the blueprint for

Achaemenid rule), bearing a bundle of sticks or grasses known as a *barsom*, which was used in religious ceremonies. The plaques were probably votive objects – that is, offerings to be given to a shrine as an act of devotion and piety.

• **Lion-griffin ornament:** an embossed ornament of exquisite workmanship, fashioned in the form of a composite lion-griffin creature, demonstrates the syncretic nature of Achaemenid art. Composite creatures were common to all the ancient cultures, but pieces such as this illustrate the cultural influence of the Scythian and Central Asian nomads to the north of the Achaemenid Empire.

• **Armlets:** the Greek writer Xenophon, a soldier who served as a mercenary with the Persians around 400 BCE, and who is an important source for knowledge of the Achaemenids, records that bracelets worn on the arm were given as gifts of honour at the Persian court. A gold armlet with ends fashioned into horned griffin-heads, probably the most iconic piece in the Oxus Treasure, is held by the British Museum in London, where the bulk of the Treasure is kept. The very similar piece purchased by Captain Burton is kept at London's Victoria and Albert Museum.

***Above** Votive gold plaque from the Oxus Treasure, showing a man in distinctive Median costume, bearing a sheaf of sticks and with short-sword, hanging from his belt.*

India and Central Asia, including the kingdom of Bactria, where the Treasure was found. The empire, founded by Cyrus the Great (ruled 559–530 BCE) in the mid-6th century BCE, was the largest the world had ever seen and arguably the first world empire, linking as it did the Mediterranean world to Asia and the East in a single kingdom.

The trove was probably gathered at the Oxus Sanctuary either as a collection of votive offerings or simply as a repository of wealth (temples were relatively secure places, especially in wild regions such as Bactria), but

the close correspondence between the designs of many of the pieces and reliefs at Persepolis, the capital of the Achaemenids, suggests they may have been associated with or even originated from the very centre of Persian power (see page 18). Another theory is that the items that make up the Oxus Treasure were originally grave goods, that were interred with kings, queens and potentates in their tombs, but were subsequently looted when the Achaemenid Empire collapsed under the onslaught of Alexander the Great, if not before.

Persepolis: city of ceremony

The Persian emperors built Persepolis as a statement of power, an engine of ceremony and ritual for the purpose of proclaiming their glory and, crucially, their authority. This engine operated on Persians and foreigners alike, from lowly subjects to visiting potentates, and the oil that lubricated its gears was treasure. Persepolis was the natural home of the Oxus Treasure (see page 16) and, quite possibly, its origin.

PERSEPOLIS AND THE ACHAEMENIDS

The Achaemenids were a kingdom of Persians in what is today Iran, who rose to power with dizzying speed in the 6th century BCE when Cyrus the Great defeated his enemies in Persia to unify the region and went on to conquer Babylon and Assyria. To these he added Syria and the Levant in the west and Bactria in the east. His successors, Cambyses, Darius and Xerxes, extended the empire to Egypt and Asia Minor until Greek resistance halted their expansionism.

Material demonstrations of power and glory were important tools for asserting the legitimacy of kingship, so the Achaemenids built a series of increasingly impressive capital cities, culminating in the construction of Persepolis, which was begun by Darius in 513 BCE, and continued and enlarged by his son Xerxes and grandson Artaxerxes I.

Persepolis was sited against a range of low, rocky hills at the edge of the Marv Dasht plain, in present-day Iran. Upon a vast platform raised above the surrounding plain sat a host of immense halls and palaces, in a style that blended the Achaemenids' Persian traditions with those of their neighbours and subjects, the Medes (see page 17) and Mesopotamians, together with an added gloss of Classical aesthetic picked up from the Greek world.

CENTRE OF CEREMONY

Ceremony and ritual were at the heart of Persepolis. Its design was calculated to awe visiting subjects and foreign potentates, and to provide a theatre against which ceremonial functions could be played out. Historians today speak of the sociocultural economy of places like Persepolis, and it was gifts, offerings, votive pieces, tribute and ornamentation that formed the currency of this economy. Rank and power were reinforced through display of personal ornamentation, and through the extravagance of the gifts and votive pieces that a person could offer. The authority of the king was asserted by his role as the receiver of tribute, and by the supremacy of his display. It is possible that many of the items in the Oxus Treasure were created specifically for use at Persepolis or similar seats of power.

THE END OF PERSEPOLIS

In 333 BCE Alexander the Great invaded the Persian Empire, driving Darius III before him, arriving at Persepolis in 330 BCE. Here Alexander held a great drunken revel for his officers, and then, possibly in revenge for the destruction of the Athenian Acropolis by Xerxes 150 years earlier, set fire to it, although not before looting its treasures. These were so great that it was said it took 20,000 mules and 5,000 camels to carry them away – perhaps some of them ended up in the hoard buried on the banks of the Oxus River more than a century later?

① PLATFORM AND BUILDINGS

Persepolis was built on a huge stone terrace 450 m (1,475 ft) long and 300 m (1,000 ft) wide, which rose 14 m (46 ft) above the plain. Giant staircases led through an immense gateroom, known as the Gate of All Lands, and from here visitors could gain access to the main buildings: the *apadana*, or audience hall; the palace of Darius; the palace of Xerxes; a long, narrow building traditionally identified as Xerxes' harem; the Hall of One Hundred Columns; and a building known as the Treasury, which probably had an administrative function.

② LIVING QUARTERS

There is evidence that Persepolis was not a residential complex, but served a mainly ceremonial purpose. Most of the year few (if any) people lived in the complex, and even when the court was in residence the main living quarters may have been offsite. Traces of less magnificent buildings around the platform show that a skeleton staff of maintenance workers and others lived around the site, and an inscribed pillar reveals that Xerxes had a palace on the plain as well.

③ TOMBS OF THE KINGS

The tombs of four kings, starting with Darius, the initial builder of Persepolis, are cut into the cliff face. The tombs were fronted by impressive buildings and by porticoes cut into the rock face itself, with reliefs of columns and friezes in classic Achaemenid style. The tombs would have been filled with rich grave goods and offerings, but were soon looted and now stand empty.

④ THE APADANA

The north and east facades were decorated with massive friezes showing 23 pairs of delegates from vassal nations of the empire, probably attending a New Year festival. Among the reliefs are depictions of Medes bearing *barsom* sheaths – bundles of sticks/grasses that were ritual gifts – which are very similar to figures embossed on some of the plaques in the Oxus Treasure. Perhaps the artists who produced them based them on the same forms or worked in the same workshops?

⑤ HALL OF ONE HUNDRED COLUMNS

Reliefs show scenes of men bringing tribute, including armlets of the sort found in the Oxus Treasure, which were a traditional gift offered to the court by Achaemenid subjects. Reliefs also show men wearing the characteristic *akinakes*, a type of short-sword with a distinctive scabbard. A gold version of such a scabbard makes up part of the Oxus Treasure.

⑥ PALACE OF DARIUS

To the south-west of the *apadana* Darius had a palace built, with suites of rooms running alongside a pillared hall. The door jambs were of stone, richly carved to show the king as a hero, fighting with beasts and monsters.

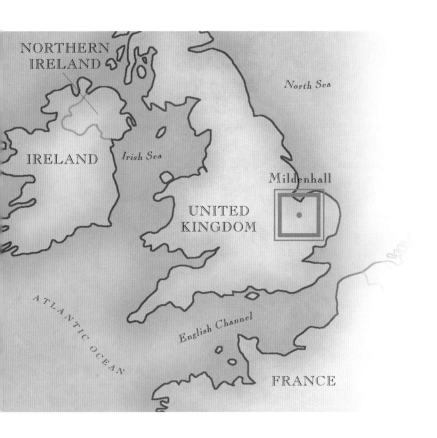

The Mildenhall Treasure

Featuring perhaps the single greatest piece of treasure from Roman times ever found in Britain, the Mildenhall hoard sheds important light on the late Roman era, but it has also raised many questions. What was the truth surrounding its discovery? Was its original finder cheated out of millions? Where was it made? And who owned and then buried it, and why?

A FORTUNE FOUND AND LOST

In 1942 Britain was facing the darkest days of the Second World War, but in rural Suffolk, a part of eastern England close to the Fens, life continued much as normal. One winter morning farmer Gordon Butcher, employed to do some ploughing for another man, was driving his tractor across a field at West Row, near the village of Mildenhall. There was a lurch and the wooden peg connecting the plough to the tractor broke. Butcher

investigated and found that the plough had struck a large metal plate, buried about 25–30 cm (10–12 in) down. The area was known to have been settled in Roman times and Butcher suspected that he had stumbled across an ancient artefact. He decided to fetch his boss, Sidney Ford, an amateur antiques collector, who might know more about the find. Together the men unearthed 34 pieces of metal, encrusted with dirt, and dulled and blackened with age and exposure.

Left *Silver ladle from the Mildenhall Treasure. The decorative dolphin handle is gilded and originally had inlays, probably of glass, in its eyes.*

Ford told Butcher they were probably pewter or lead and therefore did not need to be reported to the authorities under the Treasure Trove laws governing finds of precious metals. He convinced his employee to let him take the pieces home, where he cleaned and polished them, and for the next few years displayed them proudly on his mantelpiece, on occasion even using the biggest dish as a fruit platter. Only in 1946 did an amateur antiquarian visiting Ford's home recognize them as Roman silver. He persuaded the reluctant farmer to tell the police, who, in Ford's words, 'promptly came and pinched the lot!'

The local coroner ruled that as the find had not been properly reported, Ford and Butcher should receive only £1,000 each. Meanwhile the silver was acquired by the British Museum, where it was recognized as an extraordinary and immensely valuable service of silver plates, bowls and spoons, worth tens or hundreds of thousands of pounds (millions today). If poor Butcher had simply reported his find in the first place, he (as the finder) would have been entitled to the entire value. The woeful tale so affected the writer Roald Dahl that he immediately travelled to Suffolk to interview Butcher, publishing the tale as *The Mildenhall Treasure* and splitting the proceeds with the luckless farmer.

THE GENERAL'S TREASURE

The silver dishes and spoons dug up by Butcher and Ford were unlike anything seen in Britain before. Believed to date from the 4th century CE, they were probably produced at silversmith workshops on the Continent or in North Africa, and at first experts were sceptical that they had been found in Suffolk at all, arguing that they had been smuggled in. Only gradually did finds such as this and the Hoxne Hoard (see page 22) prove that Roman Britain had in fact been a prosperous and even wealthy province, rather than just an impoverished backwater of the empire. The original decision to bury the Mildenhall hoard, as with many other hoards in the region dating from the same era, probably reflected the instability of dangerous times, with East Anglia menaced by Saxon pirates, Pictish marauders from the north and domestic brigands.

Most of the dishes show pagan motifs and decorations, based on depictions of Bacchus, the Roman god of wine. But some of the spoons are decorated with the Chi-Rho symbol of early Christianity, suggesting that the owner was a Christian. This has led to speculation that the owner of the hoard was a Christian general, Lupicinus, sent to Britain by the emperor Julian the Apostate (ruled 360–363 CE) in 360 CE, and that the pagan dishes may have been a gift from the emperor himself. Lupicinus was later recalled to Rome in disfavour and arrested, which would explain why he never got the chance to dig up the valuables he had buried for safekeeping in his absence.

Right The head of the sea-god Oceanus is at the centre of the Great Dish, while around the outside dancing Bacchantes and satyrs accompany the gods Bacchus (at the top) and Hercules (on the left).

THE GREAT DISH

The most iconic and impressive piece of the Mildenhall Treasure is the Great Dish, a silver platter almost 60 cm (2 ft) in diameter and weighing 8 kg (18 lb). Its upper surface is covered in fine decoration, with a head of Oceanus, god of the sea, in the centre, surrounded by an inner frieze showing nereids or sea nymphs with hybrid marine monsters, including a hippocamp (half-fish, half-horse), a crab-clawed triton (a merman), a sea-stag and a *ketos* (sea-serpent). Around this is an outer frieze showing a revel with a drinking contest between Bacchus and Hercules, who is blind drunk and being supported by helpers. The Classical pagan imagery of this and several of the other pieces contrasts with the Christian symbols on some of the spoons, illustrating the religious tensions of the empire in the 4th century. Christianity had become widespread and had even been adopted as the official state religion, but the old pagan religion still informed the cultural landscape and tensions reached a head when Julian the Apostate tried to reintroduce the old ways. Perhaps the Mildenhall Treasure is a relic of this ancient culture war.

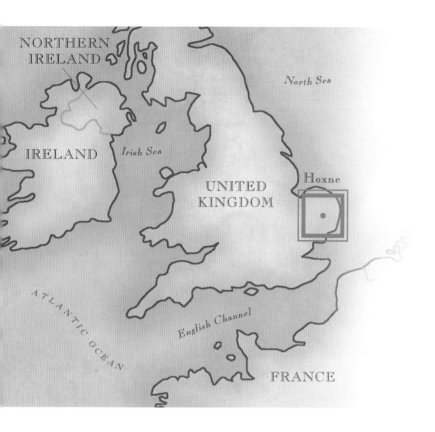

The Hoxne Hoard

The largest hoard of Roman gold and silver ever found in Britain also hails from the Suffolk area: a literal treasure chest of thousands of coins and exquisite jewellery, together with quirky and personal items that hint at their owners' identities. Above all, the Hoxne find sheds light on the murky period when Roman rule was failing and Britain slid into dark centuries of invasion and war.

Finds such as the Mildenhall Treasure (see page 20) and others show that in the late Roman era there was something of a vogue for burying treasure in East Anglia. Partly this was because East Anglia was a prosperous and settled area of Roman occupation, where there might have been many rich Romano-British families with wealth worth preserving, and partly because it was an important staging point for seafarers and travellers to the Continent. This meant that people leaving Britain might be passing through, and that the area was vulnerable to attacks from seaborne raiders – both strong motivators for the burying of wealth.

LOST: ONE HAMMER

The greatest of these buried hoards – at least, the greatest yet recovered – was found near the Suffolk village of Hoxne (pronounced 'Hoxen'), on 16 November 1992. Metal detectorist Eric Lawes was searching for a friend's lost hammer. Getting a strong signal, he began digging, but instead of a modern tool uncovered several gold and silver coins. After unearthing even more he did the right thing and stopped, alerting the Suffolk

Archeological Unit, who were thus able to excavate an almost pristine site and determine a range of important archeological data that might otherwise have been lost.

The local police were called in to stand guard over the site overnight, in case looters tried to move in, and the next morning the media descended. Local resident Tim Craven recalls that 'Reporters were in the village early the next morning, many being sent in completely the wrong direction by several helpful and gleeful schoolboys waiting for the school bus.'

TREASURE CHEST OF COINS

From the arrangement of the items and discoloration of the soil around them, the archeologists surmised that they had originally been contained in a wooden chest, which, over the course of 1,500 years, had rotted away. Other telltale signs, such as remains of straw and cloth and tiny hinges and silver padlocks, showed that parts of the treasure had been packed into smaller chests and bags, which had then been locked into the larger chest.

In other words, Lawes had stumbled across a literal treasure chest, one stuffed with the largest collection of Roman gold and silver ever found. The bulk of the treasure consisted of 14,780 coins: 565 gold, 14,191 silver and a handful of bronze. There were also 200 pieces of gold jewellery and silver tableware.

The coins helped to suggest a probable date for the burial of the treasure. The youngest of them were silver *siliquae* stamped with the name of the emperor Constantine III (ruled 407–411 CE). Constantine III was a soldier in Britain who had been acclaimed by his own troops in 407 CE, and in the following year had led his legions across the Channel to Gaul to help combat the Germanic tribesmen who had broken through the defences of the failing empire at the Rhine. His departure marked the beginning of the end for Roman Britain; the legions were not to return, and in 410 CE – the traditional end of Roman rule in Britain – the emperor Honorius (ruled 395–423 CE) wrote to the heads of the civil authorities in Britain to tell them they could expect no help from Rome against the waves of marauding Picts, Scots and Saxons.

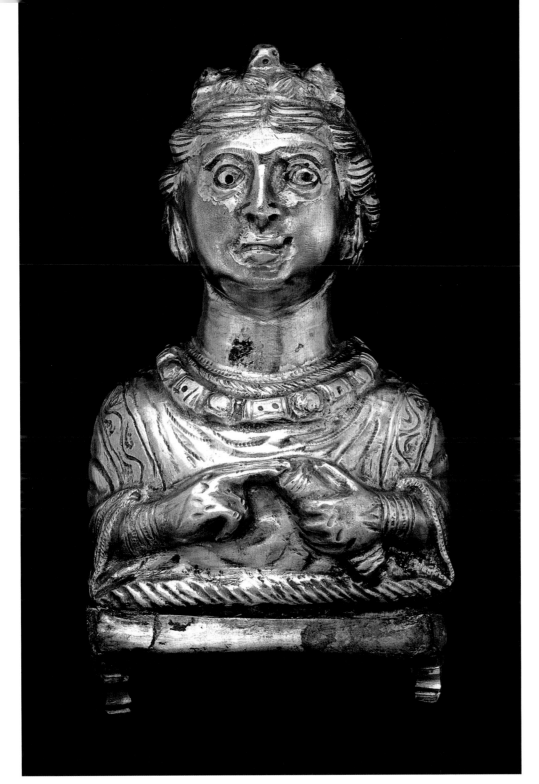

Pepper-pot – a pepper-pot in the shape of the bust of a Roman empress; a tiny statuette of a prancing tigress, which was probably originally the handle of a large vase; silver toilet instruments, which have spatulas at one end for cleaning out the ears and toothpicks at the other; and the handful of bronze coins – these are basically loose change, suggesting that whoever was compiling the chest simply threw in whatever coins he or she had in his or her pocket, as an afterthought.

Names on some of the items give clues to the identities of the owners. Some silver spoons are inscribed with the name Aurelius Ursicinus, while one of the rings bears the name Juliana. We can speculate that Aurelius was a wealthy Romano-Briton with a teenage daughter called Juliana, perhaps the owner of the body-chain. The way that spoons and bracelets were stacked together, and that other pieces were packed in straw and cloth, demonstrates that the burial was carefully planned. Obviously the owners intended to return for their possessions, but never did – were they killed by Saxons or Picts; carried off to slavery; or did they flee the disintegrating country, hoping to find refuge in Rome?

The *siliquae* of Constantine III represented the last mint of official Roman coins in Britain; the heavy clipping of their edges, where metal was clipped from the coin so that it could be melted down and used to create forgeries, bears testament to the breakdown of authority in the province. The Hoard must date from after 408 CE and is generally thought to have buried sometime around the 420s or 430s.

THE PERSONAL TOUCH

The gold and silver items lend the treasure a personal touch. The most notable piece is a rare body-chain – a slender golden chain that passed over the shoulders and under the arms and was fastened in the centre of the chest and at the back. From the small size of the chain, it is thought likely to have belonged to a very slender woman or a girl. Other notable pieces include the Empress

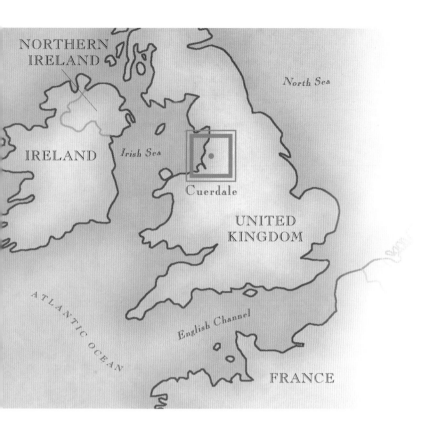

The Cuerdale Hoard

The greatest hoard of Viking silver ever discovered outside Russia – the chest of treasure discovered in Cuerdale in England in 1840 – was gathered by trade and pillage from every corner of Europe, probably with the intention of funding a military campaign, and possibly even a Viking invasion of Ireland. Its contents offer a vivid depiction of Viking wealth, power and ambition in the 10th century.

On 15 May 1840 workmen were repairing the embankment of the River Ribble, near Curedale Hall in Cuerdale, Lancashire. Digging at an exposed slice of soil, they dislodged an aged lead chest, which broke open, spilling forth a torrent of dirty grey metal, including thousands of coins. A great shout went up from the assembled labourers, but even as they scrabbled to fill their pockets with the loot, the 'hind' or bailiff of the local manor, attracted by the commotion, arrived and warned them that the find belonged to the landowner, William Asheton, and that they would have to turn it over. He mollified them somewhat by explaining that the metal

was pewter and the 'coins' merely tin counters, allowing each man to take one as a souvenir. The rest of the booty the hind removed to Curedale Hall, where it was washed in a tub and proved to be silver (as he quite possibly suspected). Much of it eventually came into the possession of the British Museum.

HACK-SILVER AND PENNIES

The Cuerdale Hoard weighed around 40 kg (88 lb), and consisted of 7,500 coins and more than a thousand pieces of silver jewellery, bullion and what is known as hack-silver – pieces of silver objects, such as plates

or ornaments, that have been chopped into small chunks. Hack-silver was a way of turning artefacts into currency, and also made silver easier to carry, share out and melt down into ingots or new artefacts. It shows that people of the time often valued objects more for their mineral value than their artistic or functional value.

The coins and artefacts (or bits of artefacts) gathered together in the chest came from every corner of Europe. There were coins from Scandinavia, France and the Netherlands, the Muslim world (known as Kufic coins, these were used in the Muslim empire that stretched from Spain and North Africa right across the Near and Middle East) and even a Byzantine coin from far-flung Constantinople, reflecting the Viking trade networks that reached across Russia to the borders of the Near and Middle Eastern world. The bulk of the coins, however, were more local – either Saxon coins, including ones minted by Alfred the Great (ruled 871–899 CE), or ones from Viking England and Ireland. At the time the Vikings were in control of a large swathe of northern England, a region known as the Danelaw, and

'The range of coins from different dates indicates that the Cuerdale Hoard was not collected all at once, but was added to (and perhaps subtracted from) over time.'

most of the coins had been minted here. From the age of the youngest coins, the Hoard has been dated to 905–910 CE.

The hack-silver and jewellery include pieces from Scandinavia, the eastern Baltic, France and Scotland, reflecting both trade and the favoured raiding targets of the Vikings. But the majority of the hack-silver is Norse Irish in origin, and it is this link that suggests the most likely rationale for the enormous assemblage.

THE WAR CHEST

In 902 CE the Vikings had been driven out of Dublin, the centre of Viking influence in Ireland, and many of them had taken refuge in the Danelaw. At the time the Ribble river valley was the main route between the Viking capital at York and the Irish Sea – an obvious staging point for Viking attempts to win back their Irish possessions. The quantity of Norse Irish hack-silver and the large number of relatively new coins from Viking York suggests that the Cuerdale Hoard had been assembled as a war chest – a pool of capital that could be used to recruit and equip a force of Vikings and mercenaries for an attempt to invade Ireland, which would be launched from the Ribble estuary.

The presence of bone pins suggests that some of the silver had originally been contained in smaller bags or parcels, and this – together with the range of coins from different dates – indicates that the Cuerdale Hoard was not collected all at once, but was added to (and perhaps subtracted from) over time. So it could also have served as a more general form of treasury for a local prince or group of leaders, at a time when banks did not exist.

The real mystery is why, whether it was intended as a war chest or a more general treasury, the Hoard was lost/abandoned? No one could have afforded to have simply forgotten such a tremendous haul of loot – perhaps its owner was killed unexpectedly, possibly even while attempting to recruit men for a campaign.

Left The Cuerdale Hoard, buried around 905 CE. Coins and whole pieces of jewellery are tumbled together with silver artefacts that have been cut into smaller pieces (hack-silver). To the Hoard's owners the value of the material lay in its weight rather than its artistic attributes.

SLOVAKIA

UKRAINE

HUNGARY

MOLDOVA

ROMANIA

SERBIA
AND
MONTENEGRO

BULGARIA

Black Sea

The Romanian National Treasure

Casting a shadow over relations between Romania and Russia is the issue of the Romanian National Treasure – a vast haul of the monetary and cultural wealth of an entire nation, sent for safekeeping from the perils of war, but caught up in the chaos and confusion of revolution. How much of the treasure is still missing, where is it and when will the Romanians ever get it back?

The outbreak of the First World War threatened upheaval and ruin on an unprecedented scale. Countries that were invaded knew they faced massive looting and despoliation. This was the threat looming over Romania in 1916. After protracted haggling with the Allied powers about territorial concessions that would increase the size of Romania when the war was won, the country signed up with the Allies against the Central Powers – the Germans and Austro-Hungarians. Unfortunately things did not go as planned and by November the German armies were threatening Bucharest, the Romanian capital.

The Romanian government relocated to a new capital at Iași, along with the headquarters of the National Bank of Romania, the institution that guarded the nation's gold reserves and many priceless historical, artistic and cultural national treasures.

As the German advance continued, the Romanians feared that even Iași would fall into the hands of the enemy, and that their national wealth would be carried back to Germany to pay for the war. It was decided that the Romanian National Treasure would have to be sent for safekeeping in another country.

MOSCOW DEPOSIT

The government agonized over where to send their precious loot. Ideally it would have been shipped off to a completely safe country, such as the United States, or to the security of the vaults of the Bank of England, or to a neutral country in Scandinavia. But the Central Powers controlled the overland routes through central and northern Europe, while their U-boat fleets threatened the sea lanes and made international shipping a dangerous option. The obvious candidate was Russia – an ally, whose armies were even now fighting alongside Romania's to protect their territory and which was easily accessible by rail. In addition, it was thought that Russia might take offence if the Romanians chose to send their treasure elsewhere. At the time Russia was still governed by the tsar, and few could have foreseen the momentous events that were to come.

Reassured by Russian guarantees and signed protocols, in December 1916 and July 1917 the Romanians shipped to Moscow two trainloads of treasure, carrying their entire reserves of gold bullion and gold coins, royal jewels, the archives of the Romanian Academy, personal valuables of the richest citizens of Romania, and national collections such as ancient jewels and artefacts, art collections and religious treasures. The first train was valued at several hundred million gold *lei* (the Romanian currency); the second at several billion. According to one estimate, the value of the first train was $1.5 billion in 2005 money; the value of the second, though much harder to estimate because of the cultural and artistic significance of its contents, must have been many billions of dollars in modern terms – perhaps $37 billion or more.

In August 1917 the Treasure was gathered together at a depository in the Kremlin, more guarantees were signed and two sets of keys to the depository were handed out – one to the Russians, the other to the representative of the National Bank of Romania.

COME THE REVOLUTION

In November 1917 the Bolshevik Revolution swept across Russia and within two months Soviet Russia was at war with the Romanians.

written guarantees, which were promptly ignored; several crates of loot were removed.

After the war vigorous protests by the Allies failed to shift the Soviets, and it was not until 1935 that the Russians returned more than a thousand crates of documents. It was obvious that they had been opened and ransacked for valuables. After the Second World War, Romania found itself behind the Iron Curtain, an ally of the Soviet Union, and in 1956 a large proportion of the artistic and cultural treasures were finally returned, including the priceless Pietroasele Treasure. This was a collection of fabulous gold artefacts believed to date back to the Goths of the 4th century CE. Artefacts from this period and culture are rare, and display a fascinating range of styles and influences, from Han Chinese to Germanic, demonstrating the wide-ranging nomadic nature of the tribes who later invaded and settled much of Europe. The Romanians were far from satisfied, however, claiming that Russia still owed them 93,000 kg (102 tons) of gold – more than $2 billion in modern terms.

Here, despite repeated negotiations and summits, the issue has remained. There are serious arguments about the exact original composition of the Treasure, which was shipped hurriedly and with poor verification, and about what happened to it once it was in Russian hands. It seems likely that much of it was moved out of Moscow during the Second World War, and parts may have been lost, pilfered or repacked. It is not even clear exactly how much has already been returned. In 2005 the Romanian president summed up the current state of play: 'Regarding the treasure, Moscow has settled the issue in the [recently signed] bilateral treaty: a joint commission of historians was formed, the commission is working, documents have been exchanged, and a search has been launched to find parts of the treasure.'

In a Resolution of 13 January 1918, signed by Vladimir Ilyich Lenin, the Soviet of the People's Commissars declared that the Romanian Treasure was 'intangible by the Romanian oligarchy' and promised that it 'would be returned to the Romanian people'. By this time the French were handling Romanian interests in Moscow and it was the French consul general who now held the key. He refused to surrender it until provided with

The Sevso Hoard

A dark saga of murder, fraud and smuggling casts its shadow over the glittering treasures of the Sevso Hoard, a remarkable but tainted collection of exquisite late Roman silver. Described as 'cursed' by the British aristocrat who owns it, the Hoard was locked away in a vault in the Channel Islands until it resurfaced recently, prompting questions in the Houses of Parliament.

In 1980 a magnificent silver ewer, identified as 4th- or 5th-century Roman, was offered for sale in London by two international antiques dealers based in Vienna. It was soon followed by 13 other pieces, including giant silver plates the size (in the rather unromantic words of the *Guardian* newspaper) of 'dustbin lids'. The largest of the plates is 71 cm (28 in) in diameter and weighs 8.15 kg (18 lb). Other highlights include a 41 cm (16 in)-high Dionysiac Ewer, gilded with a depiction of the revels of Bacchus, and a ten-sided Animal Ewer worked in niello (a technique for engraving subtle black lines), with 120 hexagonal patterns showing wild animals and hunting scenes. The collection is known as the Sevso Hoard because one of the dishes bears the inscription:

> *Hec Sevso tibi durent per saecula multa*
> *Posteris ut prosint vascula digna tuis*
> May these, O Sevso, yours for many ages be
> Small vessels fit to serve your offspring
> worthily.

UNCERTAIN PROVENANCE

The antiques dealers' story was that the dishes had been unearthed in Lebanon, in the Tyre and Sidon regions, and they apparently had the paperwork to back this up. On the advice of his accountants and a retired chairman of the auction house of Sotheby's (among others), Spencer Douglas David Compton, Marquess of Northampton bought the plates in the expectation that they would quickly be sold on to the new Getty Museum in California, for $10 million. But curators at the Getty Museum spotted that the Lebanese export papers were forgeries and the sale collapsed.

In 1990 the marquess, crippled by the huge cost of running his estates, tried to sell the Sevso collection at Sotheby's in New York for around $50 million, but a flurry of injunctions killed the auction. The Lebanese claimed that the Hoard had been smuggled illegally out of the Bekaa Valley, while the Yugoslavian government claimed it had been found on the Serbian Macedonia border. The most credible claim, however, came from Hungary.

MURDER OF THE QUARRYMAN

According to the Hungarian version of events, the Hoard was discovered by a young quarry worker, Jozsef Sumegh, in the late 1970s, who then sold the items on the black market. In 1980 he was found hanged – the official verdict was suicide, but many now believe it was murder. The incredible silver was worth millions, and in addition to the 14 known pieces it is believed there may be other pieces that have never come into public view (most hoards of this type include spoons and coins). If its doubtful provenance could be concealed – by murder, if necessary – then it could be sold for a fortune.

Many antiques experts rate the Hungarian origin as the most plausible. The Hoard resembles another collection of silver found near Lake Balaton in Hungary in the 19th century, and one of the pieces is engraved with the word *Pelso* – the Roman name for the lake. It probably belonged to a Roman general, perhaps given as a token of imperial esteem – a similar story is ascribed to the Mildenhall Treasure (see page 20).

(see page 20).

TRAPPED IN LIMBO

Unable to sell the Hoard, but facing huge legal fees to keep hold of it, the Marquess of Northampton sold many of his possessions to finance a long legal battle, which finally saw him adjudged the legal owner. The silver was spirited out of New York and locked up in a bank vault in the Channel Islands. The marquess sued his advisers for millions over the debacle, and believes the treasure has brought him nothing but trouble. Explaining his desire to sell it, he told the *Sunday Telegraph* in 2006, 'I do not want my wife or my son to inherit what has become a curse.' An exhibition of the Hoard at the London auction house Bonhams that same year was thought to be a prelude to a renewed attempt to offload the tainted silver, now valued at around £100 million (nearly $200 million), but those archeologists concerned with the trade in illegal antiquities have protested, while the Hungarian government maintains its claim. An incredible treasure worth tens of millions may prove to be impossible to sell.

Right *Many different characters and scenes from mythology are shown on the Meleager Plate, including, in the central medallion, the lovers Atalantes and Meleager.*

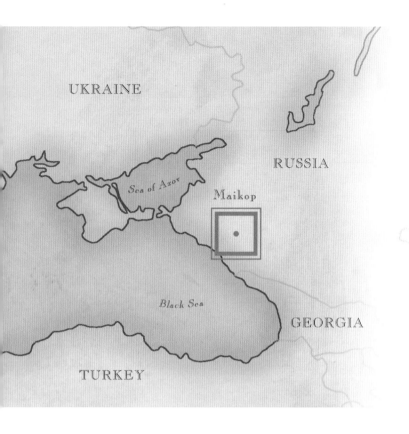

The Maikop Treasure

A large and scattered collection of antiquities from the steppes of the northern Black Sea area, the Maikop Treasure bears testament both to the extraordinarily rich and diverse culture of the nomadic peoples who lived at the fringes of the Classical world and to the perils of the looting and smuggling of antiquities and their dispersal among private collectors.

The Maikop Treasure is the name given to a large and diverse collection of grave goods from the north-western Caucasus, which includes gold, silver and bronze ornaments and weapons and more workaday items. The name of the collection suggests that it all derives from the same culture – the Bronze Age Maikop or Maykop culture – and more specifically from the Maikop Barrow that gives this culture its name.

The Maikop Barrow is a royal burial mound in the valley of the Kuban River, lying in the modern-day republic of Adygea. Around 5,000 years ago this was the centre of a nomadic steppe culture thought to be a staging post in the Indo-European 'invasion' of Europe.

In truth, however, the Maikop Treasure does not come from a single hoard, or even a single culture. It includes items spanning the period from the 3rd millennium BCE right up to 1400 CE – a span of 4,500 years – and thus provides a unique record of the cultural, artistic and spiritual evolution of a single region over a vast extent of time. But it also stands as a cautionary tale about the damage done to the archeological record by indiscriminate excavation and dispersal, and the dangers of pricelessly informative artefacts disappearing from public view and academic access for ever.

MONSIEUR DE MASSONEAU'S COLLECTION

The Maikop Treasure first surfaced into the glamorous but sometimes shady world of Belle Époque arts dealers and antiques collectors. Around the start of the 20th century a series of headline-grabbing discoveries had been made during excavations of the many barrows and mounds in the southern Russia/northern Caucasus region, which revealed great hoards of gold, silver and bronze ornaments of exquisite workmanship; the grave goods of royalty who were often interred alongside the skeletons of horses – sometimes hundreds of them. The romantic and inspiring picture of the ancient steppe cultures that emerged captured the public imagination, and, in the words of distinguished archeologist Aleksandr Leskov, 'collecting antiquities became a fashionable and prestigious activity.' Leskov went on to explain:

Unfortunately, this 'gold fever' led to a troubling increase in grave robbing and to the appearance of large amounts of archeological materials on the black market. Unlimited possibilities for private collectors were thus created, the best example of which is perhaps the collection of Merle de Massoneau.

Well-connected banker and collector M.A. Merle de Massoneau had worked for many years in the south of what was still imperial Russia, directing the royal vineyards of the Crimean and Caucasus regions, and during this time he amassed a huge collection of fabulous antiquities. Troubled by the evident instability of Russia, he sought a safer home for his treasures. In 1907 he sold off his collection, but, not wanting to flood the market and devalue it, he sold different parts to different museums, including the Berlin Museum and the Metropolitan Museum in New York – sometimes even to different departments in the same museum – thus beginning the dispersal of the treasure. Some years later another collection of artefacts from the same region was offered to the

'The treasure provides a unique record of the cultural, artistic and spiritual evolution of a single region over a vast extent of time.'

Right *This distinctive, gold, 6 cm (2 in)-high bull figurine from the 3rd century* BCE *is part of the Maikop Treasure. It is labelled as coming from the Maikop burial mound, but as with many other Maikop pieces this may be a fanciful provenance, since the date does not match.*

Berlin Museum; only decades later did it transpire that it was almost certainly related to de Massoneau's collection.

LUCKY DIP

In 1913 yet more treasures from the region arrived on the market, many of them being sold to Ercole Canessa, described by Leskov as 'the most famous antique dealer in the world at the time'. Canessa later offered these for sale as 'the famous Maikop treasure', and they were eventually bought by the museum of the University of Pennsylvania, where they are still on show today.

In 1930 the University consulted with Professor M.I. Rostovtzeff, foremost specialist

in the archeology and art of the ancient Black Sea and Caucasus cultures, who pointed out that 'The so-called Maikop find is not one find but consists of various sets which belong to various times.'

Similar sentiments were voiced 45 years later by Prudence Harper of the Metropolitan Museum, who wrote that the Maikop Treasure 'is most accurately described as an assortment of objects from the Black Sea region'. More specifically, it includes artefacts from the Bronze Age Maikop culture, the beginning of the Iron Age (8th–7th centuries BCE), Scythian times (6th–4th centuries BCE), Sarmatian times (2nd–4th centuries CE), the Age of the Great

Migrations (the name given to the period of the 4th–8th centuries CE, also known as the *Völkerwanderung*, when 'barbarian' tribes from the east overran the Western Roman Empire) and the Middle Ages (the 10th–11th and 14th–15th centuries CE). Highlights include gold plaques in the shapes of stags, wolves and hybrid animals such as griffins, *fibulae* (brooches), diadems, bracelets and earrings. The Scythian pieces in particular display the rich syncretism of the nomadic steppe cultures, which absorbed artistic and cultural influences from neighbouring cultures spanning a massive geographical range (see 'The Bactrian Hoard' on page 14).

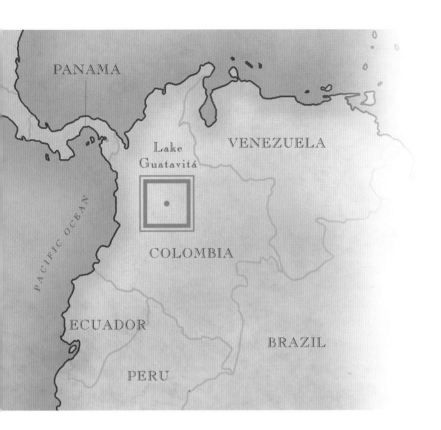

El Dorado: the legend is born

Of all the treasures sought by humans, few have promised as much and delivered as little as the fabled riches of El Dorado, the Gilded One. Both a person and a place, El Dorado drew hordes of desperate and determined treasure hunters, driving them to endure incredible hardship and commit terrible deeds in search of its illusory promise of lost Inca gold.

The Spanish conquest of the Americas brought misery and destruction to the indigenous peoples of the New World, but to the conquistadors – men whose cruelty, ruthlessness and rapaciousness were matched by their valour, fortitude and determination – it brought unimaginable wealth. Many of the conquistadors were little better than brigands and ruffians in their native lands, but in the New World they could

Right *The crater lake of Guatavitá is the probable source of the legend of El Dorado. Generations of treasure hunters have plumbed its depths for the fabled loot and many artefacts have been recovered. The lake is now protected by law from prospectors.*

join the ranks of the richest princes on Earth. All they had to do was strike gold.

GOLD FEVER

The first and most famous of the conquistadors, Hernán Cortés and Francisco Pizarro, managed just this. Cortés looted the fabulously wealthy city of Tenochtitlan in Mexico (see 'Montezuma's Hoard' on page 82), while Pizarro and his small band of

adventurers succeeded beyond their wildest imaginings when they captured the Inca emperor Atahualpa (ruled 1532–33) and he attempted to ransom himself for a roomful of gold (see 'Treasure of the Llanganatis Mountains' on page 38). But the more gold they found, the more the gold-lust of the conquistadors was inflamed. When the Spanish betrayed Atahualpa and had him garrotted, his successor Manco Inca took up the resistance, retreating with the remnants of the Inca forces to wage a bitter campaign from jungle and mountain fastnesses.

The conquistadors were convinced that they had only scratched the surface of the great wealth of the Incas, and that Manco had taken vast treasures with him when he retreated. They were reinforced in these beliefs by incidents such as that recorded in one popular legend, in which captured but defiant Indians gathered together a huge pile of maize and then presented the Spanish with a single kernel. This kernel, the Indians told them, represented the proportion of the Inca treasure they had managed to get their hands on – the rest would never be theirs.

THE LAKE AND THE CEREMONY

So the conquistadors were primed and gullible when, in 1538, a messenger from the interior fell into their hands. He was an emissary from an Indian tribe to the northeast, bringing messages for Atahualpa. The Spanish questioned him for tidings of treasure and he gratified them with an amazing story. A tribe to the east of his, he claimed, practised an annual ceremony to appease their gods. Their king was stripped naked and covered in balsam gum, whereupon priests would blow gold dust at him until he was coated with a layer of the precious substance. Embarking on a great raft, surrounded by priests and nobles, the king would be rowed out into the centre of a sacred lake and would then dive into the water to wash himself clean. Meanwhile offerings of gold and other treasures were thrown into the lake. Who knew how many years of loot might be piled up on the bottom? On hearing this tale, captain Sebastian de Benalcásar dubbed this gold-plated monarch *El Dorado* – the gilded one.

The Indian's story was probably based on truth – an account of the practices of a tribe called the Muisca, part of an agrarian culture that was a neighbour to the Inca Empire, but not at the same level of sophistication. The Muisca lived in the highlands of present-day Colombia and their worship had been based around Lake Guatavitá, a sacred lake in the hills above modern-day Bogotá, into which their gilded king would dive in an annual ritual. Unfortunately for the Spanish, the Muisca had long before been conquered by a neighbouring tribe and the ritual had not been practised for decades or more.

Tellingly, the story also concerned not the messenger's own tribe, but one further away, thus introducing perhaps the crucial and defining element of the El Dorado legend – wherever they went, the conquistadors were told that what they sought was beyond the next ridge or around the next bend of the river. No matter how deep into the mountains and the jungle they penetrated, El Dorado would always remain just out of reach.

THE SEARCH FOR LAKE GUATAVITÁ

Benalcasár set off in search of this mysterious El Dorado, a name that soon became attached to a place rather than a person, for it was believed that the gilded king lived in a city of gold, where precious metals and stones practically spilled out onto the streets. After many months of torturous travel through uncharted jungles and mountains he reached the correct area in 1539, only to discover that other conquistadors had already made it there. Another captain, Gonzalo Jiménez de Quesada, had reached Muisca territories in 1537 having battled inland from the Caribbean coast, losing many men on the way. To his European eyes, the settlements of the tribe resembled castles and forts, and he was convinced that he had stumbled upon a kingdom to rival that of the Inca – one that must surely be rich in gold. Bullying and torture elicited directions further into the interior, along with the tale of El Dorado, and eventually de Quesada became the first European to reach the sacred lake of Guatavitá.

Left The Balsa Muisca is a gold-wire votive model of a raft bearing priests and the king, and probably represents the El Dorado ceremony. Made by the pre-Columbian Muisca people, it was found in 1969 in a cave near Bogotá, although many sources claim it was recovered from the lake itself.

El Dorado: quest for the golden city

As the legend of El Dorado grew, so did its grim toll of human life. Greedy conquistadors inflamed by the legends launched expedition after expedition into the unforgiving wilderness, and many were to pay a deadly price. Epic journeys of discovery, including Francisco de Orellana's voyage down the Amazon and the crazed rampage of Lope de Aguirre, were inspired by El Dorado.

***Above** A portrait of the conquistador Pedro de Ursua (1526–61), whose brief career as governor of El Dorado was cut short when he was murdered by the notorious Lope de Aguirre.*

De Quesada followed his native guide up the side of an extinct volcano, where, 3,300 m (10,000 feet) above sea level, he discovered Lake Guatavitá brooding in the crater. But there were no signs of any settlement around the lake and he concluded that any treasure must lie beneath its murky waters. Before he could investigate further he was called away, and it was not until 1545 that his brother Hernán Pérez made the first of many attempts to empty the lake. Using a bucket chain, Pérez successfully lowered the surface by a few metres and revealed a small quantity of gold.

A more determined effort in 1580, launched by a merchant and engineer named Antonio de Sepulveda, involved cutting a deep notch in the rim of the crater and draining the lake via a ditch. The level was reduced by nearly 20 m (around 60 ft) before the workings collapsed, killing many of the workers. Enough gold had been discovered for de Sepulveda to send back to Spain – as the royal *quinto* (see page 136) – artefacts including a staff covered in gold and an emerald the size of an egg. But while this might have been enough to whet the appetites of those investigating the lake, it had long been clear that Lake Guatavitá was not the site of the fabled city of El Dorado.

DESPERATE JOURNEYS

By now El Dorado had become conflated in conquistador legend with both the city of Vilcabamba, where Manco Inca and his followers had set up a new capital in exile, and with the mythical homeland of the Inca peoples – places assumed by the Spanish to be dripping with gold. For the authorities back in Spain, launching expeditions, known as *entradas*, to explore the interior of the continent was a useful way to divert the energies of restless conquistadors, while simultaneously opening up new territories. Accordingly, a whole series of *entradas* was launched with the aim of locating El Dorado.

The first of these was a German expedition in 1541, which cost many lives, but explored new parts of the Andes and brought back legends of a city called Omagua, said to be overflowing with gold and emeralds. That same year Francisco Pizarro dispatched his brother Gonzalo on an *entrada* to cross the Andes and penetrate the rainforest on the other side. The younger Pizarro became separated from his partner Francisco de Orellana and endured a nightmare of disease, starvation, hostile natives and implacable wilderness. He lost three-quarters of his party, many of whom were reduced to cannibalism. De Orellana, meanwhile, came across a river and built some boats to explore further. Each river proved to be a tributary to a larger one, until the conquistador found himself travelling down the Amazon, the name of which derives from de Orellana's account of meeting a tribe of fierce warrior women. The Spaniard heard yet more tales of Omagua, by now assumed to be one and the same as El Dorado, and in 1546 he returned to the Amazon to search for it, only to die in the attempt.

AGUIRRE AND THE GOVERNOR OF EL DORADO

In 1560 the new Viceroy of Peru decided to launch a fresh *entrada* in an attempt to occupy the restive conquistadors and to combat Portuguese moves to expand their sphere of influence from Brazil. He appointed a young soldier named Pedro de Ursua as governor of El Dorado and

Omagua, and sent him into the wilderness with a force of unruly soldiers and a number of slaves. De Ursua made the mistake of inviting a beautiful young widow to join his expedition. Jealousy of the alluring female and extreme hardships on the difficult journey into the interior fomented discord, and on New Year's Day 1561 mutineers, led by minor nobleman Lope de Aguirre, stabbed de Ursua to death. Aguirre then proclaimed himself Prince of Peru and led his men on a deranged rampage of rape and slaughter that culminated in the murder of his own daughter, before he himself was shot and beheaded.

During the course of these adventures and the *entradas* before them, it had become clear that the treasure of El Dorado was not to be found in the area of modern-day Ecuador, Peru or Colombia. Yet always the Indian tribes questioned by the treasure hunters insisted that a land of fabulous treasure existed a little further along. The last great uncharted area in the region was in Guyana, the territory of the north-eastern side of the continent that includes modern-day Venezuela and Guyana. Here, in the remote and largely unmapped region of mountains and valleys at the headwaters of the mighty Orinoco River, the legend of El Dorado lived on.

Below Detail from a map of 1599, typical of the fanciful depictions of South American geography that inspired many explorers. It shows the fabled city of El Dorado, in its incarnation as Manoa (see page 36) in the region of Guyana.

El Dorado: the fatal inheritance

The final acts of the El Dorado drama were largely played out in Guyana, where two great adventurers would engage in an epic struggle to become masters of the lost treasure, only to meet mutual destruction and the loss of fortune, friends, loved ones and eventually their own lives.

Bogotá (originally called Bacatá) was the main settlement of the Muisca until the arrival of the Spanish under de Quesada, who founded a colonial town on the site. By 1580 it was a well-established city and the capital of a huge territory. This was the year that Don Antonio de Berrio arrived to take up an inheritance left to him by his wife's uncle – none other than de Quesada himself.

De Berrio was an old man of 60, a veteran of numerous campaigns in the Old World, but still energetic and vigorous. He would need all that energy and vigour to fulfil the stipulation in his benefactor's will: that he must use part of the estate left to him to pursue the search for the legendary kingdom and its immense treasures.

De Berrio quickly set about fulfilling his uncle-in-law's ambitions, organizing a series of *entradas* from Bogotá overland towards Guyana, where El Dorado was now believed to lie. The first set out in 1581, and after 17 months of relentless hardships de Berrio reached the Orinoco River and crossed into the mountains on the other side. Here he heard the familiar tale of a rich kingdom that lay just beyond. The Indians told of a people who had come from the west and settled by a lake in the mountains, where they lived in splendour. This fitted perfectly with the belief of the Spanish that the last Incas had fled to Guyana to found a new city, taking their vast treasures with them. De Berrio's

report back to Spain secured him the title of governor of the province of El Dorado. Subsequent *entradas* charted new territory and discovered new information – the name of the lake was Paríma, at the headwaters of the River Caroní.

THE ENGLISH ARE COMING

The tale of Juan Martínez triggered a new bout of gold fever, and de Berrio found himself competing with other greedy governors for the resources to launch new *entradas*. Now based in Trinidad, an island just off the mouth of the Orinoco, de Berrio managed to put together two more expeditions, before the arrival of a new player changed the game completely.

Spanish messages bearing tidings of El Dorado had fallen into the hands of the English, and the Elizabethan explorer and courtier Sir Walter Raleigh had seized upon them as a means of winning favour with his queen. In 1595 he arrived in the New World with a squadron of ships and captured Trinidad and de Berrio. Exploring the Orinoco, Raleigh found evidence of gold mines and learned the stories of Manoa and Lake Paríma. Returning to England, he wrote a book called *The Discoveries*, introducing the legend of El Dorado to the European mainstream, together with maps showing Paríma and Manoa, which, despite having little basis in reality, were to

JUAN MARTÍNEZ

While de Berrio was struggling with dense jungle, fierce weather and hostile Indians, confirmation of the existence of El Dorado and its treasure appeared in the form of a ragged Spaniard who emerged from the jungle in 1586 with a fantastic tale. Juan Martínez claimed to be the sole survivor of an expedition that had been attacked by Indians, and said that he had been led to a great city called Manoa, where he had met El Dorado, the gilded one, in person. Eventually he was allowed to return to his people, laden with treasures, and although he had lost most of these on the way back, he apparently possessed enough to lend credibility to his tale.

become the standard guide for explorers for centuries.

In England Raleigh scratched about for financial backing for a new expedition until he fell foul of the new monarch, James I (ruled 1603–25), and was locked in the Tower of London. Back in Guyana, de Berrio (freed by Raleigh when no one would pay a ransom for him) was contesting with Raleigh's lieutenant Lawrence Keymis to see who could find Manoa first. Their search was fruitless: each tribe they made contact with would direct them further on. In 1597 – financially, physically and spiritually exhausted – de Berrio died with the bitter epilogue, 'If you try to do too much you will end by doing nothing at all.'

In 1616 Raleigh finally secured his release from the Tower of London and returned to the New World seeking to repair his fortunes. Unfortunately, only death and misery awaited him. His son was killed in a skirmish with the Spanish, leading to a falling out with Keymis, who committed suicide. Raleigh's failure gave his enemies (the pro-Spanish faction at

court) the pretext they needed, and on his return to England, Raleigh was seized and convicted of fomenting war with the Spanish, and was executed in 1618.

THE END OF EL DORADO?

Raleigh's maps continued to inspire fruitless searching, and it was not until 1800, when the Guyanese uplands were properly charted by professional explorers like Alexander von Humboldt, that it was conclusively proved that Lake Paríma and Manoa were a figment of the imagination. Attention turned back to Lake Guatavitá, fanned by speculation on the quantity of treasure that might lurk at the bottom – up to a billion pounds sterling (around $120 billion today), according to an 1825 travel guide. In 1912 a mechanized attempt was made to drain the lake, but the muddy floor dried solid before it could be dredged and the expedition ended in failure.

In recent times the lake has been a protected zone, and the treasure of El Dorado must remain legendary and lost.

Above Sir Walter *Raleigh's conquest of St Joesph, Trinidad in 1595. Engraved for the* Universal Magazine, *1750.*

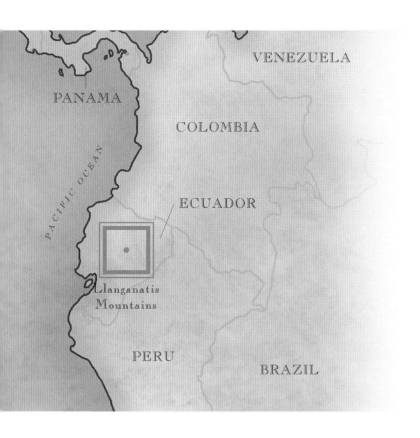

VENEZUELA

PANAMA

COLOMBIA

PACIFIC OCEAN

ECUADOR

Llanganatis
Mountains

PERU

BRAZIL

Treasure of the Llanganatis Mountains

Deep in the inaccessible reaches of a hostile Ecuadorean mountain range lies a huge cache of Inca gold, hidden from the conquistadors centuries ago and protected ever since by formidable natural barriers and, some say, by a curse that threatens all those foolish enough to seek it out.

As incredible and dangerous as the legend of El Dorado, but arguably more exciting because of the possibility that it might be for real, is the amazing story of the lost Inca gold of the Llanganatis. In 1532 the Spanish conquistadors under Pizarro captured the Inca emperor Atahualpa (see page 32). In an attempt to ransom his freedom, he promised to fill the room in which he was being held captive with gold, up to the level of his outstretched arm. Huge quantities of treasure were brought from across the Inca Empire to Cajamarca, where the emperor was held captive, but the Spanish grew anxious that Atahualpa would serve as the focus of Inca resistance and had him killed anyway. On 29 August 1533 Atahualpa was garrotted.

GOLD IN THE MOUNTAINS

The Inca general Rumiñahui ('the stone-faced') was making his way south from Quito towards Cajamarca with a huge shipment of golden artefacts and other treasure – 765 tonnes (750 tons) of it, worth more than $14 billion today in mineral value alone – when he heard the news. He promptly turned

Left The last emperor of the Inca, Atahualpa, murdered by the Spanish in 1533 despite ransoming his freedom by promising to fill a room with gold.

Left A view of the Llanganatis National Park in Ecuador. The dramatic peaks of the region so impressed the local Panzaleo people that they gave the range its name, which derives from the Quechua for 'Beautiful Mountain'.

round and marched his men and their load of loot deep into an inaccessible range of mountains high up in what is now Ecuador: the *Cordillera de Llanganates*, or the Llanganatis Mountains. Razor-sharp ridges, deep ravines and canyons, treacherous bogs and swamps, thick rainforest, constant rain and fog and lethal flash floods make this area one of the most dangerous wildernesses in the world, but the Inca were masters of their mountain realm and penetrated deep into its heart. Here, according to the main source for the legend (see below), Rumiñahui ordered his men to cast the treasure into an artificial lake (whether dug for the purpose or pre-existing is unclear). Alternatively they may have secreted the gold in a cave or in one of the many mines in the area. Rumiñahui was subsequently captured by the Spanish, and although tortured and executed, he never revealed the secret of the hidden treasure.

VALVERDE'S *DERROTERO*

The bones of this story were set out in an article published in the *Journal of the Royal Geographical Society* in 1860 by Richard Spruce, an English botanist who had travelled in the region. Spruce then introduced many other ingredients of a classic treasure tale – a treasure map; a mysterious set of directions, possibly in code; and a cast of adventurers who had perished in their attempts to find the treasure. He related how a Spanish colonial named Valverde had married an Inca princess, whose father had bequeathed to him the secret of the lost Inca treasure. Valverde journeyed into the mountains and found the huge trove, carrying off enough to make him a rich man and returning to Spain. When he died he bequeathed to the Spanish king, Charles V, his *Derrotero*, or itinerary, detailing the route to take to reach the loot. The king sent the *Derrotero* back to Ecuador with instructions for an *entrada* to be launched in search of the treasure, and a Franciscan friar named Father Longo accordingly led an expedition into the mountains. Valverde's instructions were found to correspond precisely to the real terrain, but as the expedition was nearing its goal, the unfortunate Longo disappeared during the night, presumably into one of the region's fog-shrouded ravines or swamps, and the rest turned back.

The *Derrotero* was lodged in the local archives and copied assiduously by treasure hunters over the years, until it was stolen. The copies, however, were still at large, and Spruce reproduced the text in its entirety. Modern treasure hunters agree that it seems largely accurate at first, but that flaws or inconsistencies in the text point to accidental or deliberate miscopying.

GUZMÁN'S TREASURE MAP

Spruce obtained a detailed map of the Llanganatis region, produced by a botanist and prospector named Atanasio Guzmán, who had also sought to locate the treasure and died in mysterious circumstances (he sleepwalked off a cliff). Armed with these guides, a number of treasure hunters explored the region, many of them coming to an unpleasant end. For instance, a Canadian explorer called Barth Blake claimed to have discovered an immense treasure, but later disappeared at sea. A Scotsman called Erskine Loch published an account of two disastrous expeditions undertaken in the 1930s, and then shot himself. An American called Colonel Brooks met with similar obstacles, losing his wife to pneumonia contracted in the Llanganatis and ending up in a madhouse. More recently there have been claims that the treasure was found and shipped in secret to Edinburgh in 1802, where it was either taken to the vaults of the Royal Bank of Scotland or diverted into the pockets of the Comte d'Artois, later the last Bourbon king of France as Charles X.

The Seven Cities of Cíbola

El Dorado was not the only city of gold and fabulous treasures to inspire the conquistadors. Iberian legend told of no fewer than seven such cities on a mythical island to the west, eventually identified as North America. When Spanish explorers in the region returned with tales of rich cities, an epic quest was launched to seize the wealth of Cíbola.

Before the great Voyages of Discovery of the 15th and 16th centuries, European knowledge of the West was a mix of myth and legend, much of it based on Roman and Greek reports, themselves of largely legendary provenance. A Roman story chronicled by Plutarch in around 74 CE told how a Roman consul in Spain 'met some sailors who had recently come back from the Atlantic Islands', and who fed him tall tales of an Elysium of rich soils, temperate weather and happy folk. Upon such reports was based the legend of Antillia, an island in the Atlantic that became cognate with the Isles of the Blessed and other such fantasies. In Spain and Portugal, Antillia was in turn combined with a local legend concerning seven bishops

Left An 1853 lithograph of one of the pueblos of the Zuni people, which may have misled Spanish explorers into believing they had discovered the fabled cities of Cíbola.

who had fled from Iberia in the face of the Moorish conquest and had travelled with their flocks to a wondrous island paradise, where they founded seven cities that flourished into a utopian commonwealth.

Antillia and the *Septe Cidades* of Gold were routinely featured on early maps of the Atlantic. Initially identified with the Azores and then the West Indies, they were assumed to be a real place. Gathering data for his voyage of discovery, Christopher Columbus was informed that he could measure his progress towards Japan by his arrival on Antillia, and he planned to stop there en route. A folk tale told of a Portuguese captain who encountered the island and found that the beach was one-third sand and two-thirds gold dust.

THE SEVEN CITIES IN AMERICA

Eventually it became apparent that the Seven Cities of Gold were not to be found in the Atlantic or Caribbean. But Spanish explorers were penetrating the North American continent and returned to their Mexican bases with incredible tales. A disastrous expedition of 1528 to Florida left only four survivors, who endured an epic voyage home encompassing slavery, escape and travel through the heartland of what are now the southern and south-western states of the United States. They brought with them Indian tales of great cities in the interior, and so a new *entrada* was launched in search of it.

THE BLACK MEXICAN

Guiding the *entrada* was one of the survivors of the 1528 expedition, a slave of Moorish extraction named Estebanico (a form of Esteban, itself the Spanish equivalent of Stephen, so that he is also known as Black Stephen), the first black African to feature prominently in the history of the New World. Estebanico had an amazing facility for languages and a reputation as a medicine man among the Indians, who called him the 'Black Mexican'. Estebanico was sent on ahead to scout out the route, and the story goes that he had been instructed to leave crosses of varying sizes as signs for the

Right *The Cliff Palace at Mesa Verde, one of the greatest settlements of the Ancestral Pueblo Peoples, also known as the Anasazi. Impressive multi-storey buildings like these or the ones at Chaco Canyon may have convinced the conquistadors that they had stumbled upon the fabled cities of Cíbola.*

following party to indicate what he had learned from the Indians – the larger the cross, the greater the wealth of the cities they sought. As the Spanish followed Estebanico's trail they encountered larger and larger crosses, until eventually they came across one as big as a man. A message from Estebanico told of no fewer than seven fabulous cities, the richest of which was called Cíbola.

Marcos de Niza, the friar in charge of the expedition, spurred his men on, but they discovered that Estebanico had been killed by hostile Indians. Without his guide Father Marcos did not venture too much further, although he did penetrate far enough to the north to come within sight of a city that he reported was as great as Tenochtitlan – the Aztec capital that had been looted so profitably by Cortés – and dripping with gold and jewels. Back in Mexico, it was assumed that de Niza had discovered the Seven Cities of Iberian legend.

CORONADO AND THE *PUEBLOS*

Yet another *entrada* was launched, this one under the command of Don Francisco Vásquez de Coronado. With hundreds of soldiers and slaves, he set out from Mexico to discover, subjugate and plunder Cíbola and its sister cities. This voyage was to yield the first European sighting of the Grand Canyon, and penetrated as far as Kansas, but Coronado was bitterly disappointed to discover that the wealth of Cíbola was a mirage.

The cities that had inspired the Indian reports, and which had been viewed from afar by de Niza, were the *pueblos* of the Zuni Indians. These great canyon complexes of dwellings constructed in adobe offered little to the conquistadors but dust and disillusionment. One suggestion is that de Niza was misled by the straw in the adobe mix, which glittered in the sun so that, from a distance, it looked like gold.

King Solomon's mines

The Bible speaks of a wealthy port in a distant land, from where King Solomon received huge shipments of treasure from rich gold mines, together with exotic trade goods. Later traditions link this land of gold with the Queen of Sheba. Where was this mysterious port, and was it possible that European explorers visiting new parts of the world might stumble upon the rich remains of King Solomon's mines?

Right *The Queen of Sheba offers lavish gifts to Solomon. According to the Book of Kings she brought 'spices and gold very much, and precious stones'. The source of her wealth was said to be the land of Ophir, rich in gold, gems, spices and precious woods.*

In the Book of Kings it is written that King Solomon built a great fleet of ships on the Red Sea coast and sent them to Ophir, whence they brought back a huge quantity of gold, together with ivory, apes and peacocks. Later biblical references highlight the precious woods brought from Ophir. For the Jews of biblical times and beyond, Ophir thus became a legendary land of treasure, where gold, silver and precious stones were plentiful and fabulously rich mines spewed forth the treasures of the Earth – in other words, a sort of biblical El Dorado.

Writers since ancient times have speculated on the likely location of Ophir, mainly on the basis of place names and linguistic similarities, but in the 19th century explorers penetrating into the hitherto unknown 'dark continent' of Africa stumbled across actual physical evidence – monumental ruins, which they were quick to attribute to Solomon. Had they really discovered the actual remnants of King Solomon's mines or were they simply misled by their own colonial and racist preconceptions? And where was the treasure?

OPHIR IN INDIA

Like Atlantis, locations for Ophir have been posited in every corner of the globe. Indeed, the two have even been linked, with one theory suggesting that the fleets built by Solomon and his Phoenician ally Hiram traded across the Atlantic with a mighty civilization located in South America – possibly in the Andes on the Altiplano of present-day Bolivia – which in turn inspired Plato's description of Atlantis.

A more plausible option is that Ophir was in India, and that the biblical word is a derivation of a Sanskrit word, *Abhira*, which is also similar to the Aberia mentioned by the Classical geographer Ptolemy as a port near the mouth of the River Indus. India, by Roman times renowned for its fabulous wealth, was known as a land of gold, but it seems unlikely that the pre-Classical Hebrews knew about it. Also, crucially, it seems unlikely that Solomon would have sent a fleet so far when there were rich gold mines nearer at hand.

GREAT ZIMBABWE

Another linguistic connection was between Ophir and Sofala – the coast of southern Africa opposite Madagascar. Inland from here there were rich gold fields, and the area could also have supplied the apes, ivory and woods of the biblical account. Portuguese visitors to the region reported tales of a great ruined city in the interior, and made the connection between Sofala, Ophir, the mines of Solomon and the exotic Queen of Sheba.

In 1871 this identification seemed to be dramatically confirmed when German explorer Karl Mauch finally reached the ruins of Great Zimbabwe. The expert masonry, with its massive drystone walls, and the sophisticated architecture of the site suggested to the white European that this city could not possibly have been constructed by black Africans. When he prised loose a sliver of wood from a lintel and decided that it resembled his pencil, which was made from cedar (the national tree of Lebanon), Mauch was convinced – the city was Phoenician or at least Mediterranean, probably constructed by the Queen of Sheba, Solomon himself or his ally (and builder) Hiram of Tyre.

Theories such as this inspired H. Rider Haggard to write the best-selling adventure story *King Solomon's Mines*, and the associations with Ophir were used to help recruit gullible European colonists to transplant to South Africa. In reality Europeans found little gold in the area. Only later were rich gold mines discovered around Johannesburg, which proved to be the real city of gold.

The initial archeological surveys of Great Zimbabwe were also coloured by this colonial and racist agenda, and the identification of the site's builders as northern and essentially 'white' was given a bogus academic imprimatur. Later, under the white Rhodesian government, archeologists could be fired for suggesting otherwise, and black Africans were barred from the site. But as early as 1905 an archeologist noticed that finds at the site were identical to artefacts and technology in current use by the Shona tribes of the area, and concluded that Great Zimbabwe had been built by the same people who still lived around it. It is now accepted that the city flourished in the Middle Ages, when it was the centre of the gold-trading empire of Mwene Mutapa.

OPHIR IN ARABIA

The most likely location of Ophir was on the Arabian peninsula, probably around Yemen, where the ancient Greek geographer Agatharchides claimed there were mines that produced nuggets as big as walnuts. Gold was worth less to the locals than the more utilitarian iron and copper, which made it a lucrative trading destination for merchants from the Levant. This region was ruled by a kingdom known to the ancient Egyptians as Punt, which included territories in Somalia in the Horn of Africa – perhaps the source of the ivory, apes and precious woods mentioned in the Bible. This is also the region commonly thought to be the home of the Queen of Sheba. Perhaps it is to this area that treasure hunters should turn in their quest for the real mines of King Solomon.

Below The Great Enclosure at Great Zimbabwe, the largest pre-colonial site in sub-Saharan Africa. The city was constructed by the Mwene Mutapa Empire in the 13th–15th centuries.

The Beale Ciphers

A tale of buried treasure, unbreakable codes and a pamphlet of dubious provenance – these are the ingredients for one of America's most enduring mysteries, involving a mysterious prospector who buried a huge cache of loot in Virginia and left behind three encrypted messages pointing to the location of the treasure and its rightful owners.

The Beale Ciphers are a collection of three encrypted letters (or ciphers) purported to have been written by a man named Thomas Jefferson Beale in 1820, which detail the amount, location and owners of a buried treasure. However, the letters themselves, together with the fantastic story behind their creation, derive from a single source: the pamphlet *The Beale Papers*, published in 1885 by a man named Jas (thought to be short for James) B. Ward.

THE INNKEEPER'S TRUST

The pamphlet explains that Beale and his 30 companions mined a fortune in gold and silver from a location to the north of Santa Fe in New Mexico and decided to transport it back east for safekeeping. Beale's task was to bury the loot in a secret location in Virginia, and then find a trustworthy person with whom he could leave an iron box containing three letters and three ciphers detailing exactly how to find the cache and the names of those among whom it should be shared. Beale chose an innkeeper named Robert Morriss in Bedford County and left him the box with instructions to open it only if he failed to reappear.

Beale was never seen again and eventually Morriss opened the box to discover the ciphers. After failing to decrypt them himself,

he left the letters and ciphers to a friend, who stumbled upon the fact that a particular edition of the Declaration of Independence was the key to decrypting the second cipher. This proved to be a list of the treasure buried in iron pots in a stone-lined vault. The exact composition of the treasure was given as:

The first deposit consisted of one thousand and fourteen pounds of gold, and three thousand eight hundred and twelve pounds of silver, deposited November, 1819. The second was made December, 1821, and consisted of nineteen hundred and seven pounds of gold, and twelve hundred and eighty-eight pounds of silver; also jewels, obtained in St. Louis in exchange for silver to save transportation, and valued at $13,000.

The value of the treasure comes to more than $30 million in modern terms. The first cipher describes the exact location of the vault, while the third is a list of those to whom it belongs.

TALL STORIES

The unbreakable codes are not the only fishy element of the Beale Ciphers. Apart from the overall implausibility of the tale, there are specific problems. The unencrypted letters attributed to Beale contain words such as

CRACKING THE CODE

The tale of the Beale Ciphers was a popular one and many people have tried their hands at cracking the code. The ciphers are composed of strings of digits. In the case of the second cipher, these numbers refer to specific locations – that is, letters – in the text of the Declaration of Independence. Accordingly, initial efforts to decode the other ciphers focused on finding the right cipher texts, and a wide range of historical documents has been tried. Latterly, brute computing power has been applied to the problem with an equal lack of success. In practice most experts doubt that the remaining ciphers are genuine codes – for instance, statistical analysis suggests that the codes do not correspond to the English alphabet.

'stampeded' and 'improvise' that were not current during the 1820s and did not come into use until the 1880s. Indeed, stylistic analysis suggests that the authors of the letters and the pamphlet are one and the same. Above all, there are too many holes in the tale. Why would Beale and his colleagues deem it safer to ship a wagon train of treasure across an entire continent than to find a decent bank nearer to home? And why, having done so, would they bury it where somebody else (such as the landowner) might stumble upon it? Why encrypt the three ciphers using different systems, when they are all essentially part of one letter?

Many treasure hunters have disregarded this logic, and Bedford County, Virginia has been riddled with holes. But the smart money points to a hoax, or more exactly a tall tale in the tradition of Edgar Allan Poe's *The Gold Bug*, which may well have inspired the Beale pamphlet – the two have many similarities.

115, 73, 24, 807, 37, 52, 49, 17, 31, 62, 647, 22, 7, 15, 140, 47, 29, 107, 79, 84, 56,
239, 10, 26, 811, 5, 196, 308, 85, 52, 160, 136, 59, 211, 36, 9, 46, 316, 554, 122,
106, 95, 53, 58, 2, 42, 7, 35, 122, 53, 31, 82, 77, 250, 196, 56, 96, 118, 71, 140,
287, 28, 353, 37, 1005, 65, 147, 807, 24, 3, 8, 12, 47, 43, 59, 807, 45, 316, 101, 41,
78, 154, 1005, 122, 138, 191, 16, 77, 49, 102, 57, 72, 34, 73, 85, 35, 371, 59, 196,
81, 92, 191, 106, 273, 60, 394, 620, 270, 220, 106, 388, 287, 63, 3, 191, 122, 43,
234, 400, 106, 290, 314, 47, 48, 81, 96, 26, 115, 92, 158, 191, 110, 77, 85, 197, 46,
10,113, 140, 353, 48, 120, 106, 2, 607, 61, 420, 811, 29, 125, 14, 20, 37, 105, 28,
248, 16, 159, 7, 35, 19, 301, 125, 110, 486, 287, 98, 117, 511, 62, 51, 220, 37, 113,
140, 807, 138, 540, 8, 44, 287, 388, 117, 18, 79, 344, 34, 20, 59, 511, 548, 107,
603, 220, 7, 66, 154, 41, 20, 50, 6, 575, 122, 154, 248, 110, 61, 52, 33, 30, 5, 38, 8,
14, 84, 57, 540, 217, 115, 71, 29, 84, 63, 43, 131, 29, 138, 47, 73, 239, 540, 52, 53,
79, 118, 51, 44, 63, 196, 12, 239, 112, 3, 49, 79, 353, 105, 56, 371, 557, 211, 515,
125, 360, 133, 143, 101, 15, 284, 540, 252, 14, 205, 140, 344, 26, 811, 138, 115
48, 73, 34, 205, 316, 607, 63, 220, 7, 52, 150, 44, 52, 16, 40, 37, 158, 807, 37, 121,
12, 95, 10, 15, 35, 12, 131, 62, 115, 102, 807, 49, 53, 135, 138, 30, 31, 62, 67, 41,
85, 63, 10, 106, 807, 138, 8, 113, 20, 32, 33, 37, 353, 287, 140, 47, 85, 50, 37, 49,
47, 64, 6, 7, 71, 33, 4, 43, 47, 63, 1, 27, 600, 208, 230, 15, 191, 246, 85, 94, 511, 2
270, 20, 39, 7, 33, 44, 22, 40, 7, 10, 3, 811, 106, 44, 486, 230, 353, 211, 200, 31
10, 38, 140, 297, 61, 603, 320, 302, 666, 287, 2, 44, 33, 32, 511, 548, 10, 6, 250,
557, 246, 53, 37, 52, 83, 47, 320, 38, 33, 807, 7, 44, 30, 31, 250, 10, 15, 35, 106,
160, 113, 31, 102, 406, 230, 540, 320, 29, 66, 33, 101, 807, 138, 301, 316, 353,
320, 220, 37, 52, 28, 540, 320, 33, 8, 48, 107, 50, 811, 7, 2, 113, 73, 16, 125, 11,
110, 67, 102, 807, 33, 59, 81, 158, 38, 43, 581, 138, 19, 85, 400, 38, 43, 77, 14, 27,
8, 47, 138, 63, 140, 44, 35, 22, 177, 106, 250, 314, 217, 2, 10, 7, 1005, 4, 20, 25,
44, 48, 7, 26, 46, 110, 230, 807, 191, 34, 112, 147, 44, 110, 121, 125, 96, 41, 51,
50, 140, 56, 47, 152, 540, 63, 807, 28, 42, 250, 138, 582, 98, 643, 32, 107, 140,
112, 26, 85, 138, 540, 53, 20, 125, 371, 38, 36, 10, 52, 118, 136, 102, 420, 150,
112, 71, 14, 20, 7, 24, 18, 12, 807, 37, 67, 110, 62, 33, 21, 95, 220, 511, 102, 811,
30, 83, 84, 305, 620, 15, 2, 108, 220, 106, 353, 105, 106, 60, 275, 72, 8, 50, 205,
185, 112, 125, 540, 65, 106, 807, 188, 96, 110, 16, 73, 33, 807, 150, 409, 400, 50,
154, 285, 96, 106, 316, 270, 205, 101, 811, 400, 8, 44, 37, 52, 40, 241, 34, 205,
38, 16, 46, 47, 85, 24, 44, 15, 64, 73, 138, 807, 85, 78, 110, 33, 420, 505, 53, 37,
38, 22, 31, 10, 110, 106, 101, 140, 15, 38, 3, 5, 44, 7, 98, 287, 135, 150, 96, 33, 84,
125, 807, 191, 96, 511, 118, 440, 370, 643, 466, 106, 41, 107, 603, 220, 275, 30,
150, 105, 49, 53, 287, 250, 208, 134, 7, 53, 12, 47, 85, 63, 138, 110, 21, 112, 140,
485, 486, 505, 14, 73, 84, 575, 1005, 150, 200, 16, 42, 5, 4, 25, 42, 8, 16, 811,
125, 160, 32, 205, 603, 807, 81, 96, 405, 41, 600, 136, 14, 20, 28, 26, 353, 302,
246, 8, 131, 160, 140, 84, 440, 42, 16, 811, 40, 67, 101, 102, 194, 138, 205, 51,
63, 241, 540, 122, 8, 10, 63, 140, 47, 48, 140, 288.

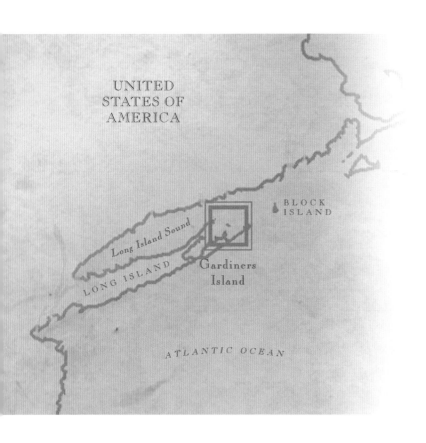

Captain Kidd: pirate gold

With the allure of a real-life Treasure Island, *the story of Captain Kidd has drawn treasure hunters and spawned legends for over 300 years. After a brief but inglorious career, the privateer-turned-pirate fell foul of the authorities, but not before secreting a cache of treasure.*

In the 17th century world trade was growing exponentially as European mastery of the seas combined with the exploitation of rich overseas territories. Ever-increasing amounts of wealth flowed back and forth across the oceans of the world, with fat merchant ships making rich pickings for those who preyed upon them. A single capture could make an entire crew rich, and could make a captain's fortune for life. But there was a crucial divide between privateers and pirates.

Privateers were captains of privately owned ships who had been issued with official letters of marque from their governments, effectively making them legal pirates. They were authorized to capture ships flying under the flag of an enemy nation. Pirates were those who preyed upon whatever ships they could catch, irrespective of nationality or affiliation. A privateer could return from a cruise to riches and acclaim; a pirate would find himself an outlaw, hunted and doomed to hang, if captured.

A PROFITABLE VENTURE

William Kidd was born and raised in Scotland, but had gone to sea and, by the late

1600s, established himself as a respected ship's captain in the flourishing colony of New York. Induced to join a consortium set up to fund a privateering expedition, Kidd put in most of his own money alongside investments from several important Englishmen, rumoured to include King William (ruled 1689–1702) himself. The intention was to purchase and outfit a ship for a cruise to the Indian Ocean, where, armed with letters of marque, Kidd would target mainly pirates, along with any legitimate (that is, French) prizes that came his way.

In 1695 Kidd sailed out of London on the *Adventure Galley*, a warship armed with 34 cannons and a match for almost any pirate. Success at sea depended as much on personnel as equipment, and Kidd had put together a decent crew of respectable sailors. Almost immediately, however, he lost most of them to the press-gang when the *Adventure Galley* was stopped by a Royal Navy ship, and Kidd was forced to recruit a new crew in New York City, a notorious den of thieves and villains. When he finally arrived in the Indian Ocean the ship was struck down by cholera,

which carried off one-third of his men, while the *Adventure Galley* proved to be leaky and unseaworthy.

FROM PRIVATEER TO PIRATE

There are conflicting accounts of what happened next. Kidd's own account comes from his trial and naturally paints him as the unfortunate victim of circumstances, but there are hints that he was far from the innocent he claimed to be. On the journey across the Atlantic he had had a run-in with a Royal Navy squadron, and once in the Indian Ocean he tangled with a convoy of merchant ships under British protection before being chased off.

According to his own account, however, Kidd simply had bad luck. No legitimate prizes came under his bows, while his largely disreputable crew grumbled at seeing rich merchants slip past them unmolested and grew mutinous. In one incident Kidd quarrelled with the ship's gunner, striking him a fatal blow with a bucket. Things looked to have turned around on 30 January 1698, when he spotted the *Quedagh Merchant*, a merchant ship that appeared to be a legitimate target. Here was a rich prize indeed, for it was loaded with a cargo of fabrics, silver and gold, but it transpired that while it sailed under a French pass, the ship itself was Indian and the captain was English. Meanwhile back in England bad reports of Kidd's conduct were accumulating. His original commission had been strictly time-limited and he had overrun it by years. Political machinations meant that his backers had lost influence and could ill afford to be embarrassed by a renegade.

Left *The body of the unfortunate William Kidd, hung in chains to deter other malefactors, after he had been hanged twice and his corpse had been tarred.*

Above right *Captain Kidd overseeing the burial of his treasure on Gardiners Island off the tip of Long Island, treasure that was soon recovered by Governor Bellomont.*

OUTLAWED

After enduring more trials and tribulations, Kidd sailed back to the Caribbean in 1699 to discover that he had been officially declared a pirate. But he did not panic, for he knew that he had a number of things on his side – he had documents that proved the *Quedagh Merchant* was a legitimate prize; he had a network of influence in the American colonies; and, most importantly, he had money. Much of the cargo of the *Quedagh Merchant* had been converted into cash and, Kidd informed the governor of Massachusetts, he possessed 'goods to the value of 30,000 pounds'.

The erstwhile pirate spent part of 1699 travelling up and down the coast between New Jersey and Connecticut, sounding out the situation, spending money and giving gifts and, famously, burying his loot. On Gardiners Island, just off the tip of Long Island, Kidd buried a large quantity of treasure, marking the spot not with an X, but with a cairn of stones.

Captain Kidd: buried treasure

Kidd's treasure, and his protestations of innocence, could not save him from a grisly end, but this merely marks the beginning of his legend, and that of his treasure. Dozens of different spots have been linked to the buried loot, but could the appearance of enigmatic treasure maps hold the real key to the mystery?

Confident that he could reason and bargain his way to freedom, Kidd finally surrendered to Governor Bellomont in Boston, but he was ill served from the start. The vital documents showing that the *Quedagh Merchant* was a legitimate prize were confiscated and sent to London, where they mysteriously disappeared (to be discovered centuries later, misfiled among government records). The unfortunate Kidd was shipped back to London in chains and put on trial for his life.

Former shipmates were marshalled against him and incidents such as the fatal bucket-blow to the ship's gunner came back to haunt him. Without the vital documents, Kidd was unable to back up his side of the story, and was duly found guilty and sentenced to death. Pleading for his life he tried one last, desperate throw of the dice. In a letter to the Speaker of the House of Commons he promised that, in return for his life being spared, he would lead a party of officials to a secret hiding place in the East

Indies, where, he wrote, 'I have lodged goods and Tresure [sic] to the value of one hundred thousand pounds' (worth more than £10 million/$20 million today). His pleas fell on deaf ears, and on 23 May 1701 he was hanged. His corpse was then tarred and exhibited in an iron cage.

UNEARTHING THE TREASURE

Exactly how much treasure did Kidd possess? His own accounts differ – in New England he had claimed to have £30,000, but to Parliament in England he upped this to £100,000. Rumours circulating in the American colonies spoke of still greater amounts: up to £400,000. All we know for sure is that shortly after taking Kidd into custody, Governor Bellomont led a small party onto Gardiners Island and dug up buried loot amounting to £20,000, and that comparison of the cargo manifest of the *Quedagh Merchant* with the recovered booty shows that most of it was accounted for.

The most likely scenario is that Kidd invented the £100,000 to bargain for his life, and that the American rumours were purely that. But there is always the chance that Kidd was a more successful pirate than he let on – it is known that he took a few lesser prizes in addition to the *Quedagh Merchant*, and perhaps he captured greater ones, but never admitted to them for obvious reasons – and

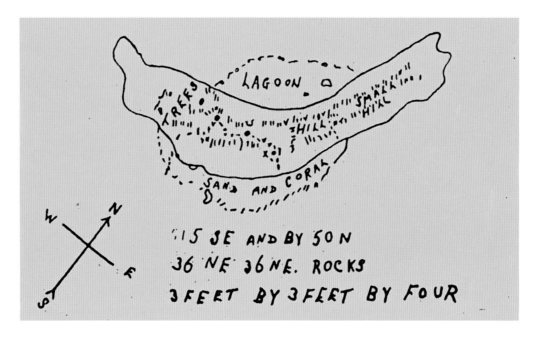

LAGOON

TREES

SMALL

HILL

SAND AND CORAL

W N E S

'IS SE AND BY 5O N
36 NE 36 NE. ROCKS
3 FEET BY 3 FEET BY FOUR

Left The treasure map that the Palmer brothers found in the Skull Chest. It is known as the Skull or Morgan Chart.

Left *Hubert Palmer displays the false bottom from one of the items of Kidd's furniture that he and his brother acquired. This chest, known as the Hardy Chest, contained a map of a mysterious island.*

Below *This chest, known as the Skull or Morgan Chest, also has a false bottom concealing yet another map of Kidd's treasure island. According to some this is the most useful map in terms of clues.*

that his voyages in the Indian Ocean, and in particular his extensive jaunts along the American coastline, included stops for secreting caches of treasure.

The legend of Captain Kidd's treasure has grown to encompass dozens of locations along the New Jersey–Connecticut coastline. Before he gave himself up to the governor, his ship is said to have stopped at many points, including places in Long Island Sound, such as Charles Island, Block Island and the Thimble Islands; locations in Raritan Bay in New Jersey, such as the now-vanished islet, Money Island; places up the Connecticut River, including Clark's Island (sometimes known as Kidd's Island); and numerous spots along the Hudson River.

THE HIDDEN MAPS

The tale of Captain Kidd enters *Treasure Island* territory with the discovery of secret pirate maps, apparently hidden inside furniture said to belong to Kidd himself. In the 1920s a pair of English brothers named Guy and Hubert Palmer, devoted collectors of pirate memorabilia, were contacted by a dealer named Arthur Hill-Cutler, who had supplied them before. Would they like to purchase some unique items: Captain Kidd's own sea chest and bureau? Of course the Palmers leaped at the chance and, on examining their new treasures, discovered four scraps of parchment hidden in secret compartments. All four showed ink-drawn maps of what appeared to be the same island, complete with atmospheric place names and markings, such as 'Smuggler's Cove' and 'Wrecks'.

Although a British Library expert at the time supposedly declared the parchment and ink authentic, subsequent experts have been understandably sceptical. The current Curator of Maps at the British Library says the maps are fakes, and Hill-Cutler was known to have a shady reputation. But Bristol man Paul Hawkins, who has devoted several years to the quest, insists that the maps are real and that he has decoded them to discover the exact whereabouts of Kidd's treasure island. He declares that it was a small atoll in the Indian Ocean, which has since sunk below the waves and now lies in about 10 m (33 ft) of water. All he needs is the financial backing to launch an expedition, says Hawkins, and the lost treasure of Captain Kidd will be recovered after 300 years.

Paul Hawkins is not the only treasure hunter who claims to have decoded the maps. George Edmunds, author of *Kidd: The Search for his Treasure*, claims to have found both the island and the burial site, although like Hawkins he is still in the process of negotiating an expedition to recover Kidd's loot.

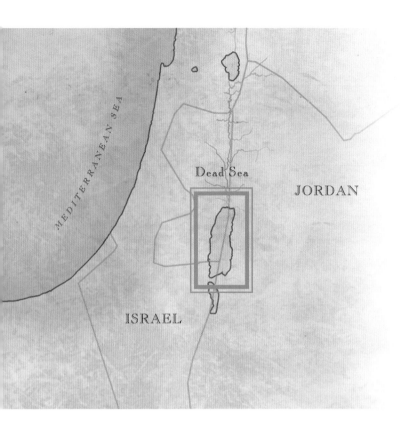

Treasure of the Dead Sea Scrolls

The Dead Sea Scrolls were discovered in caves on the desolate shores of the Dead Sea. The first cache of Scrolls was found in 1947 and many more such caches were discovered over the next few years. Most were ancient scriptures, written on papyrus and parchment, and for biblical scholars and Christians these were a great treasure in themselves, shedding new light on the early Christian era and offering new interpretations of Christianity.

But for treasure hunters the most exciting of the Scrolls was one found in 1952 at the back of a cave on a hillside about 2 km (1¼ miles) from Qumran (an ancient community, see page 52). In a pot, covered in clay, were two rolled-up sheets of copper, which proved to be the two halves of a single scroll. Marks had been made on the Scroll with a stylus and from the visible sections the archeologists could make out the words 'gold' and 'silver'.

It took four more years for the experts to work out how to unroll the Scroll (they eventually decided to cut it into strips, which could then be cleaned and analysed to recreate the whole), and even longer to translate it. But when they were finished, it became apparent that the Copper Scroll was a verbal treasure map, pointing to astonishing quantities of loot.

ENIGMATIC INSTRUCTIONS

The writing on the Copper Scroll proved to be a strange form of Hebrew, with some Greek. Even the handwriting seemed odd, leading to suggestions that it had been transcribed by an illiterate, tracing over/working from a papyrus/parchment original, as if the original author(s) did not wish to leak secrets to the scribe. The Scroll consists of a list of 64 items: 63 caches of treasure with directions to their hiding places, and a copy of the inventory with more directions and an explanation. The treasure comprises mainly quantities of silver and gold, given in an ancient unit of weight called the 'talent', together with vessels and ornaments of gold and silver, scrolls and valuable unguents and incense. How much is a talent? The answer depends on the date, and since the date of authorship of the Scroll

Right *Among the many mysteries associated with the Copper Scroll is its composition. It is 99 per cent pure copper, which would have been amazingly difficult and expensive to produce in ancient times. Clearly whoever made the Scroll was serious about it, and intended it to last.*

is uncertain, so are the quantities. But mainstream opinion puts the total listed weight of loot at 26.5 tonnes (26 tons) of gold and 66 tonnes (65 tons) of silver – worth an amazing $2 billion in today's money for its mineral value alone.

At first glance the instructions for locating this incredible wealth seem straightforward. For instance, Column VI of the Scroll has been translated as:

> *Forty-two talents of silver lie underneath a scroll in an urn. To locate the urn, dig down three cubits into the northern opening of the cave of the pillar that has two entrances and faces east. Twenty-one talents of silver can be found by digging nine cubits beneath the entrance of the eastward-looking cave at the base of the large stone. Twenty-seven talents of silver can be found by digging twelve cubits into the western side of the Queen's Mausoleum.*

But these basic directions prove to be anything but straightforward. The Scroll is ancient and completely oxidized, making it hard to read, and translators often disagree. The vast majority of the directions are either to unspecified places or to locations not familiar to modern scholars (for example, what did the Scroll's authors mean by 'the Queen's Mausoleum'?). They only make sense if one already knows the location being referred to. So far no one has successfully decoded the instructions and discovered any of the treasure.

WHO MADE THE SCROLL?

The question of who created and hid the Scroll is intimately tied up with the debate over whether the treasure really exists and where it came from. The Dead Sea Scrolls were probably hidden in around 70 CE, to protect them from the Romans who were laying waste to Judea in response to the Jewish Revolt, and it is also assumed they were linked to the people of the nearby community at Qumran (see page 52). They in turn are often presumed to have been the Essenes, a Jewish sect mentioned by ancient writers such as Josephus and Pliny. Other possibilities include that the Scroll was hidden by officials from the Temple in Jerusalem, who travelled to the Dead Sea coast by secret passages said to run from beneath the Temple Mount; or by rebels fighting the Romans during the Second Jewish Revolt (also known as the Bar-Kochba rebellion) of 132–135 CE.

Some scholars doubt there was as much treasure in the whole of ancient Israel as appears to be listed in the Copper Scroll, and it certainly seems unlikely that the Essenes, a small ascetic sect, would have accumulated such vast wealth. If they were the Scroll's authors, perhaps it was intended as an allegory of some kind. The one place in Israel that was linked with great wealth was the Temple in Jerusalem, suggesting that the authors were associated with it and that the treasure was loot removed from the Temple to keep it out of the hands of the Romans. If this were the case, it might include sacred artefacts such as the Breastplate of Aaron and perhaps even the Ark of the Covenant.

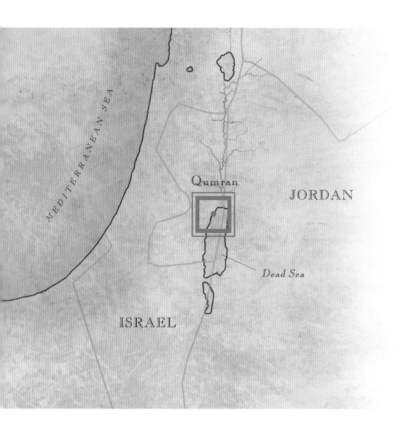

Qumran: a fortress of treasure?

Perched on a terrace overlooking a dry canyon in the midst of a barren, unforgiving region, the ancient settlement of Khirbet Qumran – 'the ruins at Qumran' – is a historical enigma that has sparked fierce controversy. Were the Dead Sea Scrolls written here and was this the staging point for the disposal of the treasures listed in the Copper Scroll?

When the Dead Sea Scrolls were discovered in caves in and around Wadi Qumran (a wadi is a dry canyon or river bed), it was assumed they might be linked with the ruins of the nearby settlement. This assumption was confirmed when pottery from the jars containing many of the Scrolls was linked to pottery from the Qumran ruins. Excavation revealed that the main phase of occupation of the site was from the 2nd century BCE up to 68 CE, when it was razed, presumably by the Romans who were putting down the First Jewish Revolt.

THE MONASTIC ESSENES

The main candidates for the inhabitants at Qumran are the Essenes, one of the four main sects of Second Temple Judaism described by ancient writers as living in desert settlements, including one near the northern end of the Dead Sea (where Qumran is located). The Essenes were a monastic, ascetic sect given to living a pious existence in communes. Many of the Dead Sea Scrolls seem to describe their belief system, obviously suggesting that they were written at Qumran by Essenes who stashed them in

the caves to hide them from the Romans. This identification, however, does not match up with the Copper Scroll, because the Essenes were unlikely to possess anything approaching the huge quantities of treasure outlined in the Scroll. One explanation has been suggested by the historian Gloria Moss, who theorizes that the Essenes ran Qumran as a sort of ancient spa/health clinic, treating those who could afford the high prices they charged for their expensive treatments, salves and unguents. This might explain how the Essenes could have earned such wealth and also ties in with the Scroll's descriptions of stashes of precious balms, oils and so on.

ALTERNATIVE INHABITANTS

More recently there has been much debate about the true inhabitants of Qumran. It has been suggested that they might actually have been Saduccees, another of the Jewish sects, associated with the priestly elite of the Temple in Jerusalem, which would provide a possible link to the Temple treasures. The fortified nature of the site may not be in keeping with the supposedly peaceful Essenes – perhaps instead it was a centre of

Jewish resistance to the Romans, in which case it may have been a staging post for rebels smuggling treasure out of the Temple ahead of the Roman advance. It has even been suggested that Qumran was a Roman villa or fort, although this seems unlikely, given its apparent links with the Jewish Dead Sea Scrolls.

① THE TOWER

The dominant building on the site was the large tower, probably built as a place of refuge in case of attack by the roving bands of marauders who haunted the desert. There was no doorway to the tower, which could only be accessed via a (presumably retractable) wooden bridge to the second floor. In case of attack, the inhabitants of Qumran could simply retreat into the tower, which probably also doubled as a food store. When the Romans attacked in 68 CE, the tower would doubtless have been the last redoubt for the defenders of Qumran. The Roman-Jewish historian Josephus describes Roman soldiers torturing captured Essenes. Perhaps the last survivors were dragged out of the tower and interrogated about the location of the Copper Scroll treasure – possibly this is why the Scroll has not been found in modern times: because it had already been recovered by the Romans.

② THE SCRIPTORIUM

The top floor of the tower proved to be one of the most interesting rooms on the site. The discovery of inkwells and writing benches led to its identification as the Scriptorium, and many experts assume this is where at least some of the Dead Sea Scrolls were penned. Perhaps it was here that the unknown scribe laboured to produce the mysterious Copper Scroll.

③ THE CEMETERY

More than a thousand people are interred at Khirbet Qumran. The gender-specific nature of the burials might support the identification of the inhabitants of Qumran as Essenes, for the Roman historian Pliny specifically describes them as living a monastic existence without wives or children. However, archeologist David Stacey argues that too many people are buried for a community the size of Qumran, which suggests that either dead or dying people must have been brought in from outside. It may simply be that other communities and settlements in the region brought their dead to Qumran for burial, or it may be that Gloria Moss is correct about Qumran being an ancient sanatorium.

④ AQUEDUCT AND CISTERNS

The Judean desert is a harsh environment, where water is the most valuable natural resource. Rain fell just a few times a year and when it did it tended to cause flash floods, where the water quickly ran off and was lost. To capture the precious substance the inhabitants of Qumran excavated cisterns in the rock, at first to gather run-off from the terrace on which the settlement sat, and later – by means of a dam across the wadi and an aqueduct system that would divert flash floods into the cisterns – from the whole Wadi Qumran catchment area. The cisterns and other basins at Qumran may have been used for ritual bathing, which would bolster the case for it being a religious community. They also raise intriguing questions about links with some of the locations mentioned in the Copper Scroll, where instructions regarding cisterns are common. Perhaps Qumran itself hid some caches of the Copper Scroll treasure.

The Stechovice Treasure

A wild tale of buried Nazi loot, secret tunnels, spies, cross-border raids and two men in the grip of an obsession, the story of the Stechovice Treasure is almost too incredible to be true. Yet a small village not far from Prague in the Czech Republic may hold the key to the greatest post-war mystery of them all.

Hitler and his generals considered the treasures of conquered and occupied nations to be theirs, and vast quantities of precious metals, artefacts, antiques and works of art were looted from every corner of Europe. Hitler planned to install the greatest of these artistic treasures in a museum known as the *Sonderauftrag* ('Special Assignment') in his native town of Linz, transforming it into the cultural capital of the world. By 1945, however, reality was intruding in the form of the imminent Allied victory, and the Germans desperately sought to first shift their ill-gotten gains to safe territory, and then simply to hide them for possible future recovery. In addition, they realized that their compulsive record-keeping might work against them, providing the Allies with evidence of their terrible crimes, and so vast archives were also secreted.

Occupied Czechoslovakia would prove to be one of the final battlegrounds of the Second World War. While the heartland of Germany was under desperate pressure from the rapid advance of the Red Army, a large and battle-ready army group of one million men was gathered in Czechoslovakia.

Hitler's lieutenants dispatched trainloads of top-secret documents, art treasures and gold to the region, deeming it safer than Berlin. Many of them found their way to Prague and the German Supreme Commander there, General Frank. With the Allies closing in, Frank picked a hiding spot not far away.

THE TUNNELS OF STECHOVICE

Today a quiet tourist town just 48 km (30 miles) from Prague, Stechovice hid a dark secret during the Second World War. It hosted training grounds for an SS weapons engineering school, together with a network of bunkers and tunnels. To excavate these, a concentration camp had been set up near by. Overseeing this complex was a die-hard Nazi, Emil Klein. On 22 April 1945 Klein was called to Prague to take charge of a consignment of dozens (perhaps hundreds) of crates, which General Frank ordered him to hide in the tunnels of Stechovice.

Left An aerial view of the town of Stechovice, wartime site of an SS weapons engineering school and purported last hiding place for hundreds of crates of looted treasures and top-secret documents.

The end of the war came soon afterwards, and the Americans in particular set about tracking down the Nazi caches of archives and loot, intent both on returning stolen treasures to their owners and on grabbing the fruits of Nazi research projects before the Soviets. In 1946 a captured SS officer in a prisoner-of-war camp revealed to his Allied interrogators the existence of the Stechovice stash, and US military intelligence launched a daring raid into Soviet-controlled territory.

Under the cover that they were retrieving the body of a downed airman, a 12-man team located one of the bunkers, negotiated explosive booby-traps and successfully retrieved 32 crates, which they managed to get across the border to the US-controlled zone of Germany. According to a journalist who was with the recovery team, the contents of the crates included Frank's journals, Gestapo reports, a list of up to 70,000 collaborators among the Czechs and a complete inventory of Czechoslovakian state treasures. The Czech authorities protested and the crates were eventually returned, although it is speculated that some of the most important contents remained in US hands.

The communist authorities then launched searches of their own, until a captured war criminal pointed out that they might turn up more lists of collaborators. Realizing that their names might well be on those lists, top-ranking officials in the new state put a stop to the investigations, which did not resume until the late 1950s.

THE SILENT PRISONER

One man knew exactly where the cache of crates was hidden. Emil Klein was languishing in a Czech jail serving a 20-year sentence, but refused to cooperate despite intimidation, torture and blandishments. Escorted to his former domain and ordered to assist, he would only frustrate his captors by drawing imaginary maps of the maze of tunnels. The authorities hit on a new plan – a young spy was infiltrated to the prison to pose as a fellow anti-communist prisoner and build up a relationship. Helmut Gaensel succeeded in starting a friendship, but Klein was too wily and revealed nothing. Eventually Klein was released and, nearing the end of his life, confided his secret to Gaensel.

Soon afterwards Gaensel left for America to make his fortune, but after the collapse of the Iron Curtain he returned to the Czech Republic and moved to Stechovice. Employing a large team and all the latest technology, he conducted searches at six different locations (some said to be decoys to put off rivals). By 2001 he had found nothing beyond a few pieces of Nazi memorabilia and his attention was diverted by a suggestion that the Amber Room – the greatest single treasure looted during the Second World War (see page 122) – had been secreted near by, and he split his team so that they could join the search for it.

Meanwhile another Czech man, Josef Muzik, has also spent more than 13 years in a hitherto fruitless search for the Stechovice Treasure. Speaking in 2004, he insisted that success was within reach: 'We selected three sites which were remembered by most of the witnesses and mentioned in historic documents. We are hundred per cent convinced that the crates with the Nazi loot are stored there.'

Muzik and Gaensel are convinced that dozens, perhaps even hundreds (Muzik claims 964), of crates await discovery, crammed with important documents such as Nazi atomic secrets, jewellery stolen from victims of the Holocaust and Czech artistic and cultural treasures. Few experts think this is likely; on the other hand, an investigation carried out by the Czech Ministry of Culture in 1994 to determine which looted treasures were still missing found that almost 10,000 objects of cultural value remained unaccounted for.

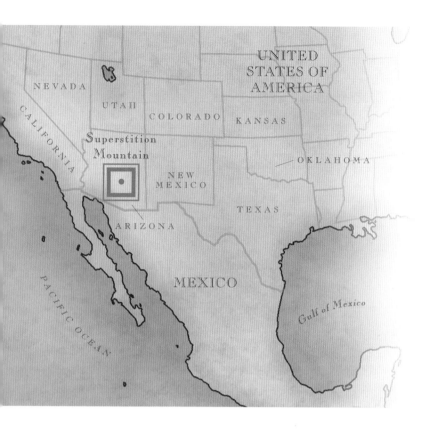

The Lost Dutchman's Gold Mine

At one time the most famous lost treasure in America, the Lost Dutchman's Gold Mine is a legendary lode supposedly located somewhere on Superstition Mountain in the Arizona desert. It features in a romantic tale of prospectors, cowboys and Indians, family feuds and mysterious desert deaths. How much of it is true is open to question.

The story of the Lost Dutchman's Gold Mine is a classic American folk tale; one that has evolved over more than a century to encompass numerous variants, while sucking in other legends so that they become woven into a richer fabric.

THE FULL STORY OF THE OLD DUTCHMAN

According to the most sprawling and lurid version of the tale, the saga begins in 1845 with the arrival of the Peralta family, descendants of the Spanish conquistadors who first came to Arizona in search of gold, at Superstition Mountain. A jagged sawback ridge of rock projecting high above the arid Valley of the Sun in the Arizona desert, Superstition Mountain was sacred to the native Apaches. The Peraltas struck gold, carting away millions of dollars worth, but also fell foul of the Apaches and in 1848 were massacred as they attempted to shift the bulk of their loot to Sonora. The pack mules, laden with heavy bags of gold, fled into the desert to meet their ends – their scattered cargo providing one source of the lost treasure of legend. At this point the Old

Dutchman himself enters the tale. Jacob Waltz (or Walz) was actually German, but the misidentification was common in 19th-century America. Having come to the United States in the 1840s, he joined the Californian gold rush of 1848–9, before turning his hand to homesteading. Having learned the secret of the Peralta mine, either from a descendant of the family or from his Apache wife, he set out into the desert with his partner, another German named Jacob Weiser, sometime in the 1870s. While Waltz returned from this trip laden with several bags of gold, Weiser was less fortunate, meeting a sticky end either at the hands of Native Americans or of Waltz himself.

Waltz made repeated trips to Superstition Mountain, returning each time with a few bags of gold, and his legend spread. Covetous eyes watched him while others pressed him for his secret, but Waltz was curmudgeonly, cagey and dangerous when riled. Two soldiers who claimed to have hit a lode in the area were murdered, and on his deathbed Waltz admitted to having killed his own nephew to preserve his secret. When he died in 1891 he confided the location of

the mine to his nurse, together with a crudely drawn map.

Over the next 50 years hundreds and perhaps even thousands of people attempted to locate the Old Dutchman's mother lode – according to one estimate, up to 8,000 people a year! Some met grisly ends, most notably the treasure hunter Adolph Ruth, who allegedly learned the mine's location from yet another Peralta descendant and arrived in Arizona in 1931, before disappearing into the desert. His skull, pierced by bullet holes, was found six months later. Other prospectors supposedly met similar fates.

TRUE LIES

According to historian Robert Blair, this lurid tale is actually the result of the amalgamation of several different stories, which have been swallowed up by the expanding Dutchman legend. The first element, concerning the Peraltas, involves a real-life gold mine transposed from California to Arizona. Apparently a Peralta family really did operate a mine in the 1860s, but it was in Valanciana, California, not Superstition Mountain, and it

Left *Superstition Mountain, Arizona, sacred peak of the Apache Indians and supposed location of the legendary Lost Dutchman's Mine. Over 900 m (3,000 ft) tall, the mountain is thought to owe its name to settlers who heard tales of spirits and gods from the indigenous people.*

THE ENIGMA OF RUTH'S DEATH

Adolph Ruth really did come to an unfortunate end in the desert, but it seems likely that he died on a wild goose chase. While there are many old gold mines in the region, it is doubtful that the Lost Dutchman's Gold Mine ever actually existed. But Ruth's death, which had many unexplained and suspicious features – such as a note apparently written in his hand claiming to have found the mine and a cover-up by the state authorities who declared him a suicide despite clear evidence to the contrary – became a national sensation. It was this that really led to the tale of the Lost Dutchman's Gold Mine becoming imprinted on the national psyche, and to the apparently unstoppable growth of the legend.

was never massively lucrative. The supposed 'Peralta Massacre' is probably a fiction.

Jacob Waltz probably did exist, as there are records of both his birth in Germany and his arrival in America, but his partner, Weiser, is doubtless a fiction – the result of confusion over Waltz's name. There is no specific evidence of Waltz striking it lucky with a gold mine of any sort, although Blair says it is true that he told a tale of lost mines to his nurse, who subsequently made a few dollars by hawking maps of the alleged mine. Other elements, such as the two dead soldiers, derive from unrelated events and have simply been absorbed into the greater legend.

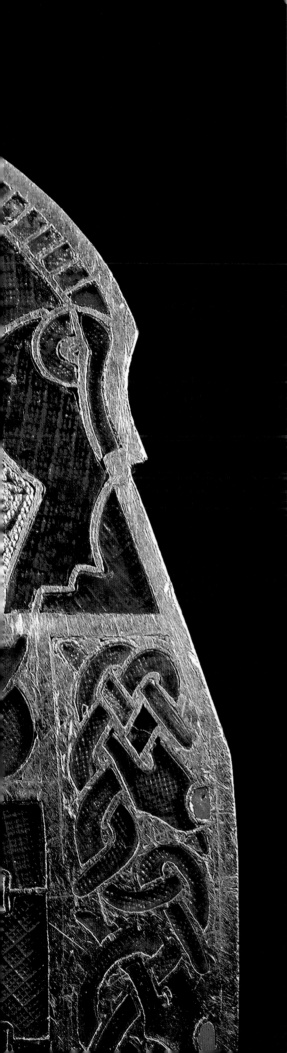

PART 2

ROYAL TREASURES

Kingship concentrated the treasure of the many in the hands of the few, and rulers needed their wealth to pay for armies, fund construction, bestow gifts, pay off enemies and, above all, maintain a suitably regal image. To this end they accumulated beautiful artefacts as well as hard cash and bullion. And because of the prevalent belief that you *could* take it with you, much of this loot was interred along with its royal owner. If it survived the depredations of looters, there was a chance it might be rediscovered centuries later. Many of the treasures in this section are royal grave goods, but some fall into the more rare category of treasures misplaced or stolen. Royal treasures can be both more interesting and more valuable than other treasures because they can be tied to a particular and significant person. Knowing who the owner of a treasure was, and his or her history, lends romance and intrigue. For the archeologist and historian the relationship often works the other way round – treasures can provide the primary source of evidence about the owner and his or her life.

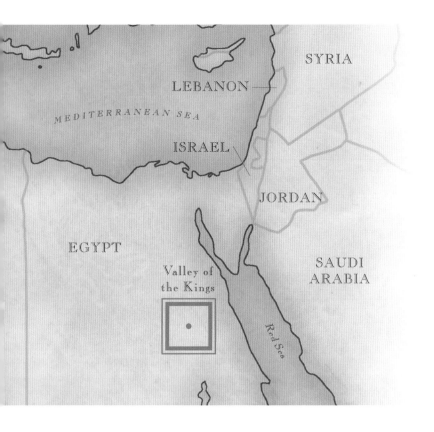

Tutankhamun: treasures of the boy-king

The story of Tutankhamun (ruled 1333–1324 BCE) is one of tragedy and glory: the sad tale of a boy-king whose early and untimely death wrenched him from the arms of his beloved and relegated him to a commoner's tomb, but who was to become the most famous of all pharaohs, thanks to the fabulous riches interred along with his mummy, the exciting tale of their discovery and the global interest they sparked.

For the ancient Egyptians he was a minor pharaoh at best, a mere footnote to those who came before and after him, but in modern times Tutankhamun and his tomb treasure completely changed the relationship between history, museums and the public. His glorious death-mask has become possibly the single most iconic image of ancient Egypt and is arguably the most valuable ancient artefact of all time.

GOLDEN BOY

Tutankhamun came to the throne in the midst of a turbulent period of Egyptian history. The pharaoh Akhenaten (ruled c.1353–1336 BCE) had overturned centuries of tradition by replacing the polytheism of ancient Egypt with a form of monotheism, making the worship of a previously minor sun-god, Aten, the state religion in what historians call the Amarna revolution. Towards the end of his reign Akhenaten had co-ruled with the pharaoh Smenkhkare, who had then briefly ruled as sole monarch, but on his death in 1333 BCE the young Tutankhaten, as he was then known, came to the throne.

Tutankhaten's parentage is the topic of much debate, but it is thought likely that he was either the son of Akhenaten or of Akhenaten's father, the pharaoh Amenhotep III. When he acceded to the throne he was a child of around eight, and probably little more than a puppet for his vizier and regent, Ay. During his short reign, Ay and other traditionalists used Tutankhaten to steer Egypt back to its old ways, restoring the polytheism (belief in more than one god) of their forefathers and erasing the cult of Aten. Accordingly, the boy-king's name was changed to Tutankhamun, the heretical 'Aten' replaced with 'Amun', a much older and more traditional sun-god.

Tutankhamun was married to his sister, Ankhesenamun. One of the most touching features of the treasure of Tutankhamun is the emphasis on the relationship between the young monarchs, with many scenes of love, romance and tenderness depicted on panels on thrones, shrines and other items. Other scenes from his sarcophagus suggest that Tutankhamun also enjoyed more masculine pursuits, including hunting, charioteering and waging war.

THE CURSE OF TUTANKHAMUN

One of the elements that fired the public imagination was the supposed curse upon those who dared to disturb the ancient tomb, which gained credence when Lord Carnarvon, the sponsor of the excavations, died not long after the opening of the tomb. In practice, however, the curse was a fiction initiated by Gothic novelist Marie Corelli and stoked by the press, and Carnarvon's premature death was caused by an infected mosquito bite. The man who first entered the tomb, archeologist Howard Carter, lived for several more decades, and analysis shows that the mortality rate among those involved with the discovery was entirely average.

Above The famous golden funerary mask of Tutankhamun. On his brow are the heads of the vulture (with a beak made of glass), symbolizing his lordship over Upper Egypt, and the cobra, symbolizing Lower Egypt.

prompted speculation that he had been murdered, with a blow to the head. However, more recent investigations (involving CT scans taken in 2005) found no evidence of a blow to the head, and suggested that the cause of death was a broken leg that swiftly, perhaps over just a few days, became fatally infected with gangrene. The break itself could easily have resulted from an accident, perhaps a fall from a horse, perhaps while on campaign.

TOMB KV-62

It was Tutankhamun's early and sudden death that indirectly led to his tomb surviving more or less intact until the modern day. Most pharaohs lavished time and attention on preparing grand tombs for themselves, but when Tutankhamun died these preparations had barely begun and a hasty compromise was reached. He was interred in a relatively humble tomb probably intended for a private individual rather than royalty.

The tomb in question, designated KV-62 in the official classification, is now the most famous of all ancient Egyptian tombs, if not the most famous in the world. It is located in the Valley of the Kings, in the main wadi of the East Valley. Its minor status meant that it was not treated with the same respect as more significant tombs and the entry ramp leading to KV-9, the tomb of the later pharaoh Rameses VI, was cut into the valley directly above the stairway leading down to KV-62. The rock-chippings from the newer construction soon filled up the stairway and its location was obscured and then forgotten. Eventually workmen's huts were built on top of the entrance and it was lost to history for more than 3,000 years.

However, it is not entirely accurate to say that it was never disturbed. The evidence from the seals on the plastered-over doorways of KV-62, and from the state of the contents, show that it was raided at least twice soon after Tutankhamun's burial. Thieves broke in and stole easily portable loot, spilling the contents of chests in their haste and greed. The sentinels of the Valley of the Kings necropolis hastily repacked the chests, but discrepancies between their contents and the inventories listed on the outsides show what happened.

CAUSE OF DEATH

It was immediately apparent to the discoverers of Tutankhamun's tomb that he had died young. Analysis of the mummy suggested that his age at death was around 19. Ancient Egyptian records place the end of his reign in the year 1324 BCE, and show that he was succeeded by his vizier Ay. This suggests the scenario that Ay, unhappy that his previously pliant puppet was starting to assert his independence as he grew to manhood, had him killed. When X-ray analysis of Tutankhamun's mummy was first attempted in the 1960s and 1970s, shadows on the skull

The tomb of Tutankhamun

When all others thought the Valley of Kings was exhausted, one man persevered and was rewarded beyond his wildest imaginings. From ornately decorated furniture and ancient board games to priceless golden shrines and the peerless funeral mask, not to mention a variety of artefacts intended to equip the dead king for his afterlife in the netherworld, Tutankhamun's tomb offered a trove of breathtaking quantity and quality.

British archeologist Howard Carter had served a long apprenticeship at various excavations and projects in Egypt. In 1907 he secured the patronage of Lord Carnarvon and turned his attentions to searching for the tomb of a minor pharaoh, Tutankhamun, whose existence had been uncovered by one of Carter's mentors, the Egyptologist Theodore M. Davis. Davis considered that Tutankhamun's resting place had already been discovered (owing to the discovery of funerary equipment bearing his cartouche in tomb KV-54, now thought to be a cache where necropolis officials stored materials found blocking the entrance to KV-62 after it had been looted). Indeed he wrote that the Valley of Kings was 'exhausted' – there was nothing more to find there. Carter disagreed, although it took 15 years of hard graft until, with his patron about to cut off his funding and in his last season of excavation, his workers uncovered the top of a flight of rock-cut stairs.

'WONDERFUL THINGS'

By the end of the next day the doorway at the bottom of the steps had been found and Carter was able to cable his patron with news of 'A magnificent tomb with seals intact'. Carnarvon arrived a few weeks later and Carter was able to show him the name of Tutankhamun on the sealed entrance to the chamber. Over the next few days the outer doorway was unblocked and, on 26 November 1907, it fell to Carter to break through to what appeared to be a uniquely undisturbed royal tomb. His diary records the climactic events of that day:

It was the day of days. The most wonderful I have ever lived through … With trembling hands I made a tiny breach in the upper left hand corner … widening the hole a little I inserted the candle and peered in … at first I could see nothing, the hot air escaping from the chamber causing the candle to flicker. Presently details of the room emerged slowly from the mist, strange animals, statues and gold – everywhere the glint of gold.

For a moment – an eternity it must have seemed to the others – I was struck dumb with amazement, and when Lord Carnarvon, unable to stand the suspense any longer, inquired anxiously, 'Can you see anything?' it was all I could do to get out the words, 'Yes, wonderful things.'

Over the next few years Carter and his team painstakingly removed and catalogued more than 3,000 objects, many of them either covered in or made of gold.

① CORRIDOR AND SEALED DOORWAYS

When the tomb was ready, the mummy had been laid to rest and all the ceremonies were completed, the ancient Egyptians would seal each doorway in the tomb with plaster. The plaster would be marked with the seals and cartouches of the interred king and of the officials responsible for the works, and these seals provide valuable information about the date of the interment and subsequent raids on the tomb.

② ANTECHAMBER

This was the room into which Carter gazed, prompting his description of 'wonderful things'. The Egyptians believed that you could take your possessions with you, and that objects interred with the dead could be used by them in the afterlife. Accordingly this room was piled high with a variety of ceremonial and practical objects. There were couches and beds, including a folding one such as those taken on campaign and a more ornate one made of gilded wood with a strung base, a footboard and legs carved in feline form. Mummified animal offerings were stacked under one couch. Against one wall were partially disassembled chariots. Statues of the king in various costumes and guises were believed to help protect and guide him – they were known as *Ushabti* figures. The contents of the room were in disarray, probably thanks to the hasty original burial and subsequent clear-ups after looting, but they were also so perfectly preserved that when Carter entered he was able to photograph garlands of flowers, which disintegrated when touched. A smaller room off the antechamber was designated 'the annex' and was filled with more grave goods, piled high and haphazardly, possibly reflecting how the sudden nature of Tutankhamun's death had left little time to prepare.

③ BURIAL CHAMBER

This room was the only one in the tomb that was decorated – painted with scenes from the Book of the Dead showing the pharaoh's voyage to the afterworld. Again, the lack of decoration in the tomb as a whole provides a conspicuous contrast with other royal tombs. The burial chamber was dominated by a huge golden shrine (actually four nested shrines) containing nested sarcophagi. Other treasures found in this chamber include exquisite calcite lamps. One particularly well-known lamp is carved in the form of a lotus flower and was intended to be filled with sesame oil and a floating wick. When this was lit, the light would radiate out through the thin walls of the lamp, making visible a scene painted on the inside that shows Tutankhamun with his wife.

④ SARCOPHAGUS AND COFFINS

The outer sarcophagus is made of red quartzite. Inside are three more coffins. The intermediate coffin is of gilded, laminated wood with inlays of glass paste and the depiction of its occupant is different from the other images of Tutankhamun in the tomb, leading to speculation that it had been intended for someone else. The inner coffin is made of solid gold and contained the mummy of Tutankhamun. The mummy itself was wrapped in bandages, among which were interleaved many amulets and ornaments. Sadly, in their impatience to get hold of these, the archeologists dismembered the mummy, chopping off the head and limbs.

⑤ THE GOLDEN FUNERARY MASK

Lying on the face of the mummy was the incredible golden funerary mask. It was made from two sheets of gold, beaten and moulded into an actual (albeit slightly stylized) portrait of Tutankhamun, accurate enough that even today it is possible to spot the family resemblance to Queen Tiye, probably his grandmother and certainly a close relative. The gold is decorated with semi-precious stones, bits of glass and bands of glass paste, and the eyes are made from quartz and obsidian, outlined with lapis lazuli to give the effect of kohl eyeliner.

⑥ THE TREASURY

Carter called this room the treasury because it contained the richest of the treasures. Chests of jewellery jostled for space with models of barges of the type used to transport goods to and fro across the Nile. Elsewhere in the tomb were three exquisite models of luxury 'royal yachts'. In total there were more than 30 model boats in the tomb. Also in the treasury was the canopic shrine, containing the canopic chest – where the king's internal organs were stored in four compartments. The chest was carved from a single block of calcite and the compartments were stoppered with elaborately carved calcite busts of the king.

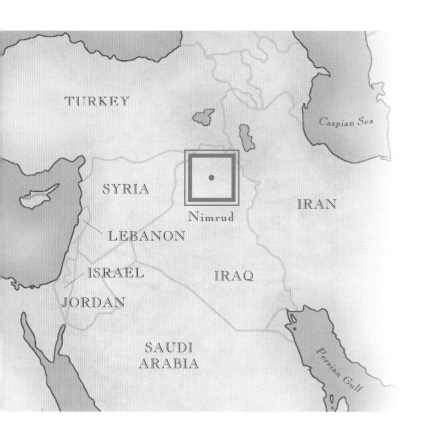

The treasures
of Nimrud

In 1988 a sharp-eyed Iraqi defied an ancient curse to unearth a treasure that had evaded looters and archeologists for 2,800 years; a treasure as great as any the pharaohs of Egypt could muster. But the war in Iraq and its aftermath threatened to do what the invading empires of old could not, until a mysterious flood seemed to have saved the treasure.

The ancient city of Nimrud, known in the Bible as Calah and to its inhabitants as Kalhu, was one of the capitals of the Assyrian Empire. Here on the banks of the River Tigris, near the modern-day city of Mosul, King Assurnasirpal II (ruled 883–859 BCE) constructed a vast palace – a monument to his glory and an edifice to awe the conquered peoples who had been transplanted to Nimrud. The Assyrians were infamous for their harsh treatment of enemies and extracting heavy tribute. They carried off both the loot of conquered nations and many of their finest craftsmen, for along with their bloodlust they also harboured a surprisingly refined taste in jewellery and ornamentation, combining aesthetic influences from conquered and neighbouring territories.

THE UNEVEN FLOOR

We know of this unexpectedly soft side to the Assyrians mainly thanks to a single discovery, which revealed one of the great treasures of antiquity. In the south wing of Assurnasirpal's palace, in a room that may have been part of the royal harem, the emperor and his successors interred a series of noble corpses,

starting with his own queen, Mullissu-mukannishat Ninua. In vaulted chambers beneath the harem chamber these people were buried along with rich grave goods, including gold and silver jewellery and ornaments, bowls, bottles, ivory plaques and boxes, mirrors and other treasures.

These burial chambers remained undisturbed (although part of one was partially looted in ancient times) as the

Above *The courtyard of the palace of Assurnasirpal II at Nimrud, constructed c.880 BCE. Nimrud is the name given to the city of Kalhu by the Arabs, who associated it with the biblical hunter Nimrod.*

Assyrian Empire waxed and waned, through the decline of Nimrud as the capital was shifted to Khorsabad, and through the Babylonian-Median conquest, which saw armies pillage and raze the city in 612 BCE. They went unnoticed by Alexander the Great, who partially rebuilt the city, and resisted the attentions of a stream of archeologists and excavations from the 19th century onwards, which cleared away the dirt of millennia and revealed the palace floor plan. Only in 1988 did Iraqi archeologist Sayid Muzahim Mahmud Hussein notice that the tiled floor of one of the rooms in the women's quarters was uneven, prompting him to start digging.

QUEEN YABA'S CURSE

Over the next two years four tombs were discovered. The first was the grave of a woman, her skull cradled in a silver bowl and her skeleton festooned with ornate golden jewellery. The second yielded a huge quantity of treasure: 14 kg (31 lb) of gold, along with a funerary tablet naming the main occupant as Queen Yaba, and calling down a curse upon any who should disturb the tomb, that the gods condemn his spirit to wander the Earth for eternity. When the archeologists broke open the sarcophagus, they discovered inside two skeletons and 157 items of gold. The third tomb, that of Queen Mullissu, was richer still, with an antechamber stuffed with 450 items of gold and silver weighing more than 22 kg (50 lb).

The haul was removed to Baghdad where highlights were briefly displayed at the National Museum before Saddam Hussein invaded Kuwait in 1990. With war and the threat of bombing, the treasure was packed up and bundled off to the vaults of the central bank for safekeeping. Here it stayed until the American-led invasion of Iraq in 2003, when it was feared that the treasure would prove to be one of the casualties of war.

THE FLOODED VAULT

The rapid collapse of Saddam Hussein's regime led to looting on a massive scale, and at first it was thought that the US failure to protect the National Museum in Baghdad had led to the disappearance of tens of

Right *Carved ivory depicting a woman at a window found by Henry Layard in the north-west palace of Assurnasirpal II at Nimrud. It is thought that she is a sacred prostitute, connected with Astarte or Ishtar, goddess of fertility.*

thousands of priceless artefacts, the Nimrud treasures among them. In fact it turned out that far-sighted curators had removed many of the artefacts before the invasion, while the Nimrud treasures had been locked in their vault all along. It transpired that they had also survived the attentions of Saddam's son, Qusay, who had visited the vaults to steal hundreds of millions of dollars in cash and gold bars, and a direct hit from an American missile that had partially ruined the building.

When the US Army eventually sent a tank to the central bank building, they discovered that looters had been making concerted efforts to break in, some of them shooting each other and one man killing himself by firing a rocket-propelled grenade at the main doors to the vaults from 3 m (10 ft) away.

Those who had managed to penetrate inside were frustrated because the vaults were flooded with more than 2 million litres (½ million gallons) of water. Ostensibly this came from a burst pipe, but it is suspected that curators or bank officials deliberately triggered the flooding to help protect the contents of the vault. When a team with the National Geographic Society finally pumped out all the water, it discovered the Nimrud treasures, intact and unharmed.

As with the Bactrian Hoard of Afghanistan (see page 14), the question now is if and when the Iraqi people will finally get to see their heritage. In fact it is entirely possible that the Nimrud treasures have finally fallen into the hands of looters, after evading them for three millennia.

Troy and King Priam's Treasure: the discovery

One of the best-known archeological finds of all time was the successful location of what was thought to be a mythical city – the Troy of Homer's epics. What made it especially significant and famous was the discovery at the site of an incredible treasure, which would change archeology for ever.

From Elizabethan times until relatively recently, any Westerner with a decent education would have been intimately familiar with Homer's epic poems, the *Iliad* and the *Odyssey*, just as the ancient Greeks and Romans were. These tales of Troy, the great city-state of Asia Minor – of how Paris, Prince of Troy, stole Helen, the most beautiful woman in the world, triggering a war with the Greeks that would end with the ruse of the wooden horse – were as well known as the most popular fairy tales or Bible stories. But while the Greeks and Romans had assumed that the tale was actual history, by the 19th century it was common knowledge that they were just myths. The chronology of Homer and his tale placed the events in the 13th century BCE, but there was no evidence that ancient Greek civilization predated the 8th century BCE, let alone the High Bronze Age magnificence of the *Iliad*, with its enormous armies, great fleets of ships and towering city walls enclosing palaces of great wealth.

Along with scepticism about the historicity of the Troy of Homer, there was ignorance of its location. The site of the city had been

known to the ancient Greeks and Romans; the latter had founded a new city there, called New Ilium (the Roman name for Troy), but this had declined in Byzantine times and passed out of memory. Heinrich Schliemann, however, was convinced that Homer's epics were based in real history and, according to his own account, he had been determined since childhood to rediscover Troy.

THE MOUND OF HISSARLIK

Homer's epics are sometimes quite precise in their descriptions of geography, and Schliemann followed his *Iliad* to a great mound known as Hissarlik, which had previously been suggested as the possible site of the real Troy. The German decided that its location matched Homer's description and set about obtaining the permission he needed from the Ottoman authorities to start excavating. He even moved to the United States for a year to obtain American

citizenship in an effort to speed up the process, while also finding time to marry a young Greek woman named Sophia.

In 1870 he launched his excavations, quickly uncovering huge stone walls beneath the dirt of the mound. The next year, impatient with the normal slow, patient procedures of professional archeologists, he ordered his workmen to dig a deep trench right across the mound at Hissarlik, which proved to be a great Tell – a hill created by the construction of settlements on one site in successive eras, with each new settlement building over the remains of the previous one. Schliemann discovered that there had been many different periods of occupancy of the site, but his brutal methods did tremendous damage to it. One of the greatest ironies was that, believing that the Troy of the *Iliad* must lie near the lowest and earliest levels, Schliemann actually dug straight through the actual home of Paris and Priam, the King of Troy in the epics (see page 68).

Left A woodcut showing Heinrich Schliemann's excavations at Troy in 1882, with the massive walls of the south-east gate in the foreground.

CUTTING OUT THE TREASURE

The most exciting phase of the excavation came in 1873, shortly after the workmen had uncovered the remains of a great building that Schliemann interpreted as Priam's palace. On 31 May, Schliemann would later claim:

> *I came upon a large copper article of the most remarkable form, which attracted my attention all the more as I thought I saw gold behind it … In order to withdraw the treasure from the greed of my workmen, and to save it for archeology … I immediately had 'paidos' (lunch break) called … While the men were eating and resting, I cut out the Treasure with a large knife … It would, however, have been impossible for me to have removed the Treasure without the help of my dear wife, who stood by me ready to pack the things which I cut out in her shawl and to carry them away.*

Schliemann claimed that this single cache included almost 9,000 golden artefacts, including fabulous headdresses and other jewellery. It was, he declared, the treasure of King Priam himself.

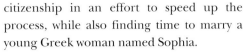

HEINRICH SCHLIEMANN

Schliemann was a German businessman and enthusiast for all things Classical, in particular the works of Homer. He became an amateur archeologist with impressive success, but questionable methods. A complex and divisive figure, he was impulsive and passionate; a self-publicist who has been accused of creativity with the truth. Born in Germany in 1822, Schliemann endured a difficult childhood thanks to an indigent and alcoholic father, who nevertheless managed to give his son a taste for ancient history. Schliemann claimed that his interest in Troy was triggered at the age of seven, when his father gave him a book with a picture of the main gate in flames.

Forced to work from an early age, Schliemann laboured as a servant and survived a shipwreck before finding employment with a shipping firm and going on to make a fortune trading in commodities and war supplies in Russia and America. In 1868 he toured Greece and Asia Minor (Turkey) and was inspired to retire from business and take up archeology, using Homer as his guide. His first foray was on Ithaca, supposed home of Odysseus (although convincing recent research suggests that the ancient Ithaca was actually another island altogether), where his cursory excavations revealed two jars of ashes that Schliemann fondly imagined were the remains of Odysseus and his wife Penelope, demonstrating the lack of academic rigour that would mark and mar his archeological findings elsewhere.

Troy and King Priam's Treasure

The story of Heinrich Schliemann and his discoveries at Troy changed the way the world looked at archeology, paving the way for everything from King Tut to Indiana Jones. At the heart of this story is a great treasure, which stirred controversy and debate when it was discovered, vanished again amid the fog of war and then reappeared to ignite a new series of rows.

Above *Sophia Schliemann wearing some of Priam's Treasure. Schliemann had created the necklace from hundreds of loose gold beads he had discovered at Troy.*

In 1874 Schliemann revealed the existence of Priam's Treasure to an astonished world, displaying some of it in photographs showing his wife modelling the jewellery (see left). His discovery captured headlines around the world – it was the first time an archeologist had found actual treasure and it changed the way people thought about the discipline, adding new tinges of excitement and romance to a dry profession. Here, Schliemann claimed, was exotic and ancient treasure from the pages of Homer, possibly the crown jewels of the last King of Troy.

BEFORE THE TROY OF PRIAM

In practice Schliemann was undone by his sloppy archeology. The layer he had plunged down to, known as Troy II because it represents the second major phase of occupation on the site, actually dates from the early Bronze Age, around the mid-3rd millennium BCE, about a thousand years before the Troy of Priam. At this time Troy was based around a small but heavily fortified citadel 100 m (330 ft) across, the inhabitants of which evidently included nobility of great wealth, probably founded on a flourishing textile industry and the control of lucrative trade routes. Troy II met its end in flames and the layer of ash this left convinced

Schliemann that he had found the Troy of Homer, the fiery end of which had made such an impression on his youthful mind.

If Priam really did exist at the period Homer described, he would have lived in one of the higher layers. For many years it was thought this was probably Troy VI, a huge citadel with massive stone walls over 4 m (13 ft) thick, which was occupied between around 1800 and 1300 BCE. But the evidence is that Troy VI was destroyed by earthquake, not fire or war, and that the inhabitants had probably managed an orderly evacuation, again not concomitant with war. On the other hand the next layer, Troy VIIa, does contain evidence of a siege and a fire, and also dates to the correct time. At this point Troy had been haphazardly reoccupied and partially rebuilt, but was a much less powerful and impressive city. No treasure has been recovered from this layer, and if Priam was indeed king, he may have been too poor to afford any.

THE BATTLE FOR THE TROJAN GOLD

After Schliemann spirited the Treasure back to his tent – allegedly with the help of his wife's skirt – he then illegally smuggled it out of the country to Greece, intending to render the treasures to the Greek government rather than to the Turks, who were legally entitled to half the finds. The Turks were outraged, and the Greeks were intimidated into refusing the gift. Eventually Schliemann sent most of it to Berlin to be exhibited in museums there.

There it remained until the Second World War. As the Red Army advanced on Berlin, Priam's Treasure (as it is still known today, although even Schliemann himself eventually accepted that it was far too old to have belonged to the Iliadic king) was stored in the massive command bunker under Zoo Station, but after the fall of Berlin it mysteriously vanished. The Soviets denied any knowledge of it, and it was widely assumed that it had been looted and probably melted down, the only evidence of it ever having existed being the photos that were taken of Sophia Schliemann draped in ancient jewels.

Trésor de Priam découvert à 8½ mètres de profondeur

Left *Schliemann presented what he termed Priam's Treasure to the world after smuggling it out of Turkey. In practice it came from the early Bronze Age phase of occupation known as Troy II and may not have been found as a single cache, contrary to Schliemann's claims.*

'After Schliemann spirited the Treasure back to his tent – allegedly with the help of his wife's skirt – he then illegally smuggled it out of the country to Greece.'

After the collapse of communism, however, the Russians began to come clean about a number of treasures looted during the war and carried back to Moscow and St Petersburg. In 1993 it was revealed that the largely intact Treasure was being held at the Pushkin Museum in Moscow, and it was put on show there in 1996. Currently the Russian, German, Greek and Turkish governments are locked in dispute over its ownership.

Controversy has also arisen over Schliemann's original account of finding the Treasure. Close examination of his diaries has proven that his wife Sophia was not at Hissarlik on the day in question and so she cannot have smuggled the treasure off the site in her skirt. In fact it is now suspected that, far from finding all the Treasure as a single cache, Schliemann combined different finds from different layers and locations on the mound.

The Mask of Agamemnon

Not content with discovering Troy (see page 66), Heinrich Schliemann followed the trail of his Homeric heroes back to Greece and determined to excavate the treasures of the greatest king of the epic era: Agamemnon of the Atreids, who led the Greek forces at Troy and whose palace would hold the key to an entire civilization.

Agamemnon was a mythic hero of the Greeks who features heavily in Homer. He was King of Mycenae and had extended his influence over much of Greece when called upon to assist his brother in recovering Helen and conquering Troy. On his return home he and his companions were murdered by his faithless wife and her lover. For the ancients there was little doubt that Agamemnon was a real person, but in the absence of solid archeological evidence specifically naming him, today it is considered more likely that he is a legendary character, perhaps based on oral traditions of genuine chiefs and kings lost in the mists of prehistory.

THE CITADEL OF MYCENAE

Sitting atop a hilltop commanding the plain of Argos in the Peloponnese, are the ruins of the ancient citadel of Mycenae. According to the ancient geographer Pausanias, this had been the palace of Agamemnon and was the location of his grave and those of his companions. Flushed with success from his triumph at Troy, but *persona non grata* in Turkey thanks to

his shady dealings over Priam's Treasure, Schliemann decided that he would now discover the greatest king of antiquity. As at Troy, however, his expectations and assumptions would threaten to overwhelm his shaky scholarship.

Previous scholars had interpreted Pausanias to mean that Agamemnon's grave would lie outside the citadel, but Schliemann demurred and in 1874 conducted test digs within the walls. The discovery of a tombstone and terracotta artefacts was encouraging, and in 1876 he returned to excavate the site on behalf of the Greek government, who, aware of his reputation, assigned Greek archeologist Panagiotis Stamatakis to supervise him. Over the course of a five-month dig the two were to clash over what Stamatakis perceived as Schliemann's cavalier disregard for Classical antiquities in his enthusiasm to discover Homeric remains, while Schliemann constantly chafed at the official bit.

Nonetheless, Schliemann's remarkable luck continued. By the end of August he had located a ring of *stelae*, or stone slabs, just within the citadel's Lion Gate, which marked

the perimeter of a grave circle. This proved to contain a series of shaft graves dating from the late Bronze Age – just the period that Schliemann was looking for. As the dig progressed, he made a series of remarkable discoveries. Interred in the shafts were the bodies of warrior princes, laden with treasure, in particular spectacular golden funerary masks.

'I HAVE GAZED UPON THE FACE OF AGAMEMNON'

The most spectacular of all was the mask from grave V, which proved to be wonderfully detailed and full of character, with a long, straight nose, curling moustache and a neat beard. The face conformed to all Schliemann's preconceptions about what a Homeric hero should look like and perhaps inevitably it was hailed as the death-mask of Agamemnon himself. According to popular legend, Schliemann telegrammed the King of Greece with the memorable boast: 'I have gazed upon the face of Agamemnon.' In practice this tale is apocryphal, but Schliemann did send a telegram along similar lines:

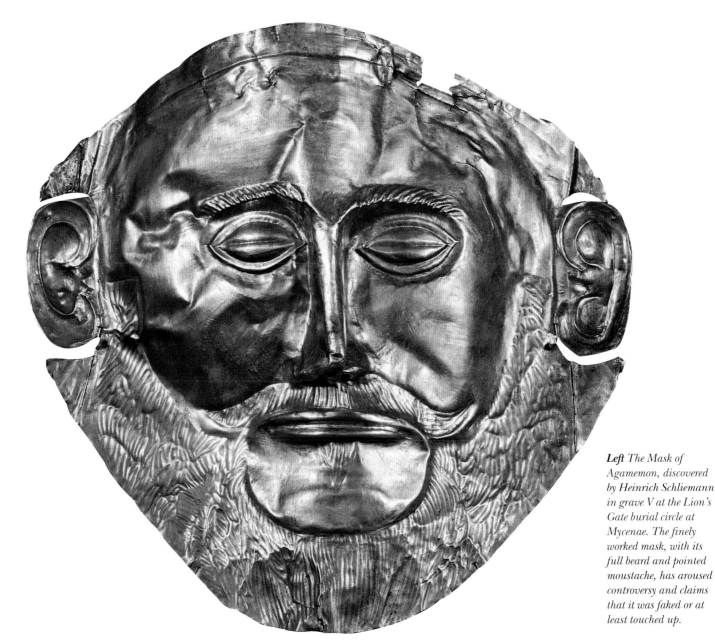

With great joy I announce to Your Majesty that I have discovered the tombs which the tradition proclaimed by Pausanias indicates to be the graves of Agamemnon, Cassandra, Eurymedon and their companions, all slain at a banquet by Clytemnestra and her lover Aegisthos.

A NEW CIVILIZATION

In fact it seems probable that Schliemann had misjudged the age of his finds. The graves he had discovered dated back to around 1600 BCE, around 400 years before the time of Agamemnon, and revealed the existence of a major Bronze Age civilization, now known as the Mycenaeans, after the site excavated by Schliemann. The Mycenaeans were the dominant power in the Aegean between 1600

and around 1100 BCE, with the first writing and other elements of high civilization in Greece. Whether or not Agamemnon and the other Homeric heroes were genuine historical figures, it seems likely that the epics evolved from oral traditions about Mycenaean heroes and exploits.

SCHLIEMANN THE SWINDLER

Recently, increasing doubts about the probity of Schliemann's archeology have led to a debate over the authenticity of the Mask of Agamemnon. Writing in the journal *Archeology*, historian William Calder marshals circumstantial evidence that it is a fake. He points out that it is stylistically different from the other masks discovered at Mycenae, with features that conveniently conform to then-

current conceptions of what a royal hero should look like, with the unusual facial hair in particular mimicking that of Germany's Hohenzollern rulers. Calder also cites the widespread suspicions that Schliemann would 'salt' his sites to provide spectacular finds that would mark the climax of a dig. He was referred to by Ernst Curtius, director of the excavations at Olympia and professor of ancient history at Berlin, as a 'swindler and con-man'. Schliemann's defenders point out that there is no concrete proof of any of this, and that Agamemnon's mask does bear strong similarities to other treasures recovered at the site. An alternative suggestion is that the mask is genuine, but was 'enhanced' by the addition of facial hair after its excavation, to produce a more impressive find.

The Pereshchepina Treasure

When a shepherd boy playing on the beach found himself stuck in the sand, he could little have realized that he had stumbled upon the colossal treasure of a long-dead khan – a collection of magnificent grave goods that bears testament both to a revered ruler and to an ancient friendship with a Byzantine emperor.

Ukraine, in the summer of 1912, and four shepherd boys are playing on a small beach on the banks of the River Vorskla, near the village of Malaya Pereshchepino (near the modern-day city of Poltava). One of them suddenly drops up to his waist in the sand, and when nearby peasants help to dig him out, they realize he is up to his waist in a large golden vessel. Digging further, they start to uncover a massive trove of gold and silver. The authorities soon get wind of the find and archeologists led by the high-ranking noble and descendant of Catherine the Great, Count Aleksey Alexandrovich Bobrinsky, descend on the village, backed by police.

Under Bobrinsky's supervision, the rest of the hoard is excavated and carried back to Kiev, from where it will later be transferred to the Hermitage in St Petersburg. There prove to be more than 800 different items. There are 16 vessels of gold and 19 of silver; two gold rhytons (drinking/pouring vessels); gold plating from a wooden jug; a staff covered in gold; an iron sword with a scabbard, hilt and crossguard of gold; other weapons; gold and silver buckles; a range of golden jewellery, all finely worked and some encrusted with

precious stones; golden plaques and coins, including a necklace of coins; and rings of gold. In all there is more than 25 kg (55 lb) of gold and more than 50 kg (110 lb) of silver.

IMPERIAL FRIENDS

Obviously this was a treasure trove befitting royalty, probably representing grave goods buried alongside a powerful king. Clues from the coins and the styles of decoration and jewellery suggested that it dated from the Age of the Great Migrations, or *Völkerwanderung* (see page 31); but when and to whom did it belong? Unusually for ancient hoards, it was possible to attribute this find to a specific person, one of the leaders of late antiquity. One of the golden rings bore the inscription *Chouvr(a)Tou patr(i)k(iou)* – 'Kubrat, Patrician'. It marked the grave as the tomb of Khan

Kubrat, an important chieftain of the early Bulgars, the founder of Old Great Bulgaria and a Patrician of the Byzantine Empire.

Kubrat (who was known by other names, including Kuvrat, Houvrat, Kurt and, by the Byzantines, as Quetrades) was born around the start of the 7th century CE. This was a period of complex and shifting territories and tribes in the region to the north of the Byzantine Empire, as waves of migrating tribes pushed others westwards. Groups such as the Avars, Huns, Croats, Slavs, Turks and Bulgars were on the move or battling for control of territories from Eastern Europe to the Aral Sea. Meanwhile, to the south of these nomadic groups, mighty empires such as the Byzantines and Sassanians contended for control of Asia Minor, the Levant and the Middle East and North Africa. Alliances

'This was a treasure trove befitting royalty, probably representing grave goods buried alongside a powerful king.'

with the groups to the north were important, and there was a complex relationship between the ancient imperium based in Constantinople and the 'barbarian' peoples beyond the borders.

Kubrat's uncle, Organa, had sent him to the court at Constantinople as a boy – possibly as a hostage, possibly in order to protect him from dynastic struggles in his homeland – and the young Bulgar had been baptized and brought up in the palace. Here he received a Roman education and became a close friend of the emperor Heraclius (ruled 610–641 CE), eventually being awarded the title of 'Patrician' – one of the highest honorifics the empire could bestow.

Around 628 CE Kubrat returned to his people, the Hunogunduri Bulgars, who were at the time vassals of the Avars. Taking over from Organa, Kubrat expelled the Avars and united the Bulgar tribes into a single confederacy, known as Old Great Bulgaria. A firm ally of the Byzantines, Kubrat ruled over a realm stretching from the Danube delta to the Volga, and his kingdom was officially recognized by a treaty of 635. When he died after a 30-year reign his sons buried him with the rich grave goods befitting his status.

HIGHLIGHTS OF THE HOARD

Many of the pieces are of Byzantine origin, and may well have been awarded to Kubrat as gifts from the Byzantine emperor, perhaps even from his friend Heraclius. For instance, the splendid iron sword with its hilt of gold surmounted by a ring, was probably made in a workshop that specialized in producing objects for the nobility of the nomadic peoples, to be given as gifts/diplomatic presents. Greek letters scratched on its hilt point to a Byzantine origin, while the crosses inscribed on it mark it as belonging to the Christian Kubrat. Other highlights include a goblet with a bulbous stem, which is hollow and contains a bell, so that it rings as it is used (probably to help scare off evil spirits); and a silver ladle and pitcher bearing the monogram of the Byzantine emperor Mauritius Tiberius (ruled 582–602), and thought to have been part of a diplomatic gift presented to Kubrat's uncle Organa.

Below A magnificent golden-hilted sword and matching sheath, from the Pereshchepina Treasure. Greek letters on the hilt suggest the sword was made in a Byzantine workshop, perhaps as a gift from the Byzantine emperor Heraclius to his friend the khan.

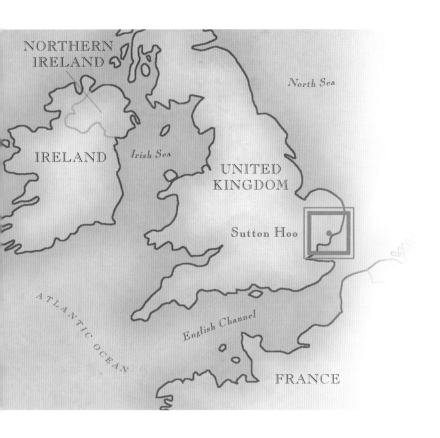

Sutton Hoo: the haunted mound

The greatest treasure of the Dark Ages – perhaps of any age – discovered in Britain was preserved against all the odds from centuries of grave robbers and was finally located thanks to the curiosity of a middle-aged lady, who may have had help from the spirit world.

Left *The burial mounds at Sutton Hoo. In addition to the great ship-burial of Mound 1, there are about 20 other burial mounds, containing cremation burials and grave goods, execution victims, a much smaller ship-burial, and even a young man buried with his horse.*

Near the village of Sutton in East Anglia, a spur, or 'hoo', of land rises above the River Deben. Here atop Sutton Hoo a series of burial mounds looks across the river to the harbour of Woodbridge, a little way inland from the North Sea, an area that in late Roman and early medieval times (or the Dark Ages) was one of the centres of the Anglo-Saxon world. In the 1930s the mounds were a well-worn and familiar part of the local landscape, but to Mrs Edith Pretty, the woman who owned the land upon which they stood, the barrows were a source of fascination and mystery. She might have known of local legends that spoke of buried treasure – folk tales possibly derived from local memory of the many intrusions and pits dug by grave robbers and tomb raiders over the centuries. Or perhaps her interest was piqued by something stranger?

BASIL BROWN INVESTIGATES

Mrs Pretty decided she wanted to know more about what lay within the mounds, and in 1938 she contacted Ipswich Museum, which recommended to her the services of an excavator named Basil Brown. She duly

Left *The outline of the longship buried in Mound 1, preserved in the earth where the disintegrated timbers had stained the soil. Note the long lines of iron rivets.*

engaged Brown, suggesting that he start his explorations with Mound 1. But Brown knew that many of the mounds had been disturbed by treasure hunters, and it was clear that Mound 1 – one of the most obvious targets – was among them. Instead he tried his luck with some of the smaller mounds. These proved to have been robbed of most of their secrets long before.

Mrs Pretty was undaunted and again prevailed upon Brown to look at Mound 1. In May 1939, helped by the gamekeeper and the gardener, he dug a trench in from the east end of the barrow. They soon started to come across rusted iron rivets and Brown realized that he had stumbled across the remnants of a buried ship of great dimensions. Digging further, they eventually reached a large burial chamber in the centre of the ship, at the exact spot where Mrs Pretty – possibly guided by unnatural forces – had asked him to dig the year before.

Incredibly, the chamber was undisturbed. By an astonishing stroke of luck it had been missed by the treasure hunter who had tried to loot it in ages past, thanks to a ditch cut across the mound in medieval times when field boundaries were being marked. The ditch had altered the apparent shape of the barrow, so that when the looter dug into its centre, reasonably assuming it to be the most

likely spot to find treasure, he was actually well off to the side and missed the burial chamber altogether.

A GIFT TO THE NATION

Professionals from various museums and societies soon moved in to complete the excavation, and the remarkable treasures found within the burial chamber were packed up and taken to the British Museum. Before long, however, they had to be brought back to Sutton village hall for a Treasure Trove inquest. Treasure Trove was the law governing the ownership of buried treasure in England, but Sutton Hoo was an anomaly. According to the Treasure Trove laws, a treasure belonged to the Crown if it was lost – that is, if its owners had buried it, but never got the chance to reclaim it. But Sutton Hoo was a grave, with treasure that was intended to stay buried for ever. The trove was duly awarded to Mrs Pretty, who could have sold it for a vast fortune. Instead she bequeathed it to the nation. This was a particularly significant act at the time, as the gathering storm of war was about to break. It was suspected that the Sutton Hoo trove was an early Anglian royal treasure, marking the start of the history of the English nation, which had obvious resonance at a time when that nation was under threat.

DOWSERS AND MEDIUMS

The period between the world wars was a time of burgeoning interest in the paranormal and in what are now called 'earth mysteries'. Popular pastimes included spiritualism and dowsing, and both of these were involved in the discovery of the treasure at Sutton Hoo.

Pretty's nephew was keen on dowsing and had run his wands over one of the largest mounds (known to archeologists as Mound 1), picking up a strong reading that he thought indicated buried gold. Mrs Pretty's spiritualist acquaintances also thought there was something special about the mounds and claimed to see mysterious figures around them.

Reports of spirits and strange powers around large mounds suggest obvious links with fairy lore, in which such artificial hills are said to be fairy palaces, where elves and other little people dwell. But this charming and quaint Victorian notion of fairies derives at least in part from much older and darker traditions. To the pagan Anglo-Saxons who built the mounds, and, as it transpired, interred kings and great wealth within them, the barrows were haunted and spirit-ridden places, where dangerous wights or living creatures, trolls, ghosts and even dragons might lurk, protecting the buried heroes and treasures. Was Mrs Pretty's circle somehow picking up on this ancient tradition of dark magic?

Treasure of the last pagan king

The burial chamber at Sutton Hoo proved to be the grave of an Anglo-Saxon king, interred in spectacular glory as a powerful statement of pagan values. Its marvellous treasures, including the famous helmet and shield decorations, also mark the birth of a uniquely English aesthetic tradition.

Excavation before and after the war revealed that Sutton Hoo was a rare example of a ship-burial. At 27 m (90 ft) long, 4.4 m (14 ft) wide and 1.5 m (4 ft 10 in) deep, the galley, with spaces for 40 oarsmen, had been dragged overland from the river up to the top of the hill and placed in a specially dug trench, so that only its fore and aft posts projected above ground level. The mast and decking had been removed, leaving just the hull and its supports, in the centre of which had been constructed a wooden cabin or house, probably with a pitched roof. Inside this cabin, possibly within a large wooden coffin, the body of the occupant had been lain out, dressed, ornamented and surrounded by treasures and grave goods from the exotic to the everyday. These included artefacts probably made in England, possibly by an artist in the employ of the king; some made in Scandinavia; and others from further afield, such as Byzantium and Egypt.

FIT FOR A KING

One of the most glorious pieces was a purse lid, made of horn with a gold frame of exquisite workmanship depicting birds of prey, man-eating wolves and other animals. The purse it covered had rotted away, but its contents lay near by: 37 carefully selected coins from Europe, together with three blank coins. Perhaps these 40 coins were intended as payment for the 40 phantom oarsmen who would row the ship's occupant to Valhalla. The dates of the coins help to pinpoint the burial to around 620–630 CE.

Given that the grave was of such quality and wealth that it must have been that of a king, it was speculated, and is widely accepted, that it was the grave of King Raedwald of the East Angles (ruled 599–624 CE), whose seat of royal power was located near by. According to the Venerable Bede, Raedwald was one of the first kings of all England. He had been baptized by St Augustine, but later reverted to paganism. His successor, Edwin, would later go on to confirm Christianity as the official religion of England. If Sutton Hoo is the burial of Raedwald, it seems to mark a last hurrah for the pagan religion of the Anglo-Saxons.

THE BEOWULF CONNECTION

One of the most famous items in the treasure is a helmet that closely resembles ones from the same period found in Scandinavia, as do many other aspects of the burial (for instance, strips of metal sheet on a magnificent shield found in the tomb bear the imprints of dyes that had also been used on grave goods recovered from a cemetery at Vendel in Sweden). This might suggest that

Right *The purse lid constructed from gold, garnets and millefiore glass. The animals portrayed include two pairs of wolves attacking hapless victims and stylized birds of prey facing each other in the centre.*

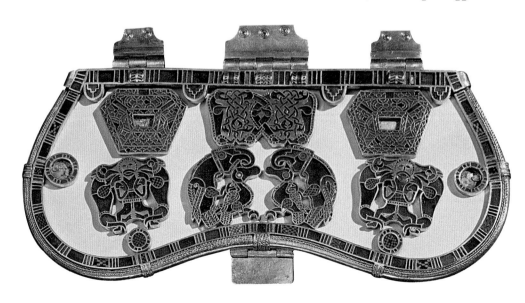

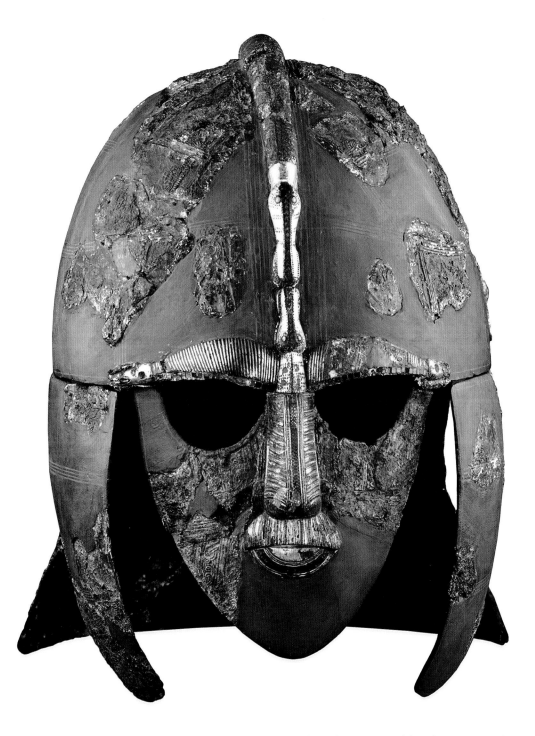

Raedwald spent his childhood being fostered in a royal court in Scandinavia, underlining the way that the emerging kingdom of England was linked to the wider Anglo-Saxon world.

A further link is provided by the epic Old English poem *Beowulf*, which tells a tale of heroes, kings and monsters in 6th-century Scandinavia. Although it is a fictional, exaggerated world, many of the things described in it have direct parallels with the Sutton Hoo burial. For instance, the marvellous sword buried alongside the Sutton Hoo king. This is pattern-welded, which means it is made from bundles of iron rods hammered together to give a herringbone-patterned blade, to which a hard cutting edge of carbon steel was added. Compare this to the description in *Beowulf* of Unferth's blade, which the eponymous hero wields against Grendel's mother: 'the curious sword with a wavy pattern, hard of its edge'.

More generally, the burial at Sutton Hoo seems almost to have been based on the mighty ship-burials described in *Beowulf*, while there is evidence that Raedwald would have traced his ancestry back to the Wulfing clan mentioned in the poem. Historians suggest that in staging the elaborate ship-burial, the Angles were emphasizing their pagan origins and heritage, as celebrated in *Beowulf*, in the face of the increasing influence of Roman Christianity.

THE ROMAN CONNECTION

At the same time, the Sutton Hoo treasures suggest that the new rulers of what had been Roman Britain were still modelling themselves on the (by now) legendary glories of the Romans. When Raedwald won overlordship over the other English princes,

he was said to have claimed the *imperium*, and the evidence of his grave suggests that the trappings of a Roman lord were an essential element in the way he presented himself and constructed his kingly persona. For instance, the magnificent shoulder-clasps found where his torso would have lain suggest that his body armour would have included a close-fitting Roman-style cuirass, while two enigmatic artefacts found alongside the body are also suggestive. One is a whetstone staff

carved so that it resembles the sceptre of a Roman consul; the other is a strange iron stand, which might have formed a frame for cloth, so that it could function as a standard – reminiscent of Roman standards.

Many of the pieces, however, combine diverse influences to produce a new style, so that the Sutton Hoo treasures are considered a landmark in English art history. They mark the emergence of a truly Insular style (that is, one specific to the British Isles).

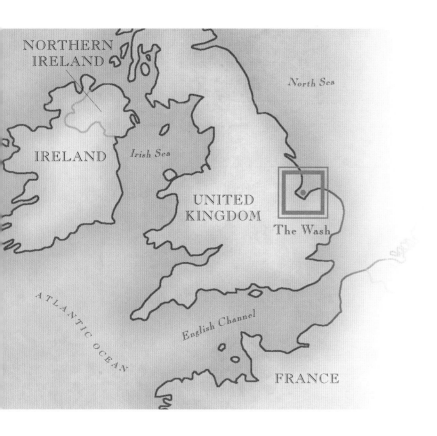

King John's Crown Jewels

Best known as Robin Hood's arch-nemesis, King John (ruled 1199–1216) is also famous for having lost his royal treasure in the Wash, a river estuary in England, shortly before he died. Although treasure hunters have sought this royal cache for centuries, there are many questions about where and what was lost and the circumstances surrounding John's death.

In late 1216 King John of England was travelling from Lincolnshire to Norfolk in the east of the country, together with the baggage train that normally accompanied a royal progress. Reaching Bishop's (now King's) Lynn in Norfolk, he fell ill and it was decided that he should recuperate back in Lincolnshire. The shortest route back to the north-west was to cross the Wash, a large square bay that indents the coastline, into which several rivers empty. The broad expanse of shallow water changes with the tides, and in medieval times low tide revealed fords and causeways that could shave many miles off a journey, but also mudflats and marshes, quicksand and sudden changes in water level that could catch out the unwary or incautious traveller.

On 12 October King John successfully forded the Wellstream, one of the rivers that fed into the Wash. His baggage train, however, was surprised by the rising tide and, to his horror, the carriages were overwhelmed by the waves or lost in quicksand. According to the traditional version of the story, the baggage train included the king's Crown Jewels. Devastated

by the loss of his loot, for he was renowned as a greedy and covetous king, John was taken to a nearby abbey at Swineshead in Lincolnshire, where the monks served him 'quantities of pears, and peaches, and new cider'. Evidently this did not agree with him, for he fell ill with dysentery and died on 18 October at Newark.

WHERE WAS KING JOHN'S LOOT LOST?

While medieval scribes described King John's crossing point – at Wisbech on the Wellstream – there are serious problems for modern-day treasure hunters hoping to locate his drowned loot. In medieval times the Wash extended further inland and the coastline was very different. Land reclamation and changes to the water courses have resulted in significant retreat of the sea and deposition of soil. The Wellstream no longer exists, although the current River Nene flows along a similar route. Wisbech, which was close to the coast, is now several kilometres inland, and it may be that wherever the baggage train was lost is now under up to 10 m (33 ft) of soil, beyond the range of metal detectors.

Also, since it is not certain that John was actually travelling with his baggage train (which moved slowly, which in turn could explain why it was taking a dangerous shortcut), it is not clear whether the location of the disaster is the same as the location of John's crossing point.

Traditionally it has been assumed that the baggage train crossed the Wash from Cross Keys to Long Sutton and was lost near present-day Sutton Bridge, which has formed the focus of most treasure-hunting efforts. If the baggage train *was* with John (and it can be argued that he would not have let it out of his sight), it may have been lost between Wisbech and Walsoken, perhaps overwhelmed by a tidal bore.

A reconstruction of tide tables for the date of the disaster suggests that the baggage train would have had plenty of time to cross the Wellstream and is more likely to have come to grief crossing the mouth of the Welland River, near modern-day Fosdyke.

Left A rare depiction of King John, from the chronicle Flores Historiarum *('Flowers of History'), one of the primary sources of the tale of King John's royal treasure.*

WHAT WAS REALLY LOST?

Is it worth treasure hunters searching at any of these locations? The popular legend has it that John lost his Crown Jewels, but there is a great deal of uncertainty about this. The main contemporary source for the story is Roger of Wendover's *Flores Historiarum* ('Flowers of History'), written around 1230, which says merely, '*regium apparatum amisit*' – 'royal apparel or furnishings were lost'. At the time *apparatum* did *not* mean treasure. This suggests that John simply lost some of the tents and furnishings that accompanied him around the country.

John had instituted official inventories known as the Rolls. Although there is evidence that the baggage train included large quantities of the silver that made up his personal treasury, the Rolls do not record any significant damage to the treasury at this time. On the other hand, they do show that when John's successor Henry III (ruled 1216–72) was crowned, the regalia that had

previously been present were no longer listed. These included the imperial regalia he had inherited from his grandmother, the Empress of Germany, which made up part of his Crown Jewels, so perhaps the popular legend is right after all.

KING JOHN'S HOLE AND BARON TIPTOFT

Many other questions surround the whole affair. There have been suggestions that John, having previously put the Crown Jewels up as collateral for a loan, faked the incident as a kind of fraud; or alternatively that John's death was due to poisoning and the Crown Jewels were stolen after this. Some local legends claim that the lost treasure was hidden in a pool in the Sutton area known as King John's Hole; others that it was discovered in the 14th century by local baron Robert, the 3rd Lord Tiptoft, who suddenly became enormously wealthy, but with no apparent source.

RUSSIA

MONGOLIA

CHINA

Yellow Sea

The lost loot of Genghis Khan

Genghis Khan (ruled 1206–27) was possibly the greatest conqueror in history, and his Mongol hordes looted and pillaged empires from the Pacific to the Mediterranean, including some of the richest kingdoms that had ever existed. Yet no trace of this incalculable booty has ever been found. Legend has it that much was buried with the great khan himself, but his last resting place is a mystery.

Left The Genghis Khan Mausoleum in Inner Mongolia, which is actually part of China. The mausoleum is a political tool, intended to help China harness the political energies associated with Genghis' legacy and legitimize its claim to be the true caretaker of Mongolian heritage.

At the start of the 13th century, one name filled the world with dread. Genghis Khan was feared from the shores of the Pacific to the fields of Europe, and with good reason. He had forged the disparate nomadic tribes of the Central Asian steppes into the most fearsome fighting force that had ever been known, and with it he had conquered

and despoiled the empires of China, India and Persia and the kingdoms of Russia and the Caucasus up to the borders of Eastern Europe. Genghis must have accumulated staggering quantities of loot, much of which was carried back in triumph to Mongolia, but no one knows what became of it. One possibility is that it was buried with him.

When Genghis died in 1227, on campaign in western China, he too was carried back to Mongolia. Exactly what happened next is uncertain. According to one legend, a river was diverted and he was buried in its bed, so that his tomb would be covered over when it resumed its course. According to another legend, after his tomb was raised, the slaves who had built it were slaughtered and then the soldiers who killed them were executed in turn, so that none could reveal its location. A herd of horses was driven across the mound to flatten it and a forest of trees was planted on top to hide all trace of it – and of the huge hoard of looted treasure and tribute buried alongside him.

ON THE TRAIL OF GENGHIS KHAN

Today the location of the tomb of Genghis Khan is one of the great mysteries of archeology. Little is known of the early Mongol era because by nature it has left few traces – Genghis and most of his people were probably illiterate, while their nomadic culture left few long-lasting remains. But enough details of his biography have come down to us to suggest a number of locations where he might have been buried, because they were significant in his life.

His birthplace is an obvious candidate. It is thought to be Hentiy Aymag, in northern Mongolia, near the sources of the Onon and Kerulen Rivers. A place that is known to have held special significance for him is a mountain called Burkhan Khaldun, in the Hentiyn Nuruu range, where he took refuge from enemy tribes and spent much of his youth. He was acclaimed Great Khan in 1206 at the Kurultai, or Great Convention, thought to have taken place near the present-day town of Batirsheet, close to Mongolia's border with Russia, and this is another candidate location.

Yet another is suggested by writings that date to not long after his death, which speak of a mausoleum to Genghis' memory that was constructed on the site of his former palace. Supposedly court officials would process from the mausoleum to his nearby tomb for ceremonial purposes, suggesting not only that the site of the tomb was not always a mystery, but also that locating the site of his former palace or mausoleum will put treasure hunters on the track of the grave.

THE GOLD TRADER AND THE KHAN

Leading the hunt for the elusive tomb is an eccentric and bombastic Chicago gold-trader and self-made millionaire, Maury Kravitz,

Right *A Chinese portrait of Genghis Khan from the National Palace Museum in Taipei, Taiwan. Or rather, this is what the artist imagined him to look like as there are no authentic contemporary portraits of him.*

who has been interested in Genghis Khan since reading about him when he was doing national service, an interest that has turned into an obsession. With the collapse of the Soviet Union and the lifting of the Iron Curtain, Inner Mongolia was opened up to potential tomb-raiders, and in the late 1990s Kravitz put together a board of specialists and approached the Mongolian government with a proposition. He would track down the lost tomb of Genghis Khan, winning eternal glory, and any treasure, artefacts or remains located there would go to the government. They would be getting, Kravitz told them, a haul of loot that would 'eat the Tut[ankhamun] exhibit for breakfast'.

In the course of several years of expeditions, Kravitz and his team have located various important sites. First they found the site of the Kurultai, or Great Convention. Then they explored Burkhan Khaldun, the mountain that held a special place in Genghis' heart, but were beaten back by hordes of biting black flies. In 2001 they

discovered a highly significant site called Ölögchiin Kherem, or the Almsgivers' Wall, also known as the Ulaan Khad (Red Rock), and, most suggestively, as Chinggis' Wall (Chinggis is the Mongolian rendering of Genghis). Near the locations of both Genghis' birth and the Kurultai, the Kherem site is a hill surrounded on three sides by a ruined wall, a structure unique in Mongolia. Initial surveys suggest there are up to 40 graves on the site and analysis of some remains suggests that they date to the early imperial era – the time of Ghengis. Investigations at the site continue, while Kravitz himself is hard at work on a screenplay about his exploits.

Kravitz's is not the only team searching for the tomb of Genghis Khan. A Japanese group claimed to have found the site of his former palace, while the Chinese have constructed a massive mausoleum to him in Inner Mongolia, which they claim is the real deal. Despite all these efforts, however, the tomb and its treasure have still not been located.

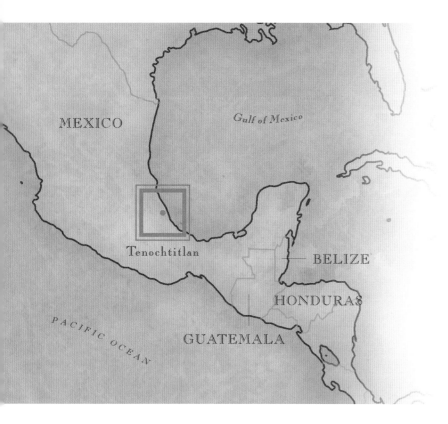

Montezuma's Hoard: the last emperor's gold

One of the oldest legends of post-Columbian Mexico is of the treasure popularly known as Montezuma's Hoard, after the name given by the Spanish to the last Aztec emperor. Most details of this popular legend, however, are wrong.

The conquistadors of Peru and the lands to the north of Mexico, whose greed blinded them to reality and led them to chase the fatal figments of El Dorado (see page 34) and the Seven Cities of Cíbola (see page 40), were simply following a pattern established by the first of the conquistadors. Hernán Cortés, who began the Spanish Empire in the New World by conquering Mexico and overthrowing the Aztecs, was similarly blinded by greed and obsessed with the idea that great treasures were being denied to him.

From this obsession grew the legend of Montezuma's Hoard. The most prevalent version of the legend today is that in 1519 Montezuma (ruled c.1502–20), the last Aztec emperor, fearing the advance of the conquistadors, packed up the great bulk of his royal treasury and dispatched it to the remote northern reaches of the Aztec world – today the southern states of the United States. Here it lies, awaiting discovery by the intrepid treasure hunter lucky enough to locate a cache that could be worth hundreds of billions of dollars. The legend of Montezuma's Hoard thus ranks alongside the Lost Dutchman's Gold Mine (see page 56) and the treasure of Captain Kidd (see page 46) as one of the keystones of American treasure folklore.

The popular legend is probably wrong on all counts. Firstly, the Aztec emperor's name was not Montezuma – this is a later Spanish version of a more difficult original, which modern scholars render as Moctezuma. Furthermore, Moctezuma was not really the last emperor, as he was succeeded by at least two others before the Spanish finally destroyed the Aztec Empire.

HOW THE HOARD WAS LOST

More important is the issue of whether there really was a lost hoard of Aztec gold, and if so, how did it become lost? There are four different answers to this pair of questions.

• **The traditional version:** there are conflicting accounts of Moctezuma's reaction to the Spanish arrival in 1519. On the one hand, the Aztecs considered Cortés to be a latter-day incarnation of the god Quetzalcóatl, a culture hero who had founded Aztec civilization and then sailed off into the east, but who was prophesied to return as a bearded white man. On the other hand, Moctezuma was wary, attempting to divert the conquistadors from approaching the capital and delay their progress. Perhaps he was suspicious enough to hide much of his treasury, just as the legend says. The Spanish certainly believed this to be the case and later tortured many Indians to learn more, but there is no actual evidence to back this up.

• **The Spanish:** the small force of conquistadors installed itself in Moctezuma's palace in the centre of the great Aztec city of Tenochtitlan, which was built on a series of interconnected islands in the marsh-like Lake Texcoco. They ordered the Indians to bring them treasure and accumulated huge quantities (much of which they melted down into ingots), but also managed to antagonize the populace until a siege situation developed. On the evening of

1 July 1520, loaded with as much loot as they could carry, the Spanish tried to slip out of the city, but were harried by an army of angry Indians. Hundreds of Spaniards were killed in what the Spanish called *La Noche Triste* or the 'Night of Tears'. Crammed onto a narrow causeway, many of the Spanish conquistadors fell into the water and were dragged down by the gold they carried; others were forced to ditch their loot. Ironically it may be the Spanish who were the source of the lost Aztec gold.

• **Cuauhtemoc:** after the Spanish fled Tenochtitlan, Moctezuma's nephew Cuauhtemoc (ruled 1520–21) took the throne, making him the true last Aztec emperor. He must have known that the Spanish would return in force and it is possible that, if there was Aztec treasure left, it was he who dispatched it to the far north to keep it out of their hands.

• **Dumped:** sure enough, the Spanish returned and invested Tenochtitlan, which finally fell on 13 August 1521 after an 80-day siege. Cuauhtemoc was captured and the Spanish tortured him by roasting his feet over a fire. They demanded to know the whereabouts of the missing Aztec treasure, but all he would tell them was that what little treasure was left had gone to the bottom of the lake. Again, it seems possible that Montezuma's Hoard was to be found on the bottom of Lake Texcoco.

Left A depiction of the first meeting between Cortés and Moctezuma, on 8 November 1519. The meeting took place on one of the causeways leading to Tenochtitlan.

'*Hernán Cortés was blinded by greed and obsessed with the idea that great treasures were being denied to him.*'

Montezuma's Hoard: Aztec ghosts

Cortés was only the first – though possibly the most brutal – in a long line of treasure hunters who have sought the lost Aztec gold of the 'last' emperor. From Mexico City to the badlands of Utah, prospectors have sought it underground and underwater, even facing ghostly guardians in the process.

The first man to hunt for Montezuma's Hoard was Cortés himself. In addition to handing Cuauhtemoc over to his treasurer for interrogation under torture, he had all the captured Indians searched, even making the women strip and checking inside their mouths. When this failed to divulge any loot, he pressed native divers into service to scour the bed of Lake Texcoco, but all that was recovered was a disc, described by the Spanish as a 'golden sun' – probably an Aztec calendar wheel. Eventually Cortés had the lake drained and founded Mexico City on top of it, now one of the world's largest cities.

FOUND AND LOST

Whatever loot was in Lake Texcoco may well have been found over the last five centuries. Montezuma's Hoard has long been a feature of local legend and it is not difficult to imagine poor Mexicans neglecting to report any finds. In 1981 a single artefact was recovered from the former lake bed – workers excavating the foundations of the Bank of Mexico found a pre-Columbian gold disc (recalling the calendar wheel found by Cortés) that was described as 'the first discovery of Moctezuma's treasure'.

A tenuous theory that has been advanced is that the treasure was recovered as long ago as 1528, by a Castilian adventurer named Figueroa, who met disaster as he tried to ship it back to Spain when his ship was caught in a storm off Veracruz. In August 1976 newspaper reports told of a remarkable find at Río Medio, near Veracruz, with divers recovering a huge haul of gold, including many Aztec artefacts. This booty was linked to Montezuma's Hoard – although it is unclear on what evidence – but it mysteriously disappeared almost as soon as it had reappeared. Shipped off to the Bank of Mexico, it promptly vanished and was never seen again, having presumably been illegally sold off to private collectors.

Right A disc of beaten gold inlaid and edged with turquoise pieces. This is actually a disc from the Mixtec culture, a neighbouring and rival culture to the Aztecs, but similar to the disc that Cortés found and the one dug up from beneath the Bank of Mexico.

UTAH GOLD

Despite the total lack of evidence for the legend of the Aztec expedition to the southwestern states (as they now are), many American treasure hunters have sought Montezuma's Hoard in this area. Just as local legend links Captain Kidd with every other coastal town between New Jersey and Connecticut, so Montezuma is linked to places from California and Colorado to Texas and Utah. In particular a region of south-west Utah near Kanab and the Three Lakes has been a fertile hunting ground, at least in terms of tall tales.

One yarn involves a prospector named Freddie Crystal, who in 1914 turned up in Utah with a newspaper clipping showing a petroglyph (a rock painting or carving made by the pre-Columbian Indians) in Johnson Canyon, near Kanab. Crystal was convinced that the glyph pointed the way to Montezuma's hidden stash. Apparently his enthusiasm was infectious, for within a few years most of the town had moved to a tent city at the head of Johnson Canyon to join in the search.

Their efforts were fruitless, but more recently other petroglyphs set in motion an even more incredible chain of events. In 1989 a treasure hunter named Grandt Child

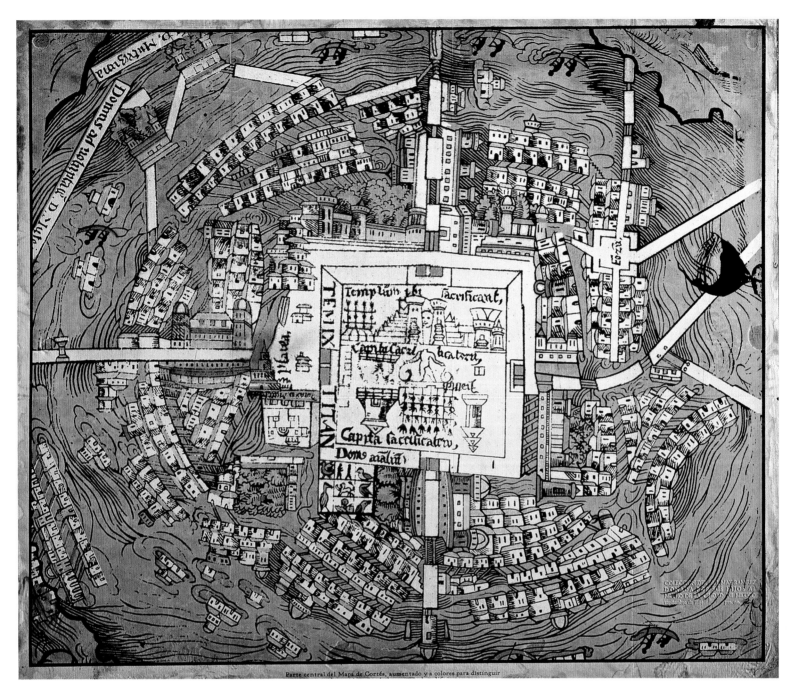

Parte central del Mapa de Cortés, aumentado y a colores para distinguir

decoded a petroglyph that he claimed pointed to an Aztec water-trap in one of the Three Lakes chain. When divers explored they found a tunnel, but here things began to turn strange. First, a diver exploring the tunnel with a safety line reported that the line had gone mysteriously slack when the assistant at the surface insisted it had been taut all along. The team brought in sonar equipment, which indicated that there was a chamber at the end of the tunnel, while their metal detectors registered the presence of a dense metal – gold? The next day divers attempted to reach the chamber, but were blocked by an invisible force that tried to choke them. The previous night one diver had dreamed of an Aztec warrior brandishing a spear – were spirit guardians protecting the lost treasure of the last emperor?

The region remains rich in caves and pre-Columbian Indian sites, but no one has yet uncovered the vast trove of legend, and given the facts of the last days of the Aztecs, it seems unlikely they ever will.

Above A map of *Tenochtitlan, capital of the Aztec Empire, supposedly based on a design penned by Hernán Cortés himself. It was one of the illustrations in a letter he sent to Charles V and it shows the causeways and the central sacred district with its twin pyramids.*

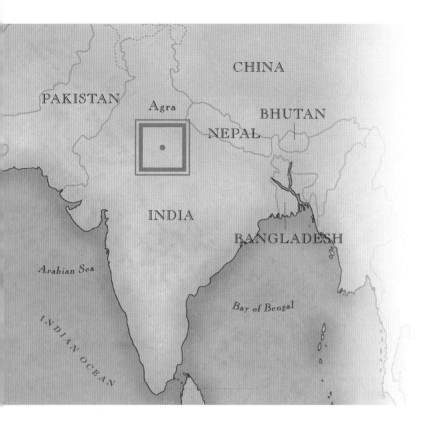

The Peacock Throne of the Mughals

Created for an emperor with tastes of unparalleled extravagance and crafted from the treasures of many nations, the Peacock Throne was possibly the most valuable artefact ever created. Made from more than 1,000 kg (2,200 lb) of solid gold, encrusted with priceless jewels and dripping with the finest pearls, it became the ultimate prize for a war-crazed despot who trampled across the corpses of thousands to obtain it.

The Peacock Throne of the Mughals was a great golden, jewel-encrusted throne commissioned by the Mughal emperor Shah Jahan (ruled 1628–58), which sat in the audience hall of the Red Fort at Agra until 1739, when the Persian emperor Nadir Shah (ruled 1736–47) overran India and carried it back to Iran.

'KING OF THE WORLD'
Shah Jahan was the fifth Mughal emperor, ruler of a vast region of the Indian subcontinent and of territory that stretched into Afghanistan and beyond. Although his most famous legacy was the Taj Mahal, a magnificent mausoleum for his beloved wife Mumtaz Mahal, his most extravagant creation was the Peacock Throne. By some reckonings it is the most valuable artefact ever created, costing *twice as much* as the Taj Mahal. In 1999 the modern-day value of the materials alone was conservatively estimated to be $804 million.

Shah Jahan planned the throne as an expression of his glory (his name meant 'King of the World', while his titles included *Zille-i-Illahi*, 'Shadow of God on Earth') and it

was said to have been modelled on the throne of King Solomon.

DIAMONDS AND PEARLS
The cream of the imperial treasury was selected, along with 230 kg (507 lb) of precious and semi-precious jewels from around the kingdom and 1,150 kg (2,535 lb) of pure gold, and these were given over to Bebadal Khan, the superintendent of the royal goldsmiths. The throne was designed in the shape of a bed or couch, about 2.3 m (6–9 feet) long and 1.7 m (4–7 ft) wide (sources differ), seated on four golden feet, with 12 columns supporting a canopy around 4.6 m (15 ft) high.

According to a French jeweller, Jean-Baptiste Tavernier, who was lucky enough to see this marvel when he visited Delhi in 1665, it was adorned with 108 large rubies (one of which, the Timur ruby, was 283 carats), 116 emeralds and many huge diamonds, several of which are now famous in their own right, such as the 186-carat Koh-i-noor and the 95-carat Akbar Shah. Despite this, Tavernier was of the opinion that the most valuable jewels were the rows of pearls set on the columns.

The outside of the canopy was of enamel set with precious stones, and each column was topped by a pair of peacocks set with gems and interleaved by jewelled Trees of Life. Embedded in the throne was a poem praising the emperor, spelt out in letters of emerald.

THE NAPOLEON OF PERSIA
The throne resided in one of the two great audience halls of the fortress palace of Agra, where the Mughal emperors had effectively made their capital. For private audiences it was kept in the Diwan-i-Khas, and for larger audiences at the Diwan-i-Am. Here it sat until 1739 when Nadir Shah, a military genius with an insatiable appetite for war, known in the West as 'the Napoleon of Persia' for his exploits, invaded India and looted Delhi of treasures estimated to be worth many billions of dollars in modern terms. He carried the throne back to Iran, but when he was assassinated by his own tribesmen (for fear of his increasingly psychotic behaviour) the Persian Empire fell into chaos, and it is thought likely that the Peacock Throne was broken up and its constituent jewels carried off to various corners of the Earth.

① THE RED FORT

The first fortifications on the site were of brick, but in 1565 the Mughal emperor Akbar (ruled 1556–1605) decided to make it his capital and had it rebuilt in red sandstone, leading to it being known as the Red Fort. His grandson Shah Jahan undertook extensive redevelopment, replacing much of the red sandstone with white marble buildings. The walls of the fort are up to 21 m (70 ft) high, with double ramparts and massive circular bastions, and they describe a perimeter 2.4 km (1½ miles) long. A moat, 9 m (30 ft) wide and 10 m (33 ft) deep, surrounds them.

② THE MUASAMMAN BURJ

There was something of a tradition among Mughal emperors of sons winning power by revolting against their fathers. This was how Shah Jahan had come to the throne, and in due course his own son Aurangzeb (ruled 1658–1707) overthrew him. Shah Jahan spent the last seven years of his life immured in luxurious house arrest within Agra fort, living and eventually dying in the Muasamman Burj, a tower with a splendid marble balcony offering views across to the Taj Mahal, the crowning glory of his reign.

③ DIWAN-I-AM

The Hall of Public Audience was where the emperor gave audience to the general public. One of the earliest manifestations of Shah Jahan's obsession with white marble as a building material, the Diwan-i-Am is constructed from red sandstone plastered with a white veneer to resemble marble. It is 61 m (201 ft) long and 20 m (67 ft) wide, with a flat roof, a facade of nine arches and arched gates of red sandstone at either end. Within is a raised platform from where the emperor would address his subjects – perhaps this is where the Peacock Throne sat when it was in residence.

④ DIWAN-I-KHAS

The Hall of Private Audience was completed in 1635, the same year that the Peacock Throne itself was finished. Here Shah Jahan and his successors would receive the nobility, foreign potentates and ambassadors. The exterior is of red sandstone, while within were three halls — the innermost one, known as the Tambi khana, decorated with ornate carvings, inscriptions and inlays. The flat wooden ceiling was covered in leaves of gold and silver meant to represent the rays of the sun, which itself was personified in the body of the emperor.

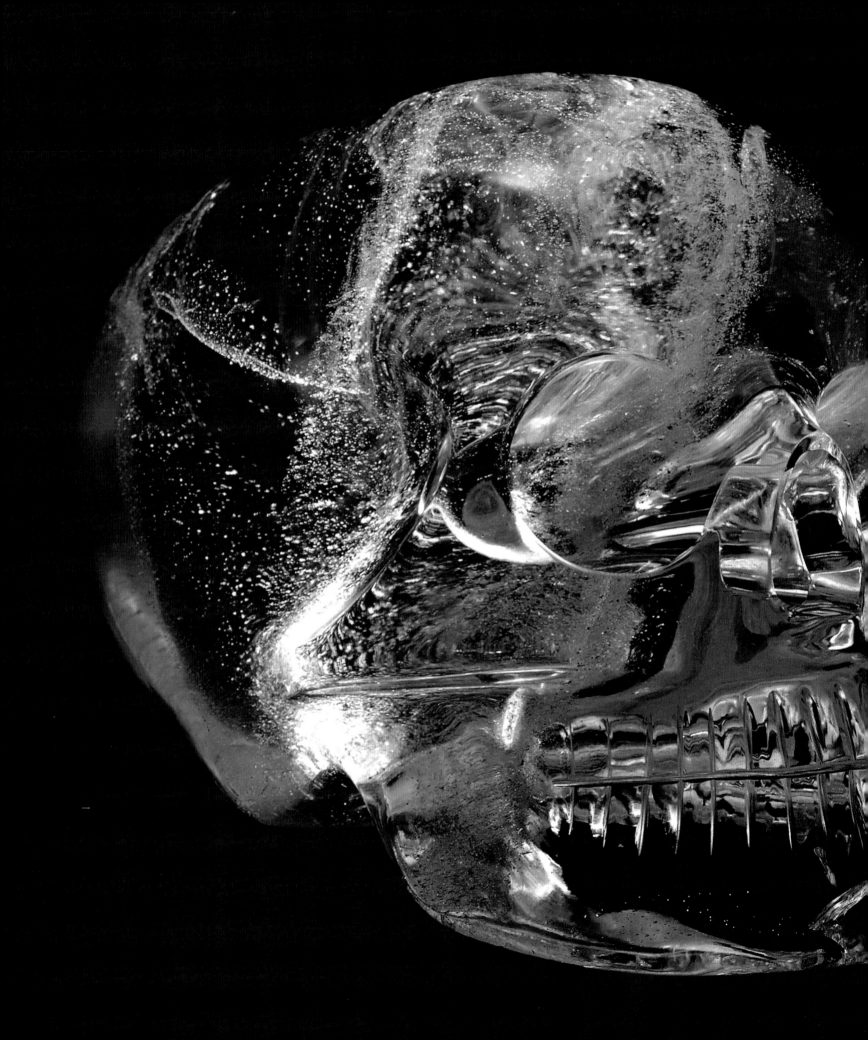

PART 3

ARTEFACTS AND RELICS

Few of the objects discussed in this section conform to the popular notion of treasure; on the whole they push the boundary of the definition of 'treasure', illustrating how it can mean different things to different people. To historians of science, for instance, something as prosaic as a clay jar (the Baghdad Battery) or a disc (the Phaistos Disc) can be priceless, while to peoples and nations anything from a set of chess pieces (the Lewis Chessmen) to a statue (Athena Parthenos, Zeus and the Colossus of Rhodes) can be a cultural treasure. Some of the topics covered here – the Buddhas of Bamiyan, the sacred Warka Vase – also serve to illustrate the perils and pitfalls that threaten treasure, and which mean that so little of the past survives. Examples such as the Ark of the Covenant and the Amber Room also show how the promise of treasure can blind people, and even nation states, into fruitless searches – quests that can consume lives.

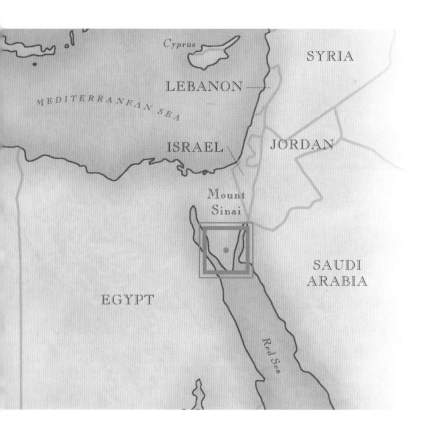

The Ark of the Covenant

Described as the most holy piece of furniture ever made, the Ark of the Covenant was a great chest built to house the Tablets of the Law that Moses brought down from Mount Sinai. Stored in a specially constructed portable temple, it was an artefact of terrible power, but ornate beauty. But was it the actual manifestation of God, or a sophisticated technical marvel millennia ahead of its time?

Left *A medieval Italian fresco depicting an episode in the history of the Ark. Here the Ark rests in the house of leading Levite Amminadab during its journey to Jerusalem.*

Exodus records how Moses was instructed by God to build a chest to house the stone tablets upon which the Ten Commandments had been inscribed. Variously known in the Bible as the Ark of the Testimony, the Ark of the Covenant and the Ark of the Lord, it was to be two and a half cubits long and a cubit and a half wide and long. The ancient Hebrews of the time of Moses probably used the royal cubit of Egypt, from where they had just fled, which was 53.3 cm (20⅞ in), making the Ark 1.3 m (4 ft 4 in) long and 76 cm (2 ft 7 in) wide and deep – roughly the size of a coffee table. God gave further specific instructions: the Ark was to be built of setim (or shittim) wood, a type of very high-grade and long-lasting acacia, and was to be covered inside and out with pure gold, with a band or crown of pure gold around the rim. Set into the golden covering, probably high up on the sides of the chest, were four golden rings, through which passed two rods of setim wood, also covered with gold. These poles allowed the Ark to be picked up and carried, and were never supposed to be removed.

God also specified where the Ark was to be stored, and the Hebrews built an elaborate tent-shrine known as the Tabernacle to house it whenever they made camp. The Tabernacle was constructed from drapes of linen, goat's hair and leather over a frame of setim-wood planks and pillars, with fixtures of brass, silver and gold, and could be collapsed when the Hebrews were on the move, with parts of it being used to cover and protect the Ark.

THE MERCY SEAT

The cover of the Ark was of solid gold and was known as the Mercy Seat or 'propitiary', because the Hebrew word for cover also means 'propitious'. Sitting atop the Mercy Seat were two cherubim of beaten gold, facing each other with their wings outstretched until they almost touched. Exactly what these cherubim would have looked like is unclear (and they are not to be confused with the chubby baby cherubs of more recent times), but it seems likely that the Ark itself was modelled closely on Egyptian temple furniture of the period, specifically chests known as *naos*, in which were stored images of the gods and their sacred emblems, or perhaps the sacred *bari* – representations of river boats in which the idols of the Egyptian pantheon were carried during ceremonial processions. This in turn suggests that the cherubim would have been hybrid man-beasts, like winged sphinxes.

WHAT WAS IN THE ARK?

Initially only the Tablets of the Law were placed inside the Ark, but later Moses was commanded to place within the Tabernacle a golden vessel holding manna (the miraculous foodstuff that God commanded to rain down from the heavens to feed the Hebrews on their long quest through the desert) and the rod of Aaron (Moses'

THE LEYDEN JAR THEORY

The strange powers attributed to the Ark, and the specifics of its construction, have led to speculation that the ancient Hebrews had somehow created an early version of a powerful technology known as the Leyden Jar. Not officially invented until 1747, a Leyden Jar is a type of capacitor – a device for storing electrical charge. The charge that is stored can be discharged as a single spark or as a continuous glow, and the ionizing effects of the charge can create a mist or cloud – all effects associated with the Ark. A pint jar (570 ml) can store enough electricity to kill a man, so the Ark, which was considerably larger, would be able to store tremendous amounts of energy.

This theory sounds incredible, but there are intriguing parallels between the design of the Ark and Tabernacle and the specifications needed for a Leyden Jar. The wooden parts would act as insulators, helping to store the charge, while the golden parts would be conductors, with the cherubim as positive and negative terminals; the gap between their outstretched wingtips would cause a corona-like discharge (a glow), manifesting 'divine' power. The way that the Ark was stored between curtains and drapes of linen, goat's hair and leather would help to generate charge by static build-up, and the poles – which God specifically instructed should always remain in place – would enable the highly charged artefact to be carried without danger, because those holding them would be earthed.

brother), which had blossomed as the result of an earlier miracle. Jewish traditions and one of the books of the New Testament suggest that these items were actually stored inside the Ark. The Bible also says that the book of Law written by Moses (either Deuteronomy or the whole Pentateuch) was to be placed 'in the side of the Ark', although it is not clear whether this means 'inside' or simply 'alongside'. By the time the Ark was placed in the Temple built by Solomon, however, the Book of Kings suggests that it contained only the Tablets of the Law.

THE POWER OF GOD

According to the various accounts in the Bible, the Ark was an incredibly powerful artefact. It was not simply a storage chest – God himself would manifest in the space between the wings of the cherubim on the Mercy Seat, which was called the oracle, because it was from here that God would speak to Moses. The divine presence, or *Shekinah*, would appear as a cloud over the oracle and issue commands and proclamations. In fact in some passages God seems to identify himself as being one and the same as the Ark, while in other traditions the Ark seems to have a mind and will of its own.

Divine power made the Ark both a potent weapon and a danger even to those who ministered to it. It could smite enemy armies and fortifications (as when the Israelites toppled the walls of Jericho), bring misfortune and plague (as when it was captured by the enemy Philistines) and kill any who touched it. It could consume with fire those who displeased it.

'God would manifest in the space between the wings of the cherubim.'

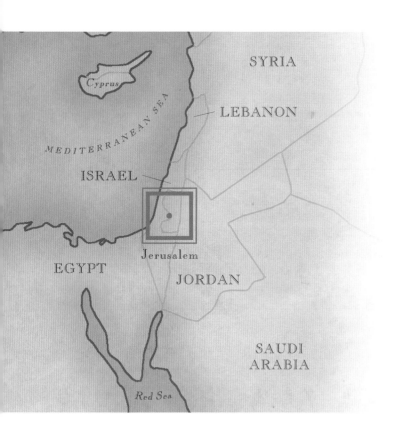

The Ark, the Temple and the Holy of Holies

The accession of the greatest of the kings of Israel brought a new era for the Ark, and a new home. It was to form the centrepiece, most precious treasure and animating spirit of the Temple in Jerusalem. The chamber where it was stored was considered the most holy place on Earth, and only one man was allowed to enter, once a year.

THE HISTORY OF THE ARK

While they were wandering in the desert in Sinai the ancient Hebrews carried the Ark with them, and when they made camp it was stored in an elaborate tent shrine known as the Tabernacle. When Solomon built the great Temple in Jerusalem, the Tabernacle was recreated in the form of the Holy of Holies – the innermost sanctum of the Temple, where the Ark was to be stored as a physical manifestation of the spirit of God.

Here it remained for hundreds of years, only occasionally taken out to be paraded or used as a weapon in military campaigns. It may also have been temporarily removed and hidden to preserve it from misuse at the hands of wicked kings. The Book of Chronicles provides the last biblical mention of the Ark, recording that King Josiah ordered it be brought back to the Temple (according to the accepted chronology, this was in 623 BCE).

After this the Ark disappears from the pages of history and it is assumed that it was stolen/destroyed by one of the many invaders who conquered Jerusalem, probably during the Babylonian conquest of 586 BCE,

when the First Temple was destroyed. The Second Temple was constructed 70 years later, but the Ark is not mentioned. When the Romans conquered Jerusalem in 70 CE, the victorious general Titus marched into the Holy of Holies of the Second Temple to discover that it was empty, and it is generally assumed that it had been empty all along.

DATING THE ARK

From the Bible accounts it is possible to follow the history of the Ark from its creation over a period of several centuries, but equating this with a historical chronology is difficult. Traditionally the date of construction of the Ark is taken from a passage in the Book of Kings, which states that the Exodus happened 480 years before Solomon built the Temple, while the reign of Solomon itself is dated by correspondence with a contemporaneous Egyptian pharaoh mentioned in the Bible. Putting them together gives the year of the Exodus, which included Moses' encounter with God on Mount Sinai and the construction of the Ark and the Tabernacle, as 1446 BCE. However, archeological and other evidence points to a

more realistic date around 1250 BCE (although it should be noted that many scholars dispute the historical reality of the Exodus). The last mention of the Ark in the Bible is the reign of Josiah, whose rule can be dated with much more certainty than the earlier events, to 640–609 BCE. The destruction of the First Temple is firmly dated at 586 BCE, which is the most probable date for the demise of the Ark.

① THE TEMPLE OF SOLOMON

King David had decided that it was appropriate to the glory of his capital at Jerusalem that the Ark be housed in a special Temple and set about gathering the materials to construct it. The task itself was left to his successor Solomon, who built a huge complex on Mount Moriah in Jerusalem around 3,000 years ago. Great courts surrounded a central building composed of an outer ring of storage chambers around a long, rectangular building of three main segments. The easternmost was the *Ulam* – the entrance, composed of a great porch surmounted by two great pillars. This led into the *Hekhal*, or Holy Place, a rectangular chamber, which in turn led on to the *Kadosh haKadoshim*, or Holy of Holies. The walls and floors of the Temple were covered in the finest wood and gold, and the fittings were of gold and fine cloth.

② THE HOLY OF HOLIES

The Holy of Holies was modelled on the equivalent chamber in the original Tabernacle, the *Kadosh haKadoshim* was a windowless cuboid chamber 20 cubits on each side (8.56 m/28 ft). It was screened off from the *Hekhal* by a two-leaved door that was made of wood covered in gold, and by drapes of fine cloth. The only thing that was stored inside the Holy of Holies was the Ark of the Covenant, which sat on the *Even Shetiyah*, or Foundation Stone, which was considered to be the centre of the world where Creation had begun. Thanks to the *Shekinah*, which would manifest between the wings of the cherubim on the lid of the Ark, the Holy of Holies was considered to be the actual dwelling place of the presence of God.

③ ENTRY BARRED

The Holy of Holies was too holy for anyone except the High Priest to enter, and even he was allowed in only once a year, on Yom Kippur. He would sprinkle onto the Ark the blood of sacrificial animals and offer incense. Then he would prostate himself face down on the ground and utter the name of God (Yahweh). When he came out of the chamber, his face was said to be radiant.

The hunt for the lost Ark

The fate of the Ark of the Covenant is one of history's most enduring mysteries. Why does the Bible not record what happened to it? Was it carried off by one of the invading armies that periodically marched into Jerusalem, or did it direct its own fate and escape to another continent? Could it be sensationally rediscovered by a real-life Indiana Jones?

TO THE VICTOR THE SPOILS

The most likely version of events is that the Ark was destroyed by one of the armies that conquered Jerusalem and probably looted the Temple, and the finger is usually pointed at the Babylonians and their emperor Nebuchadnezzar (ruled c.605–562 BCE). It was common practice at the time to carry the 'gods' (that is, the idols) of defeated nations back to the capital, where they would be installed in the sacred precinct and would thus, literally and conceptually, fall under the sway of the Babylonian gods. Evidence for this scenario comes from the *Apocalypse of Ezra*, one of the Apocrypha (scriptures that did not make it into the canonical version of the Bible for various reasons), which

Right An aerial view of Jerusalem, with the Mount of Olives in the background. In the centre is the Dome of the Rock and towards the bottom right is the Wailing Wall, one of the last traces of the original Temple of Solomon.

specifically lists the Ark as being among the loot carted off by the Babylonians, although it was not written until 500 years after the fall of the First Temple.

Other invaders who might have carried off the Ark include an Egyptian pharaoh, thought to be Sheshonq I (ruled 942–922 BCE), who invaded Israel in 925 BCE, not long after the Temple was built; the Syrian king Antiochus Epiphanes (ruled 174–164 BCE), who looted the Second Temple; and the Romans under Titus in 70 CE, who razed the Temple to the ground after his soldiers carried off vast quantities of loot. Although Titus is generally assumed to have found the Holy of Holies empty when he marched in, one theory is that in fact the Romans spirited the Ark off to Rome, where it was captured by the Visigoths and taken to Constantinople, falling into the hands of the Knights Templar after the city was sacked during the Fourth Crusade in 1204. Alas, there is no evidence for this tale, nor for the even more fantastical claim that the Templars found the Ark when delving beneath the Temple Mound (see page 160).

Left The Chapel of the Tablet of Moses in the grounds of the cathedral of Our Lady Mary of Zion in Axum, Ethiopia. The Ethiopian Church claims that the Ark of the Covenant rests within, guarded by a priest who spends his whole life within the chapel compound.

UNDER THE MOUNTAIN

Most Ark hunters concentrate on theories that it was hidden by the Hebrews to keep it out of the hands of invaders, either in one of the many tunnels and caves that riddle the Temple Mount or somewhere else in the Holy Land. One tradition is that the prophet Jeremiah hid the Ark in a cave on Mount Nebo, now on the Jordanian side of the Dead Sea. Similar traditions link the Ark to the Copper Scroll – one of the Dead Sea Scrolls (see page 50), which seems to detail the whereabouts of a fantastic quantity of treasure, possibly including sacred artefacts from the Temple. This avenue also suggests a hiding place somewhere in the hills around the Dead Sea. A more radical suggestion is that the Ark fell into the hands of the Jurhum, the Arabic tribe that controlled the Kaaba, now the holiest shrine in Islam, but then a focal point of polytheistic worship, and that it might still lie in or near the Kaaba. Other locations suggested for the hiding place of the Ark range from Ireland's Hill of Tara to the state of Utah in the United States.

THE SECRET OF AXUM

Ethiopia has a tradition, recorded in its national saga the *Glory of Kings*, that the Ark was spirited away from Jerusalem by Menelik, the King of Ethiopia and the son of Solomon and Queen Sheba. Supposedly the Ark itself asked him to take it, and he swapped it for a copy before carrying the holy chest back to his homeland, where it still resides within a locked and guarded chapel in the town of Axum. Visitors to Axum over the centuries claim to have been allowed access to this Ark, some even reporting stone tablets stored within, but they often concluded that they had been shown copies or crude fakes, which is not surprising given that the guardian of the Chapel of the Tablet of Moses, a post handed down through the generations, adamantly refuses to let anyone (from researchers to emperors and generals) see the artefact. Is the Menelik story plausible? Menelik himself is a legendary rather than historical figure, while Sheba, the kingdom that is said to link Menelik to Israel and the Ark, was probably in Arabia rather than East Africa. Menelik is not mentioned in the Bible, while the Ark continues to appear after the period of his supposed visit (although this could simply mean that the Hebrews fell for his copy of the Ark).

MULTIPLE ARKS?

Even during the period of its biblically attested existence, there is something strange and confusing about accounts of the Ark. At times it seems to be described as simultaneously residing in its Tabernacle or Temple and roaming abroad in a military or ritual capacity. The tale of Menelik explicitly talks of copies of the Ark, while the various fates suggested for it suggest that there was more than one Ark. In Ethiopia today the alleged 'original' is kept locked up in a chapel in Axum, but there are many copies that are used for processions and the like, each of which is considered to be holy in its own right. Perhaps the situation in ancient Israel was similar.

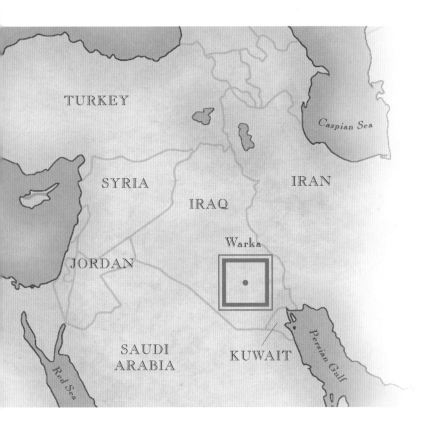

The sacred Warka Vase

One of the oldest surviving artefacts produced by civilization, the Warka Vase bears testament to the artistic skills, cultural achievements and religious universe of the people of Uruk, the world's first city. In recent times its story has been sadly emblematic of the chaos and tragedy of Iraq.

On 2 January 1934 German archeologists excavating the ancient Sumerian city of Uruk (a site now occupied by the village of Warka) unearthed an extraordinary artefact. It was an alabaster vase, more than 1 m (3¼ ft) tall, elaborately decorated with four tiers of carving. The bottom level shows plants of the Tigris and Euphrates delta, including reeds and grain stalks. The second tier shows oxen and sheep marching around the Vase. The third tier shows a line of nude males, also in profile, bearing vessels of fruit and grain intended as offerings for the goddess Inanna, whose temple is shown in the top tier.

INANNA OF URUK

Here the carvings show a scene in which offerings are made to Inanna, the chief goddess of Uruk, later to become better known as Ishtar. Inanna was the goddess of both war and fertility, bringing conquest and abundance, and her worship was the central preoccupation of Uruk, a city in southern Mesopotamia near the delta where the two great rivers reach the sea. Uruk was arguably the first city in the world, but it was also something even more significant. Here, around 4000–3500 BCE, at the uttermost beginnings of civilization, a pair of simple farming villages coalesced into a new stage in human evolution: a conglomeration of people different not simply by virtue of their numbers, but in many other ways. By 3300 BCE Uruk was home to 40,000 people, organized into an entirely new social model, with specialized artisans and craftsmen, priests and merchants, slaves and farmers.

The centre of this ancient world was the sacred precinct of Eanna, the 'house of heaven', where a number of huge buildings raised up on platforms and terraces hosted the worship of Inanna, the mother goddess. One

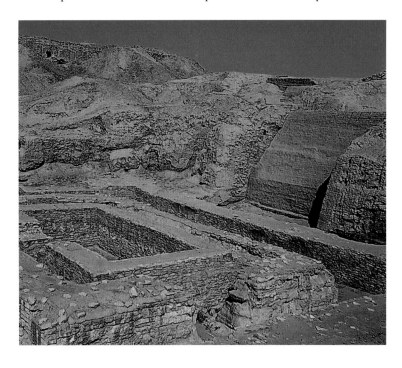

Right *Part of the excavations at Uruk, showing the White Temple complex – one of the earliest of the great Sumerian ziggurats, constructed over 5,000 years ago at around the same time that the Warka Vase was being crafted.*

of these shrines is depicted in the top register of carvings on the Warka Vase, which shows a naked man – possibly a priest or chief – making an offering to a female figure in a horned headdress, who represents either the goddess herself or her chief priestess. Behind her are two bundles of reeds, which were standard emblems of the goddess, also known as *asherah* – phallic posts. Looking on are figures in ceremonial clothing, probably priests.

The Vase itself has been dated from the period 3200–3000 BCE, when the city of Uruk was approaching its greatest magnificence. By 2800 BCE it covered 5.5 sq km (2.1 sq miles) and its influence spread to Asia Minor, Persia and beyond. But the period of the Vase's manufacture also saw Uruk approaching a seismic cultural and social shift, for it was in the 3rd millennium that the ancient tradition of rule by community elders was supplanted by the dictat of a king.

SHATTERED REMNANTS

For many years after its discovery the Warka Vase was the prize exhibit of the Iraqi National Museum in Baghdad, one of the oldest pieces of Iraq's national heritage. But its fate since the US invasion of 2003 reflects the recent history of this troubled nation. In the aftermath of the initial invasion, the museum's guards fled and the US forces, despite warnings and desperate appeals, failed to protect it against looters. Hundreds of treasures were stolen, including the Vase, which was snapped off at the pedestal in the chaos. On 23 June it was returned to the museum, wrapped up in a blanket and broken into 14 pieces. Its recovery was hailed as a landmark and it was to form the central exhibit in a revitalized museum.

Four years later, however, this dream lies in tatters. The director of the museum was forced to flee because of death-threats, and the museum itself was bricked up and surrounded by concrete walls in a desperate attempt to keep out raiders. Recently the museum has reopened to small groups of people but it is still closed to the general public due to the security situation. At present there is no way of knowing when the Vase might be restored and exhibited again.

Right The Warka Vase, showing the four tiers or registers of carving. The Vase is one of the greatest surviving cultural achievements of arguably the first – and for several centuries the largest – city on Earth.

97

Athena Parthenos

Second only to the statue of Zeus at Olympia in its ability to inspire awe, the colossal chryselephantine (gold and ivory) statue of Athena in the Parthenon was the centre point of the Acropolis in Athens and a statement of Athenian hegemony over the Mediterranean world. It represented the start of one of the most influential aesthetic movements of all time, as well as a complex discourse on religion and politics.

Right *An artist's reconstruction of Athena Parthenos inside the Parthenon. Note the winged Nike in her right hand and the coiled serpent Erichthonius that supports the great bronze shield to her left. Her totemic bird, the owl, is absent.*

The Persian Wars of the 5th century BCE pitted the mighty Persian Empire against a loose confederation of Greek city-states. It is the Spartans who are perhaps best remembered today for their exploits at the Battle of Thermopylae, but it was the Athenians who emerged from the overall war with most credit and found themselves the pre-eminent power in Greece. They were the driving force behind the setting up of the Delian League, a confederation of city-states in which each promised to field naval units as part of a defensive and offensive alliance against Persia. Those polities (self-governing units) unable or unwilling to construct and man galleys could contribute financially instead, and the treasury of the League was initially set up on the island of Delos, with strict guarantees of impartiality and fair dealings.

But things did not turn out this way. The Athenians supplied the bulk of the actual fighting forces, in return soaking up most of the funds. When they started to flex their muscles, members of the League found that it was harder to leave than to join, and that they had unwittingly subsidized the creation of an Athenian navy, which soon turned the Delian League into a de facto Athenian Empire. The turning point came in 454 BCE when the Athenians decreed that the treasury would be safer in Athens and carried it back to their city. Suspicious rivals suspected that Pericles, the leading man in Athens, intended to use the League's funds for the aggrandisement of his own city, and they were soon proved right.

TO THE GLORY OF ATHENS

The tutelary deity of Athens was Athena, the Greek goddess of wisdom, worshipped in many guises and under many names. In particular she was known as Athena Parthenos ('the Virgin') because she had no consort among the gods (Hephaestos had tried to rape her, but succeeded only in spilling his seed onto the ground, where it gave rise to Erichthonius, who became Athena's foster-child).

Keen to pay homage to her glory, especially since she had just inspired the city to military glory, Pericles instituted a set of building works of unequalled magnificence, including a great temple, the Parthenon.

Appointed to oversee the project and create the decoration and ornamentation was Phidias, the master sculptor who would later go on to build the statue of Zeus at Olympia. At the Parthenon, his masterpiece would be a colossal statue of Athena Parthenos, made of chryselephantine. The statue, finished in 438 BCE, was 12 m (40 ft) high and constructed from a wooden frame to which plates of bronze had been fixed, with plates of gold and ivory laid over the bronze. It depicted the goddess standing, in a long tunic, wearing a helm high on her head and the aegis or breastplate given to her by Zeus, with a spear in the crook of her left arm while her hand rested on the top edge of a mighty shield. In her outstretched right hand stood a statue of winged Nike (Victory), while between her sandalled feet and the shield coiled her son Erichthonius in the form of a threatening serpent (in practice the snake was positioned to help support the weight of the great bronze shield). An owl, Athena's totem bird, completed the

Left The Parthenon atop the Acropolis in Athens, looking at the West Facade. Built between 447 and 432 BCE, the temple was constructed in the Doric style and is considered to be the finest example of Doric architecture ever achieved.

ensemble, although it is not clear where this creature sat.

Her skin where it was exposed was of creamy-white ivory plates, preserved from cracking by the humidity coming off a great pool of water in front of the statue. Her robes and armour were covered in sheets of gold; according to ancient sources, 44 talents of it (1,134 kg/2,500 lb) – so much that Pericles and Phidias were accused of having looted the Delian treasury to pay for their art.

THE CLASH OF ART AND POLITICS

Ancient writers testify to the extraordinary power of Phidias' sculptures – it was said that he alone had looked upon the actual likenesses of the gods and revealed them to humans – and Athena Parthenos must have been a potent statement of Athenian

hegemony. Stylistically Phidias' efforts at the Parthenon represent the touchstone for the idealized Classical style that would inspire almost all subsequent generations of artists in the West. But his masterpiece proved his downfall. He had included a self-portrait among the reliefs on Athena's shield and his enemies used this against him, accusing him of impiety and exiling him from Athens.

The statue itself stood for nearly a thousand years. In 296 BCE the gold plates were stripped off to pay soldiers, but the bronze was then gilded. It survived a fire and was repaired, and was still in the Parthenon in the 5th century CE. After this it is not clear what became of it. It may have perished in fire, or been removed to Constantinople as a curio of ancient times, but if so, it did not survive the sack of the city in 1204.

The statue of Zeus

One of the great artistic achievements of the ancient world, the statue of Zeus at Olympia, was one of the original Seven Wonders of the World. Composed of ivory and gold and detailed with astonishing virtuosity, it was said to be so magnificent that it could lift the weariest soul from despondency, and that no one's life was fulfilled until they had gazed upon it.

Olympia, near Elis in the south-west of the Greek mainland, was the cult site of the god Zeus, head of the Greek pantheon and greatest of their gods. Here were held the Olympics, pan-Hellenic games where citizens from every polity in the Greek world would collect to compete for acclaim as an Olympic champion. Protected by a sacred truce, up to 40,000 Greeks would stream towards Olympia every four years, competing in the Olympic stadium and honouring the gods in the *Altis*, the sacred grove where the Temple of Zeus was located.

At first his shrine was relatively modest, but in the 5th century BCE it was decided that Zeus merited a more impressive home. By 456 BCE the architect Libon of Elis had finished constructing a massive temple similar to the Parthenon, and Phidias, the artist responsible for that temple's great statue of Athena (see page 98), was recruited to create something even grander.

THE STATUE IS DESTROYED

There is debate over the exact date of the destruction of the statue. It presided over the sanctuary at Olympia until at least the late 4th century CE, when it was caught up in the anti-pagan crusades of the now-Christian Roman emperors. In 392 CE Emperor Theodosius of Rome decreed that the Olympic Games were a pagan rite and should be suppressed, while the Temple itself – possibly with the statue still inside – was demolished on the orders of Theodosius II in 426 CE. However, there is also a tradition that the statue was removed and shipped to Constantinople by Greek merchants, surviving there until it perished in a great fire in 462 CE.

① ZEUS THE GREAT

From the descriptions of ancient writers, we know what the statue looked like. It was in the form of a bearded, robed giant, seated on a throne. It was 12 m (40 ft) tall, and occupied the whole width of the inside of the Temple (6.7 m/22 ft). The exposed skin of the figure was in ivory, with robes of gold. According to the Greek traveller Pausanias: 'On his head is a sculpted wreath of olive sprays. In his right hand he holds a figure of Victory made from ivory and gold ... In his left hand, he holds a sceptre inlaid with every kind of metal, with an eagle perched on the sceptre. His sandals are made of gold, and his robe is also gold. His garments are carved with animals and with lilies.'

② CHRYSELEPHANTINE CRACKING

The statue was probably constructed by fixing plates of ivory and gold to a wooden framework. This combination of gold and ivory was known as chryselephantine. In the moist climate of Olympia the ivory used to make the 'skin' of the statue was in danger of cracking, so it had to be continuously anointed with olive oil, which collected in a pool beneath Zeus' feet.

③ REACHING THE ROOF

The statue filled the interior, so that Strabo commented, 'If Zeus were to stand up, he would unroof the temple.' To the Greeks this was notable, for the statue was viewed as the actual embodiment of the god, with the Temple as his literal home, leading some to criticize Phidias for not allowing the deity enough space. However, it is likely that Phidias knew exactly what he was doing, as the cramped conditions emphasized the scale of the statue and boosted the impression it left.

④ THE THRONE

Zeus' throne was made of gold, ebony and ivory and inlaid with precious stones. It was carved with the figures from Greek myth, including gods and sphinxes. Phidias left this part of the work to his students, Panainos and Kolotis. The feet of Zeus were supported by a stool held up by lions.

The Antikythera Mechanism

An unheralded find from an ancient Roman shipwreck proved to be one of the most extraordinary artefacts in the history of technology, an ancient astronomical computer 'more valuable than the Mona Lisa' and more than 1,700 years ahead of its time, which has completely rewritten the history books.

Science began in the 17th century, at least according to the accepted, mainstream history of science. In particular, sophisticated technology at the level of intricate clockwork, cogs and gears, calculating machines and similar devices is assumed to have been the preserve of the 17th century onwards, with the advent of complex clocks, factory machines and the like. The roots of this technology could be traced back further – to impressive but cumbersome clocks created for monasteries in the 14th century, and even to the 'Box of the Moon', a mechanical astronomical calculator that used eight gear wheels, built by the Islamic astronomer al-Biruni in the early 11th century. But in the conventional story of science, it was only in the 17th and 18th centuries that technology became sophisticated enough to produce machines with large numbers of intricate gears, which in turn stimulated an inevitable snowball of inventions and applications to produce the Industrial Revolution.

THE ENIGMA OF ITEM 15087

This standard view of the history of science was based in part on the absence of any surviving technology from the ancient Greek and Roman worlds that even approached the complexity of the clocks and calculating devices of the 17th century. But this received wisdom was to be turned upside down by one of the most extraordinary discoveries ever in the archeology of technology.

The discovery began inauspiciously. In 1900 a party of Greek sponge divers sheltering from a storm off the island of Antikythera discovered an ancient Roman shipwreck from the 1st century BCE, perched on a ledge 43 m (140 ft) underwater. Statuary, coins and other valuable and important artefacts were recovered from the wreck, which was the first (and still one of the only) of such ancient ships to be explored. Nobody paid much attention to Item 15087, which at first glance appeared to be a lump of rock and barnacles accreted to a small piece of bronze.

Two years later an archeologist reviewing the finds at the National Museum of Greece noticed that there was more to Item 15087 than initially thought. It was part of a wooden frame containing fused pieces of bronze, and although most of the details were obscured

Right The Antikythera Ephebe (youth), a Greek bronze statue attributed to Euphranor and thought to have been sculpted around 340 BCE, from the same shipwreck that yielded the Mechanism.

Left *The Antikythera Mechanism, showing some of the calcification accreted by the ancient bronze during its long immersion, which meant that on discovery it resembled little more than a lump of rock.*

by the centuries, it was possible to make out some fascinating features. There appeared to be several fine-toothed gear wheels and something that looked like a dial. Other pieces, some with what looked like Greek inscriptions, were identified as belonging to the same device.

The museum archeologists suggested that it might be some sort of astrolabe, a relatively simple device for calculating the motions of heavenly bodies, which could help to determine dates, latitude and related information (for instance, Muslim sailors would use them to work out the direction of Mecca for their prayers). The evidence that the Antikythera Mechanism was actually much more advanced and sophisticated than a simple astrolabe was not taken seriously, because it was regarded as impossible for such a device to have existed 1,700 years ahead of its time.

UNDERSTANDING THE MECHANISM

Not everyone agreed with this opinion, and there have been a number of research efforts over the years, culminating in the work of the Antikythera Mechanism Research Project, which used specially made high-tech imaging equipment to study the interior of the Mechanism in unprecedented detail and read the ancient inscriptions. These investigations have revealed that it was in fact a highly sophisticated astronomical calculator or orrery, operated by setting dials and turning a handle so that its 37 gears would interact and display the desired information on one of a number of other dials and indicators. It was capable of calculating the position of the Sun, the Moon and possibly up to five of the planets; of allowing for leap years; of predicting eclipses; of showing the phases of the Moon; and even, thanks to an ingenious technical adaptation called a pin-and-slot, of compensating for an anomaly of lunar movement caused by the Moon's elliptical orbit – a feat that outfoxed Isaac Newton and shows that whoever built the Mechanism not only understood complex orbital mechanics, but had the technical skill to apply that knowledge.

THE WIZARDS OF RHODES

Who had constructed this amazing device? Evidence from the Antikythera shipwreck shows that it was sailing from Rhodes to Rome, possibly carrying merchandise and loot for a grand Triumph in honour of Julius Caesar. Rhodes was known as the home of a school of philosophers and craftsmen of marvellous technical ingenuity, and it was probably here that the Mechanism was constructed some years before, possibly even by the great philosopher and astronomer Hipparchos.

The Roman writer Cicero mentions a device that sounds remarkably similar, which had been constructed on Rhodes, but modern scholars had dismissed his account as fanciful. Now they are having to revise everything they thought they knew about ancient technology, for the Mechanism cannot have been a one-off – the sophistication of its conception and execution shows that its makers would have had lots of experience. Perhaps the real question now is, given that the ancients had apparently reached a level of technological sophistication comparable with Europe in the 18th century, why were they not launched into an Industrial Revolution of their own? In this sense the Antikythera Mechanism, a treasure described by Professor Mike Edmunds of the Antikythera Mechanism Research Project as being 'more valuable than the *Mona Lisa*', could tell us as much about the differences between us and the ancients as about the similarities.

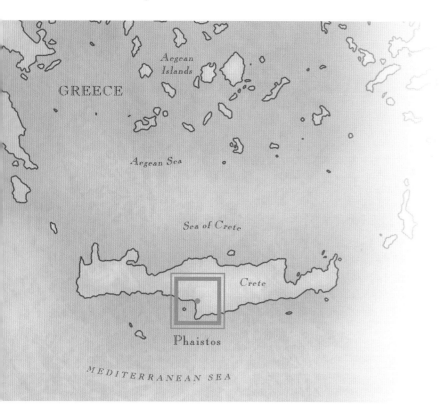

The Phaistos Disc

One of the greatest archeological mysteries of all time, the Phaistos Disc has resisted all attempts to break its ancient code, while historians of science can only guess at how an artefact 2,500 years ahead of its time could have been lost beneath a Minoan palace floor, along with the secret of its creation.

On 3 July 1908 Italian archeologists excavating the site of a Minoan palace at Phaistos, on the south coast of Crete, found a remarkable ancient artefact. Deliberately sealed into a small chamber below the floor of the palace's basement, packed in among soil, ashes and burned bones, was a small clay disc. It was circular, 16.5 cm (6½ in) across and about 1 cm (⅜ in) thick, and both sides were inscribed with spiral patterns of symbols, apparently produced by pressing specially carved stamps into the wet clay, which was then fired to harden it. This was an extraordinary find, because while the date generally attributed to the ruins where the Disc was found is c.1700 BCE, the technology used to make it – moveable type – was not thought to have been invented until 2,500 years later and many thousands of kilometres away, in 9th-century CE China.

ANOMALOUS ARTEFACT

Moveable type is best known to Westerners today from Johannes Gutenberg's invention of the printing press c.1450 CE, which used metal, cast into small stamps with raised symbols (in this case, letters of the Roman alphabet) on the end, which could then be locked together to create whole blocks of type, which could in turn be covered in ink and used to print the type onto sheets of paper. But Gutenberg himself was only building on a much older Chinese technology, which used individual stamps carved from small blocks of wood. It appears that the technology that created the Phaistos Disc was similar to this, but instead of printing with ink on paper, the ancient printer practised 'blind-printing' directly onto the medium of clay.

Making the stamps must have been a laborious and demanding job, and they are unlikely to have been created simply to produce a one-off curio. Rather, the Phaistos Disc must be the only surviving example of something that was produced regularly, indicating that moveable type was an established technology in ancient Minoan Crete. This in turn raised other important questions: where did the technology come from and why was it lost so completely that it did not resurface for millennia? Most intriguingly of all, what does it say?

DECIPHERING THE DISC

The text on the Disc is in the form of pictograms (pictorial representations) and symbols resembling hieroglyphs. It is arranged in a line that starts on the outer edge of the Disc and spirals inwards towards the centre (or the other way round, depending on your interpretation) along a base line, in a clockwise direction. Groups of symbols are separated by vertical lines into what are assumed to be words. There are 241 characters on the Disc, but many of them are repeated, so that the whole is made up of only 45 different symbols, which are arranged into 61 'words'. Most experts agree that the signs probably represent syllables rather than letters, perhaps with some ideograms (symbols representing whole words) mixed in.

Deciphering what language the writing represents and what it might mean are tasks made difficult – impossible, according to many authorities – by the relatively small number of words and by the fact that nothing comparable to the Disc has ever been discovered. Most of the signs on it have never been seen anywhere else, although there are

UNINVENTING THE WHEEL

The Phaistos Disc would appear to contradict the generally held dictum that it is impossible to uninvent something. Rather it underlines that technological progress is not a simple and inevitable progression. Historian Jared Diamond suggests that although the Phaistos Disc demonstrates that a relatively advanced writing technology had been fully developed in ancient Minoan Crete, it also shows that without the right conditions inventions can easily be lost.

Perhaps too few people could read, or the process of producing and using the stamps did not offer a significant advantage over writing by hand – for whatever reason, the technology was not sufficiently popular, widespread or useful to survive, and only the Phaistos Disc bears witness to its brief existence. Putting a value on something so utterly unique is impossible, but there is no doubt that the Disc, which resides at the Iraklion Archeological Museum on Crete, is one of the great treasures of history.

some highly suggestive correspondences with other ancient writing systems. For instance, there are some similarities with the ancient Minoan writing called Linear A, which itself has not been fully deciphered. There may also be similarities with Egyptian hieroglyphics, Hieroglyphic Luwian and proto-Byblic script. Dozens of different interpretations have been offered, including a magical curse, a religious ritual, a mathematical proof and a prayer.

It has also been suggested that the Disc is actually a board game, of the type known as 'chase' games, in which game pieces chase each other along a board, like today's Snakes and Ladders. The ancient Egyptians, who interacted heavily with the Minoans, had a board game called Mehen, 'the coiled one', which might link to the spiral nature of the text on the Disc. Such ancient game boards were often two-sided, just like the Disc.

Right *The Phaistos Disc. On this side 122 stamped hieroglyphs are visible. Note how some of the characters are repeated many times, and how groups of characters are separated by vertical lines into what are presumably words.*

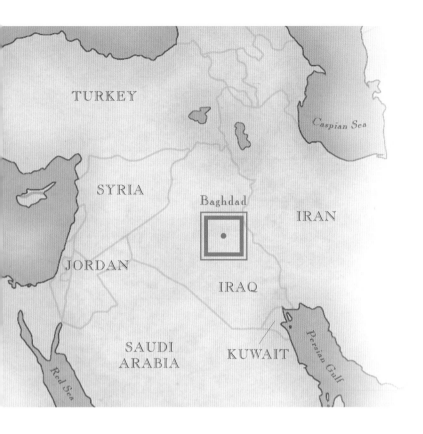

The Baghdad Battery

Perhaps the most famous piece of anachronistic technology, the Baghdad Battery is widely seen as a scientific treasure as well as an historical enigma. A simple but intriguing device, it may be evidence of electrical technology, a conjuror's ruse unearthed or simply a warning of the dangers of over-interpretation.

There are many mysteries surrounding the Baghdad Battery. The basic premise of the story is that an ancient jar was unearthed from a site near Baghdad and was found to contain a copper cylinder, within which was an iron rod, both of them held in place in the neck of the jar by an asphalt plug. In 1940 the German former director of the National Museum of Iraq, Wilhelm Köning, first suggested that the strange contraption might have been an early form of battery, possibly used to generate electricity for the process of electroplating (where a very thin layer of one metal, such as gold or silver, is deposited onto the surface of another metal, in order to gild or silver it).

A NUMBER OF MYSTERIES

Many of the details of this story are unclear. Firstly, there is confusion over how many 'batteries' there actually are. The original jar that triggered König's interest was said to have been dug up from the village of Khujut Rabu in 1938, but whether it was the German who had discovered it, or whether he simply stumbled across it in the archives of the museum, is unclear. In addition to

this 'original', however, several other apparently similar devices were found, so it may be more correct to speak of around a dozen Batteries.

The original Battery was a small, fat clay jar about 13 cm (5 in) tall. The copper cylinder that it enclosed – about 9 cm (3½ in) tall and 2.5 cm (1 in) across – was made of a rolled-up sheet of beaten copper with a separate base crimped onto the bottom and sealed with more asphalt. The iron rod was heavily corroded. Tests on the inside of the jar found acidic residue. To König, the resemblance to a battery was obvious. Alessandro Volta was previously thought to have invented the battery in 1800 when he discovered that two metals of differing electrical potentials, put into a conducting medium such as vinegar, will generate a current.

In the case of the Baghdad Battery it seemed likely that the jar, when filled with vinegar, lemon juice or grape juice, would generate a small but measurable current, and that if several of the jars were connected in a series, a big enough current would be generated to have an application. This interpretation seemed to be confirmed after

the Second World War when an American engineer built a replica of the Battery and filled it with grape juice, producing a current of about one volt.

König knew of copper vases coated with a thin layer of silver, which had been dug up elsewhere in Iraq. Perhaps, he speculated, devices like the Baghdad Batteries had been used to deposit that film of silver. Again, this interpretation seemed to be backed up by experiments in the 1970s by German researcher Dr Arne Eggebrecht, who claimed to have used a series of replicas to successfully perform electroplating. The site where the Battery had been discovered was a Parthian settlement, leading König to attribute the jar and the precocious electrical technology to the ancient Parthians (c.250 BCE–225 CE), and the date of the Battery is usually given as c.200 BCE.

UNDERCURRENT OF DOUBT

Many of these attributions have proved doubtful. For instance, the clay jar that forms the housing of the Battery is Sassanian in design, suggesting that the records of its discovery may not be accurate, and that in

'Wilhelm Köning, first suggested that this strange contraption might have been an early form of battery.'

Left *Reconstruction of one of the Baghdad Batteries, cut away and faced with glass so that it is possible to see how a working model looked when filled with electrolyte. Note that the cap on the bottom of the inner copper cylinder, described as part of the original Battery is missing in this reconstruction.*

fact it dates from the Sassanian era (225 CE–640 CE). Dr Eggebrecht's claims of successful electroplating are also doubtful, given that there seems to be no record of his tests. Many experts doubt that even a series of the jars could generate enough power to do useful electroplating and point out that all the examples of gilding and silvering known from the ancient world can be explained using 'conventional' methods (such as mercury gilding). The original Battery may not even be properly set up to work as a

battery, as the copper cylinder needs to be open at the bottom in order to allow oxygen to get into the electrolyte.

Alternative theories about the Battery include the suggestion that it is an electrical device, but was used either for electrotherapy (the ancient Greeks wrote about applying electric eels to the soles of the feet for this purpose), electro-acupuncture, or to pass a very small current through a metal idol so as to create a supernatural effect for worshippers touching it. The gathering

consensus, however, is that the Battery is not a battery at all. Similar contraptions have been found in Seleucia and Ctesiphon in Iraq and proved to be containers for sacred scrolls of papyrus or bronze. Perhaps the Baghdad Battery was simply an eccentric filing cabinet – the breakdown of its papyrus contents could explain the acidic residue found inside it. The Baghdad Battery(ies) reside at the National Museum in Baghdad, which means that at present their fate is uncertain (see 'The sacred Warka Vase' on page 96).

The Spear of Destiny

A holy relic claimed to be the actual blade of the spear or lance that pierced Jesus' side while he was on the cross, the Spear of Destiny was said to control the fate of nations and bestow greatness upon its bearer. In practice, however, there are at least four different versions of the Spear – which is the real treasure?

The Spear of Destiny, also known as the Holy Lance or the Spear of Longinus, is commonly held to be the spear referred to in the Gospel of St John, chapter 19, verse 34, which records that after Christ had died on the cross, 'one of the soldiers with a spear [*lancea*] opened his side and immediately there came out blood and water'. Other Gospels mention an unnamed centurion who remarks of Jesus, 'Truly this man was the Son of God' – a line best known today for being the one line that John Wayne gets to utter in the film *The Greatest Story Ever Told*.

MYSTICAL POWERS

In later years this centurion acquired a name, Gaius Cassius Longinus (Longinus probably being a variation of the Greek word *longke*, meaning 'spear'), and was said to have been converted and cured of partial blindness by a drop of Christ's blood, before becoming a martyr in Asia Minor. His spear was reputed to have been wielded deliberately to help put Jesus out of his misery as an act of mercy. What is more, the spear in question was not simply an ordinary soldier's weapon.

The Spear accrued a phenomenal provenance, and was said to be the Spear of Herod Antipas, which in turn was an ancient sacred weapon forged from meteoric iron by Tubal Cain, wielded by Joshua at Jericho and later by Saul and David, used by Brutus to assassinate Caesar and in Herod's slaying of the first-born. Later it was carried by Emperor Constantine, helping him to win battles and assert his authority over the squabbling clergy, and he bore it before him as he marked out the bounds of the New Rome he was founding at Constantinople. Like so much of the story of the Spear, however, these are all later additions to the legend.

Over the centuries a body of legend and folklore grew up around the Spear, which was said to possess mystical powers that could change the course of history, guaranteeing victory and world domination to whoever wielded it. It was this reputation that supposedly led Adolf Hitler to obsess about the version of the Spear that was stored in the Hofburg Museum in Vienna, where it still lies today.

MULTIPLE SPEARS

Like many holy relics, there are multiple claimants to the title of the Holy Lance. The first-recorded mentions date from the 6th century CE, when pilgrims to Jerusalem described seeing the lance that pierced Jesus. In 615 CE Jerusalem fell to the armies of King Chosroes of Persia and from this point on different spears diverge into history, possibly because it was impiously broken in two by the heathens. A shard from the point of the blade was given to the Christians and taken to Constantinople, and was presented to the

Right The Holy Lance from Vienna. The blade is Carolingian and was first recorded in 961. At that time it was not linked with the Spear of Longinus, although it was said that shards of nails from the Cross had been used to forge crosses onto the blade.

Crusader king St Louis of France in 1244. It was placed in Saint-Chapelle in Paris, but vanished during the French Revolution. The larger fragment may have stayed in Jerusalem for some time, but also turned up in Constantinople. It was supposedly sent by Sultan Beyazit II to Pope Innocent VIII in 1492, who had it placed in the column of Longinus in St Peter's in Rome, where it still resides today.

Meanwhile a third version was dug up in 1098 by Crusaders in Antioch after a divinely inspired dream and also made its way to Constantinople (which seems to have been a clearing house for holy relics). This may be the Spear that is now preserved at Etchmiadzin in Armenia, although the Armenian Church claims that its provenance descends from the disciple Thaddeus.

HITLER'S SPEAR

The most famous version, said to have passed through the hands of a martyred Roman centurion called Mauritius (or St Maurice), and thus known as the Spear of St Maurice or more simply as *die Heilige Lanze* (the Holy Lance), made its way to the court of the Holy Roman Emperors after inspiring the victories of a succession of post-Roman kings, culminating in Charlemagne. This version, complete with a nail from the True Cross, became part of the imperial regalia and was used in the coronation ceremony for new emperors. It lived at Nuremberg until 1794, when the threat of looting by Napoleon Bonaparte occasioned its removal to the Hofburg in Vienna.

By the 20th century the Spear had accreted many legends – those mentioned above and others, including a walk-on role in the tale of Joseph of Arimathea, who was said to have brought the Spear to Britain along with the Holy Grail (see page 150). Perhaps it was inevitable that Hitler, who combined a degree of interest in the occult (exactly how much is questionable) with a covetous fascination for artistic and cultural treasures, should be attracted to the Spear.

The main source for the lurid tales of Hitler's fascination with the Spear is the occult writer Trevor Ravenscroft and his

book *The Spear of Destiny*. Unfortunately Ravenscroft had no qualms about mixing serious research with less convincing material (including some gleaned by clairvoyance). According to his version of events, Hitler's first act on marching into Vienna in 1938 was to spend an hour alone with the Spear, which was then removed to Nuremberg, as part of the Führer's evil occult plan for world domination. Supposedly it fell into the hands of the Allies at the exact same moment of Hitler's suicide in Berlin, thus working its dangerous influence on fate. On 6 January 1946 it was returned to the Hofburg, where it can still be seen to this day.

Above *Bernini's statue of St Longinus holding his famous spear, at the base of the Column of Longinus in St Peter's in the Vatican, one of the four columns supporting the great dome. A fragment of the Spear of Destiny is said to have been placed inside the column.*

The Visby Lenses

Excavated from a Viking grave on the Baltic island of Gotland, the Visby Lenses are a sophisticated Viking treasure. Marvellous and mysterious, they seem too close to modern lenses to have been simply jewellery. Could the Vikings have invented modern optics centuries before the official birth of the telescope?

FIRE-STARTER, TELESCOPE OR MAGNIFYING GLASSES?

The advanced optical properties of the Visby Lenses mean that they could have been used for a number of functions. With their power to concentrate rays of sunlight to a very fine point, they could have been used as fire-lighters or perhaps even a primitive form of surgical laser for cauterizing wounds. According to some experts, however, the extreme precision of the Lenses would have been wasted on this task.

There has been speculation that they could have been used to create the first telescopes, 500 years before the recognized birth of the telescope in early 17th-century Holland, when Dutch lens-makers put together two lenses to achieve high levels of magnification. The greatest flaw in these early Dutch

telescopes, however, was a phenomenon known as chromatic aberration, caused by imperfectly ground lenses. Different wavelengths of light refract by differing degrees on passing through glass, so unless a lens is perfect the different colours of light passing through it will not be focused onto precisely the same point and a blurred image will result. The Visby Lenses, however, are so good that they could have overcome this flaw and made high-quality telescopes.

The most likely scenario, however, is that the Lenses were used as reading stones (known elsewhere in Europe from the 11th century), or single magnifying glasses for craftsmen involved in fine close-work that required optimum imaging.

In 1990 German scientist Karl-Heinz Wilms stumbled across a strange artefact that had been discovered on the island of Gotland (in the Baltic Sea to the east of Sweden). Named the Visby Lens, after the island's capital, it appeared to be a highly polished piece of rock crystal mounted on a silver backing. Wilms died before he could investigate further, but in 1997 a team of three German scientists, inspired by his initial curiosity, made the trip to Gotland to the local museum where the lens, which proved to be one of ten, was kept.

OPTICAL ODDITY

It had initially been assumed that the highly polished pieces of rock crystal had been intended for use as part of some jewellery, to be inserted into a necklace or other ornament, as with any other polished semi-precious stone. But the German team quickly realized that the quality of workmanship and the very specific shape and properties of the pieces indicated that they must have been made intentionally to function as lenses. The Lenses were aspherical – that is, not shaped like a sphere, but with an ellipsoid cross-section on one side and a flattened

cross-section on the other – which make them perfect for refracting light in the way that modern telescope or corrective lenses do. But here were lenses from a Viking site dating back to around the 10th–11th centuries CE.

Closer examination produced even more extraordinary results. The best of the lenses is so perfectly ground that it exceeds even the finest modern correctional lenses. According to one Harley Street ophthalmologist, 'Only special lenses for scientific or professional use are made to an optic resolution as high as the Visby Lenses.' It has a refractive power more than twice the strength of the thickest correctional lenses. Specifically, the bulging sides of the Lenses display almost perfectly elliptical cross-sections.

The Lenses must have been ground on a turning lathe by a genuine master craftsman, but what baffles modern optical experts is how the grinder knew what shape to aim for. The exact shape necessary for a lens of this type was not worked out until René Descartes calculated it in the 17th century, and even then he was not able to execute his theory because the right equipment did not exist. Presumably the medieval artisan who produced the Visby Lenses must have arrived at their shape through trial-and-error.

FROM DISTANT BYZANTIUM

Another mystery surrounding the Lenses is where they came from. Gotland was a trading centre with links across the Baltic to the rivers that penetrated deep into Russia, and which the Vikings had used to engage in substantial trade with the Byzantine Empire and the Muslim world. Since rock crystal is not found on Gotland, the material for the Visby Lenses must have been imported, but where were they ground?

It was assumed that they had been produced by workshops in sophisticated Constantinople or the lands of the Caliphate (the Islamic world in particular was the home of optical knowledge at this point in history). But excavations on Gotland have discovered many intermediate stages of rock-crystal manufacture, including raw crystals, polished beads and lenses, which suggests there was some sort of rock-crystal industry on the island. Gotland must then have been home to a lens-grinder of unequalled skill. As with other technological anomalies, however, such as the Phaistos Disc (see page 104) and the Antikythera Mechanism (see page 102), the existence of the Lenses raises important questions. Why wasn't more use made of corrective lenses if they could be produced at this quality, and why was this technology and all knowledge of it lost, not to reappear for more than 500 years?

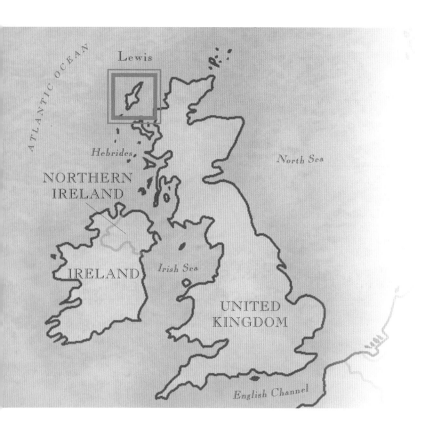

The Lewis Chessmen

Sometimes described as Scotland's greatest treasure, and featuring in the British Museum's list of the top-ten treasures in the whole of Britain, the Lewis Chessmen are enchanting and strange. Uncertainty surrounds their discovery and their original owner.

The Lewis Chessmen are a large collection of mainly walrus-ivory chess pieces discovered on the Isle of Lewis in the Outer Hebrides, islands off the north-west coast of Scotland. Probably made in 12th-century Norway, they are considered to be among the finest surviving art treasures of the period.

ELVES AND TROLLS

Mystery surrounds the discovery of the Chessmen, and in the absence of solid evidence, a number of picturesque legends have developed. According to one tale, they were stolen by a sailor in around 1600, but he was then murdered by a shepherd named Ghillie Ruadh. Fearing that the loot would incriminate him, he buried the pieces in a small stone cairn or chamber on the southern shore of Uig Bay, on the western coast of Lewis. The cairn was then covered with a sand dune, either deliberately or through natural processes, and its secret was lost when the shepherd was hanged for another crime.

An even more popular tale recounts what happened next. In early 1831 a local man, Calum nan Sprot, came across the cairn after the sand dune had been washed away. Breaking it open, he beheld the collection of tiny, grim-faced figures. The islands were steeped in superstition and folklore, and local people retained a strong belief in the supernatural world of their Gaelic and Viking ancestors. Accordingly poor Calum thought he had stumbled upon a fairy mound filled with elves and trolls and was overcome with terror and fled. His wife induced him to return and salvage the pieces, which were sold to a collector.

THE SUPERSTITION LIVES ON

Although entertaining, these accounts are probably largely fictional. All that is known for certain is that on 11 April 1831 the Chessmen were exhibited to the Society of Antiquaries of Scotland. There were 93 pieces, comprising the better parts of four chess sets, together with some playing counters for chequers or a related game, and a belt-buckle. Ten pieces were bought by a collector named Kirkpatrick Sharpe, who eventually obtained another one, and this group of 11 ended up with the Royal Museum in Edinburgh and is now on display at the Museum of Scotland. The rest were bought by London's British Museum, where they are still exhibited today. According to the folklorist Katharine Briggs, in her *Encyclopaedia of Fairies*:

> *A tradition has arisen about [the Lewis Chessmen]. It is said that the guards who take the guard-dogs around at night cannot get them to pass the Celtic chessmen. They bristle and drag back on their haunches. So, perhaps the Highlander's [Calum nan Sprot's] superstition can be excused.*

A more recent development has seen calls for the pieces at the British Museum to be repatriated. In March 2005 the leader of the Scottish Nationalist Party tabled a motion at Parliament calling for the Lewis Chessmen to be returned to the Western Isles. In 2007 the SNP won power in Scotland, so the Chessmen may not yet have finished their travels.

KINGDOM OF THE ISLES

The Chessmen are beautifully carved from walrus ivory (although a handful are of whale bone), and staining indicates that some of them would have been red, showing that red and white (rather than black and white) were the conventional colours at the time. They are wonderfully expressive, with gloomy faces for the most part, except for some of the 'warders' (equivalent to rooks), who are berserker warriors biting their shields in crazed fashion. Only the pawns are not in human form and are simply gravestone-shaped objects.

A number of clues point to the pieces' origin in Norway. The kings and queens sit on ornate thrones carved in almost identical fashion to actual chairs and church pews in Norway from the same period, while the small ponies that the knights sit astride are similar to those seen in other Scandinavian carvings. Fragments and drawings of similar chessmen found in Trondheim in Norway point to the specific place of manufacture.

How did they come to be in the remote Western Isles? From around the 9th to the mid-13th centuries this region of Scotland was part of the Viking realm. Lewis was part of the Kingdom of Mann and the Isles, which owed notional fealty to the King of Norway, but in reality was a playground for warring nobles and princelings. The blending of Norse and Gaelic cultures produced a rich cultural brew, in which men were admired for both war-like and artistic traits, including an appreciation of fine sets for chess, the game of kings. Perhaps the Lewis Chessmen were a gift to a lord of Lewis, or perhaps they were lost en route from Norway to Viking outposts in Ireland.

Below *Lewis Chessmen. The two pieces in the centre of the picture are both warders (rooks). On the left the warder takes the form of a berserker warrior, biting his shield, while on the right is a rather more sedate version, although when he is seen from an angle it becomes apparent that he has wildly staring eyes.*

The Colossus of Rhodes

The shortest-lived of the Seven Wonders of the World, the Colossus of Rhodes (a Greek island off the coast of Turkey) was a titanic statue erected to commemorate a famous victory. A testament to the engineering and ingenuity of the ancients, in its day the Colossus was the biggest statue in the world, and even its ruins inspired awe for nearly a thousand years.

At the end of the 4th century BCE the generals of the deceased Alexander the Great were vying for control of his legacy. In the Mediterranean, the Greek state of Rhodes had allied itself with Ptolemy of Egypt but in 305 BCE Antigonus Monophthalmus – Alexander's successor in Macedonia – called upon it to join him in war against his Egyptian rival. The Rhodians demurred, prompting Antigonus to dispatch his son Demetrius Poliorcetes (the Besieger) to punish them.

Demetrius arrived at the principal port and capital of the island, also called Rhodes, with a force of 40,000 men. Faced with the high city walls Demetrius constructed massive siege towers, the first of which was mounted on six ships, lashed together. The elements intervened and the ship-borne tower was lost in a storm, whereupon he constructed an even greater one on land – Helepolis (Taker of Cities), which was 41 m (130 ft) high and moved on eight great wheels, each 3.7 m (12 ft) across.

The cunning Rhodians, however, defeated this tower too, according to some accounts by diverting a stream so that it got bogged down in mud, according to others by dislodging some of its protective metal plates so that it was in danger of being set alight.

The Rhodians withstood long enough for relief to arrive, in the shape of a fleet sent by Ptolemy, and Demetrius withdrew, leaving behind his siege engines out of respect for the valour and tenacity of the defenders. The city decided to use Helepolis as scaffolding to construct a statue in honour of the patron deity of Rhodes, Helios (the sun-god). Sculptor Chares of Lyndos was given the task, creating an enormous figure out of bronze. According to the ancient writer Pliny it was finished in 282 BCE after 12 years of construction.

The Colossus was the shortest-lived of the Seven Wonders, for it was toppled by a massive earthquake in 224 BCE, snapping off at the knees, the weakest point of the structure. But even the remains of the statue inspired wonder for more than 800 years and were a major tourist attraction during the Roman era. When the Arabs conquered Rhodes in 656 CE the remains were shipped to Syria for scrap; reputedly 900 camels were required to carry them away.

① BRONZE PLATES
The Colossus was built around a central stack of stone blocks, into which iron bars were driven to construct a skeleton. Bronze plates were then fixed to these bars (a similar method, using copper over a steel frame, was used to create the Statue of Liberty). So much bronze was used that it was said to have created a shortage across the ancient world.

② HEROIC STANCE
In many artistic representations of the Colossus it is shown with its legs dramatically spanning the entrance to the harbour at Rhodes, but in practice this would have been unfeasible. It actually stood on a marble pedestal 15 m (50 ft) high either on the harbour mole or on a breakwater in front of the harbour. The statue was probably sculpted into a Classical pose.

③ MONUMENTAL SIZE
Pliny the Elder visited the fallen giant in the mid-1st century CE and wrote that: 'Even as it lies, it excites our wonder and admiration. Few men can clasp the thumb in their arms, and its fingers are larger than most statues. Where the limbs are broken asunder, vast caverns are seen yawning in the interior. Within it, too, are to be seen large masses of rock, by the weight of which the artist steadied it while erecting it...'

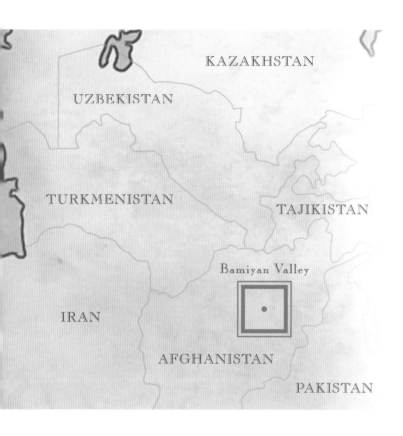

The Buddhas of Bamiyan

Previously the best-known archeological treasures in Afghanistan, the colossal statues of the Buddha carved into the mountainside at Bamiyan gained global notoriety as the most high-profile victims of the Taliban regime, when they were blasted into rubble in early 2001.

The Buddhas of Bamiyan were two colossal statues of the Buddha, carved into the sandstone cliffs of the Bamiyan Valley in central Afghanistan, 230 km (143 miles) north-west of Kabul. The largest of the pair, known in antiquity as the Red Buddha, stood 53 m (174 ft) tall, making it the tallest standing Buddha in the world, while the nearby Moon-White Buddha was 37 m (121 ft) tall.

SILK ROAD HUB

Today Bamiyan is a remote town in a high mountain valley 2,500 m (8,202 ft) above sea level, but in ancient times it was a thriving trade centre on the Silk Road. The region had seen a series of empires come and go, with Alexander the Great's passage leaving a particularly long-lasting cultural legacy of Hellenistic influence. It was the heart of the ancient kingdom of Gandhara (which spent most of its history subject to grander empires), and by the 5th century CE was the capital of the Hepthalite peoples (sometimes known as the White Huns). They followed a form of religion known as Greco-Buddhism, very much a product of the rich cultural and

Right One of the giant Buddhas before its destruction. Note the flat facial area and the holes down the front of the Buddha's sides – these are where the additional plaster-adobe crafted elements would originally have been attached.

Opposite Panoramic view of Bamiyan and the escarpment with hundreds of caves and the niche that contained the large Buddha.

RECONSTRUCTION OF THE BUDDHAS

Since the fall of the Taliban, much work has been done to stabilize the site and protect the remains. About 40 per cent of the statues are thought to have been pulverized to dust, but there is talk of using the remaining fragments for anastylosis – rebuilding using the original material. This is contentious, partly because it would involve spending millions that might arguably be better spent on relieving Afghan poverty. Similar objections are raised to a Japanese plan to create a laser-show replica of the fallen giants. Meanwhile archeologists continue their search for what may be an even greater treasure – the largest Buddha in the world. The Chinese pilgrim Xuan Zing also described a 300 m (1,000 ft)-long reclining or seating Buddha near by, and Professor Zemaryali Tarzi believes he has found the temple complex where it lies buried and is only a year or two from uncovering it.

religious traditions of the region, and the giant Buddhas were the most notable expressions of this.

Traditionally there has been some uncertainty over the exact date of construction of the Buddhas, which was given as anywhere between the 2nd and 6th centuries CE. Thanks, ironically, to the Taliban's destruction of the statues, a lot of detailed archeology has been possible as experts have picked over the rubble, and dating of plaster fragments has revealed that the smaller Buddha was built in 507 CE and the larger in 554 CE.

Originally the Buddhas would have looked quite different from their modern pre-destruction appearance. The main bodies were hewn directly from the rock face, with additional elements, such as the forearms and face, crafted from a mud-straw-horsehair mix coated with plaster or perhaps with giant masks of wood. The larger Buddha was painted red and the smaller one in many colours, and they were 'glittering with gold and many precious ornaments', in the words of the Chinese pilgrim Xuan Zing who visited them in 632 CE. He described how Bamiyan was a thriving centre for worship and pilgrimage, with more than ten monasteries and over a thousand monks, many of whom lived in niches and caves that still honeycomb the cliffside and decorated them with colourful murals.

Over the centuries the Buddhas suffered from relentless weathering and the unsympathetic attentions of earlier fanatics. The Mughal emperor Aurangzeb had cannons fired at the face of the Red Buddha in the 17th century, as did Nadir Shah of Persia in the 18th century. A Taliban commander fired rockets at the statues and blew off the Moon-White Buddha's face in 1998. By 2001 they were battered, faceless and armless, with none of their original plaster covering or ornamentation, but the characteristic folds of their robes were still largely intact.

CULTURAL VANDALISM

The destruction of the Buddhas in March 2001 is considered to be one of the great cultural crimes of our time. Ostensibly this act of vandalism was sanctioned in an edict debated by Islamic clergy of the Taliban regime, who decided that the Muslim prohibition against graven images applied and that the statues were un-Islamic. The demolition began on 2 March as tanks and rocket-launchers peppered the statues, and then local men were coerced into planting dynamite around and behind them; the work was completed by 11 March. Condemnation was global, but the Taliban dismissed it, insisting that their motives were pure and Islamic. 'All we are breaking are stones. I don't care about anything but Islam,' said the Taliban commander Mullah Omar. In practice it seems there may have been political motives. Bamiyan is the power-centre of the Hazara tribe, a Shiite minority opposed to the Taliban, and the destruction may have been a way of asserting dominance while attacking their distinct cultural identity, and even of attempting to erase all traces of Afghanistan's pre-Islamic past. In addition, the Taliban are thought to have been angered by Western concern for the monuments and by anti-Taliban sanctions.

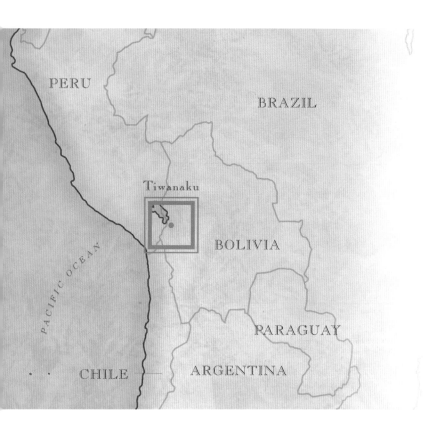

PERU

BRAZIL

Tiwanaku

BOLIVIA

PACIFIC OCEAN

PARAGUAY

CHILE — ARGENTINA

The Fuente Magna Bowl

Proponents of the Bowl's authenticity claim that it is the most spectacular archeological find ever in the Americas, if not the entire world, and that it proves there was pre-Columbian transatlantic contact, perhaps even that South America was settled by the Sumerians, or vice versa. Sceptics are dismissive.

The Fuente Magna Bowl (strictly speaking, this is a tautology, since *Fuente Magna* means 'great dish') is a brown stone dish or bowl allegedly discovered near the ruins of the ancient civilization of Tiwanaku in Bolivia, which is heavily inscribed with what looks like cuneiform writing that has been variously identified as Phoenician, Sumerian and proto-Sumerian, together with animal motifs and humanoid figures. If this is true it might date the Bowl to c.3500 BCE, and raises obvious questions about how it got there, some 5,000 years before the conventionally accepted first contact between Old and New World civilizations.

THE ROSETTA STONE OF THE AMERICAS

Proponents of its authenticity label the Bowl 'the Rosetta Stone of the Americas', although somewhat inaccurately, because they also claim that the languages inscribed on it are known and already decipherable. What they really mean to say is that it could be the key to an entirely new history of the Americas.

One of the main sources for information on the Fuente Magna is the work of Bernado Biadós Yacovazzo and Freddy Arce, independent Bolivian investigators. They describe meeting a 98-year-old Indian named Maximiliano, who explained that the Bowl, which he called *El Plato del Chancho* ('the pig's dish'), was found among a group of ziggurats or mounds near Lake Titicaca. He also claimed there were others. The Bowl first came to the attention of historians in the 1950s and is currently said to reside in a museum in La Paz.

There is no doubt that the inscriptions on the bowl do resemble cuneiform. According to a translation by one Dr C. Winters, they concern the ritual use of the dish, which was probably used to pour libations – offerings to a deity or idol. In fact, Yacovazzo and Arce also claim to have uncovered this idol: a stone statue from Pokotia, which also bears suggestive inscriptions. Other interpretations of the cuneiform point to a Semitic language, possibly Phoenician.

ATLANTIS IN AMERICA

The Fuente Magna has primarily caught the attention of the Atlantology community and other fringe historians, who argue that there is proof of extensive pre-Columbian transatlantic contact, such as similarities between Old and New World languages, correspondences between Old and New World religion and myths (such as the ubiquity of Sun worship and pyramid building), hard evidence of the transmission of goods and plants (such as traces of coca plants found in Egyptian mummies) and otherwise inexplicable archeological discoveries, such as Phoenician coins in the Americas. This evidence all points to a common origin for Old and New World civilizations, either because one was settled by the other, or because they both descend from an original mother civilization – that is, Atlantis.

The Fuente Magna has been specifically interpreted as proving previous suggestions that Aymara, the language spoken by the Indians of Bolivia's Altiplano region, is closely related to Sumerian. Both are what are known as 'agglutinative languages', and if the Sumerians settled or originally came from South America, it would explain this correspondence. In this reading, South American words such as 'Inca' are actually related to Sumerian terms such as *Enki* (the name of a major Sumerian deity, it means 'great lord').

If the language on the Fuente Magna is actually Phoenician, this ties in with extensive theories identifying the pre-Inca civilization of Peru and Bolivia as the actual site of the land of Tarshish, mentioned in the Bible as the destination of trading expeditions by King Solomon and his Phoenician ally, Hiram of Tyre. The Phoenicians were known to trade across the seas for metals such as copper, tin and silver, all of which are plentiful in South America. Perhaps this was the route by which the Fuente Magna arrived in Bolivia.

HARMLESS FAKE?

Artefacts such as the Fuente Magna can also serve a darker agenda, because proof that people from the Old World may have colonized or at least ruled over the New World since ancient times are politically and racially loaded. The post-Columbian colonization of the Americas resulted in the subjugation and genocide of many Native American nations, and in recent years these groups have made significant strides in asserting their moral and legal rights for land, special status and forms of compensation or restitution. Many racist,

right-wing Christian and white-supremacist groups resent this deeply and would love to be able to show that people from the Old World have an equal claim to be Native Americans. If the Fuente Magna were proved to be genuine, it would advance their agenda.

Mainstream archeology has taken little notice of the Fuente Magna, and in the absence of any serious research to back up its provenance, it seems unlikely to be genuine. But given the sinister ends to which claims about such artefacts can be put if left unchallenged, it might be wise for experts to take a proper look at the Bowl.

'Proponents of its authenticity label the Bowl 'the Rosetta Stone of the Americas' … it could be the key to an entirely new history of the Americas.'

Left A top view of the mysterious Fuente Magna Bowl, showing some of the inscriptions and carvings on its inner surface. The heavily pitted bottom suggests that it may have seen service as a working dish.

The Crystal Skulls

For the New Age community, the Crystal Skulls – a series of human skulls carved from rock crystals and other minerals – are among the most famous and important historical treasures in the world, gifted with strange powers and arcane significance. But sceptics argue that they are simply the result of a clever scam.

The Crystal Skulls are known throughout the New Age and fringe historical community. They are said to be proof of the use of advanced technologies by ancient civilizations, and even to have been handed down by aliens or from Atlantis. They are reputed to possess strange optical and sonic properties, to give off or enhance psychic energy and to contain information of Earth-shattering importance, the legacy of lost super-civilizations.

THE SKULL OF DOOM

The most famous of the Crystal Skulls is the Mitchell-Hedges skull, sometimes known as the Skull of Doom. The story put about by its 'discoverers', Frederick Mitchell-Hedges and his daughter Anna, is that it was discovered by the latter during a dig at the Mayan site of Lubaantun in Belize in 1924 (or possibly later; their accounts differ). Cut from a large piece of rock crystal, it is a remarkably well-crafted simulacrum of a human skull (slightly smaller than an adult male, leading to speculation that it is meant to be female), with a separate jaw piece that attaches by a hinge. According to the mythology that has grown up around it, extensive testing has shown that it was not produced by modern-era machine tools, but cut with diamonds and finished by polishing with sand over the course of centuries. Psychics insist that it has

mystical properties, while Mitchell-Hedges claimed it was at least 3,600 years old, and his daughter has suggested that it was made by aliens.

Other well-known Crystal Skulls include a specimen belonging to the British Museum (bought from Tiffany's in 1897) and one in the Musée de l'Homme in Paris. The British Museum skull was said to move around in its case and be associated with other paranormal phenomena. Several other skulls exist, supposedly recovered from various Meso-American sites, but the picture is now confused because hundreds, if not thousands, of replicas have been produced for the so-called 'para-trinket' market.

Believers in the mystical properties of these skulls say that Native American legends speak of 13 copies, which somehow store the wisdom and lore of the ancients, and which will be brought together by fate when the time is right to reveal great secrets. In the meantime the skulls can be used for scrying, divination, consciousness expansion, healing and other psychic or paranormal ends. Here is a typical explanation by a psychic 'researcher', Marianne Zezelic:

Crystal serves as an accumulator of terrestrial magnetism. By gazing at the crystal [skull], the eyes set up a harmonic relation stimulating the magnetism collected in that portion of the brain known as the cerebellum … contributing to psychic phenomena.

This is pseudo-scientific jargon without the remotest basis in fact.

SKULDUGGERY UNCOVERED

In 1996 a BBC documentary team submitted the British Museum and Paris skulls to electromicroscopic investigation and found marks produced by modern polishing wheels. They concluded that the skulls had probably been made in the 19th century, possibly by craftsmen in Germany. Further detective work by the Smithsonian Institute traced the skulls back to a 19th-century antiques dealer named Eugene Boban, who dealt in Mexican antiques, but probably obtained the skulls from Germany, passing them off as Native American.

Anna Mitchell-Hedges declined to have the Skull of Doom tested by the BBC, but there are serious doubts about its provenance. Her father was known to be an inveterate self-mythologizer, and he was not running the dig at Lubaantun, but reporting on it for the *Daily Mail*. Anna herself was probably not present at the time claimed for its discovery, while records show that in 1936 it belonged to a gallery owner named Sidney Burney, and that Mitchell-Hedges bought it from him at an auction at Sotheby's in 1943. His daughter claims that this was because he had given it to Burney for safekeeping in the 1930s and only bought it at auction because he could not get it back; but, given the suspect provenance of the British Museum and Paris skulls, it does not seem implausible that the Skull of Doom was also a fake. Even its evocative moniker may be a mistake: it may originally have been nicknamed the Skull of Dunn, after a member of the expedition to Lubaantun. The crystal from which the skull is made is thought to have come from Brazil, as there are no suitable sources in Belize, while the skull was not a major feature of Mayan culture, but rather of the Aztecs to the north.

Having said all of that, it is possible that some of the Crystal Skulls touted as mystical

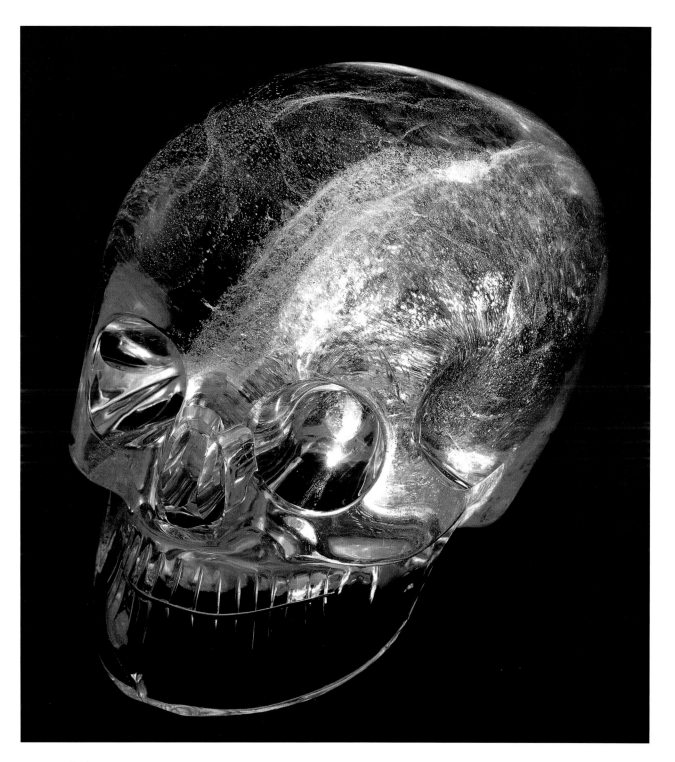

Right The British Museum's Crystal Skull, revealed by testing to have been made with relatively modern machinery and probably created by craftsmen in Germany in the 19th century.

objects genuinely were created by pre-Columbian American civilizations. More to the point, there is little doubt that, whatever their true background, many of these Crystal Skulls – including the Skull of Doom and the British Museum skull – have caused people to experience strange and even paranormal phenomena (though these may be purely subjective).

'The skulls are said to be proof of the use of advanced technology by ancient civilizations, and even to have been handed down by aliens or from Atlantis.'

The story of the Amber Room

The Amber Room was a room in the Catherine Palace in Russia that was covered in panels of beautifully crafted amber. Described as the Eighth Wonder of the World, this priceless artefact was looted by the Nazis during the Second World War, triggering one of the greatest treasure hunts of all time.

Superlatives abound when the Amber Room is discussed, whether in reference to its value, its splendour or the saga of its loss and pursuit. The *Daily Telegraph*, for instance, describes it as 'one of the greatest art mysteries of the century', but it is much more than that. For legions of treasure hunters it is the holy grail of post-war treasure, the epitome of lost Nazi loot and the ultimate prize. For the Russians it symbolizes their loss and suffering at the hands of the Nazis, representing all that was taken; it is also a valuable political and moral stick with which to beat the West – and the Germans in particular.

FIT FOR A QUEEN

The history of the Amber Room dates back to Prussia, 1701, when an ambitious court sculptor/architect saw his chance to catch the eye of a young queen. Andreas Schlüter had fallen out of favour with Queen Sophie Charlotte, the wife of Prussian king Frederick I (ruled 1701–13), and was seeking a way to win back her patronage. In the cellars of the Royal Palace, Schlüter stumbled across a huge store of amber, a precious substance that he knew held great significance for the Prussian monarchy. Amber, known as the Gold of the North, is fossilized pine resin laid down by the prehistoric forests that covered much of Europe 40 million years ago. Much of it was washed into the Baltic, where millions of years later it was collected with nets and used to create small, but immensely valuable ornaments, including some of the Prussian Crown Jewels.

Schlüter conceived the idea of fitting out in amber a room in one of the palaces that Sophie Charlotte was having refurbished. He recruited master craftsmen, who had to use a new method of working with amber to realize his ambitious vision. Fragments of amber were heated, soaked in an infusion of honey, linseed and resin, and moulded into flat leaves, which could then be pieced together like a mosaic or stained-glass window, on a backing of wood covered in gold or silver leaf. The intention was to create a set of panels and boards of amber, which could then be fitted onto the walls of a room, together with other suitably magnificent ornaments, to create an unprecedented spectacle that would blaze with golden light.

PETER'S JIGSAW PUZZLE

Schlüter never finished his project – Queen Sophie Charlotte died of pneumonia, he himself was exiled over a construction scandal, his replacement argued with the craftsmen who were creating the room and then Frederick I also died. His successor, Frederick William I, had little interest in the project and it languished incomplete until 1716, when the Prussian king unloaded it onto the visiting Russian tsar, Peter the Great (ruled 1682–1725), who was known to love amber. Peter had the Amber Room shipped to the new city he had founded, St Petersburg.

Unfortunately there was no one in Russia able to fit together the jigsaw puzzle of the uncompleted room, which had suffered serious damage in transit. It remained in storage until 1743 when the Empress Elizabeth (ruled 1741–62) revived the project and had the room moved to the Catherine Palace in Tsarskoye Selo (a village outside St Petersburg). It was only finally completed in 1782 by Catherine the Great (ruled 1762–96), who added new panels and ornamentation, including four Florentine stone mosaics.

STOLEN BY THE NAZIS

The Amber Room dazzled and awed visitors to the palace through the 19th century, the fall of the monarchy and the Russian Revolution. Along with the other treasures of the imperial palaces, it was displayed to the Russian people and cared for by curators until the Second World War. With the Nazis advancing rapidly towards Leningrad (as St Petersburg was now called), head curator Anatoly Kuchumov was ordered to pack up what he could for evacuation to the east. To his dismay, he could not find a way to take down the amber panels without breaking them, and in desperation he had them covered with fake walls, in the hope that the Germans would pass over the greatest art treasure in Russia.

The ruse failed, and the Nazis quickly managed to dismantle the Amber Room and ship it back to Königsberg, ancient seat of the Teutonic Knights and, the Germans considered, the spiritual home of the room. Here it was displayed in Königsberg Castle until the Russians began to close in, when it was packed up once more and plans to ship it elsewhere for safekeeping were discussed.

On 31 May 1945, just three weeks after the German surrender (but more than six weeks after the fall of Königsberg), Professor Alexander Brusov of the State Historical Museum in Moscow arrived in Königsberg to find out what had happened to the Amber Room. To his horror, he found the city in ruins and most of the castle a burned-out shell. Penetrating to the cellars, Brusov discovered that an intense fire had swept through this part of the castle. Amid the ashes were the carbonized remains of three of the four Florentine mosaics from the Amber Room – of the rest of the room, there was no sign.

'For legions of treasure hunters the Amber Room is the holy grail of post-war treasure.'

Below *After a quarter of a century of painstaking reconstruction, the new Amber Room at the Catherine Palace, was finally unveiled to the world in 2003.*

The search for the Amber Room

The KGB and the East German Stasi, or secret police, spent decades searching for the Amber Room. Treasure hunters from Russia to the Czech Republic are still looking. Academics and amateur historians have devoted their lives, and sometimes their sanity, to the search. But have they all been looking in vain?

Below *Detail of one of the panels from the restored Amber Room, begun in 1979 and completed with the help of German money, and reopened amid great fanfare in 2003.*

Opposite *Königsberg Castle, home of the Amber Room for most of the Second World War after it was looted by the Nazis, and probable scene of its destruction, when a fire swept through the castle.*

The Nazis had perpetrated many outrages on Russia, including the theft of thousands of art treasures. Recovering these was an important way for the Soviets to salvage some pride and repair, while those artefacts that were not recovered would make powerful ammunition for the steadily escalating propaganda battle with the West.

SCOURING THE RUINS

The evidence of the cellars did not look good, but Professor Brusov was determined to explore all options. He knew from interrogation of Germans who had worked at Königsberg Castle that the Amber Room had been packed up with the intention of shipping it off to a safer spot. The former curator of the castle's art collection led him to a bunker across town, but there was no sign of the room. Eventually he returned home with the conclusion that the Amber Room had probably been destroyed in the castle fire.

But Anatoly Kuchumov, the Catherine Palace curator who had looked after the room for so many years, refused to accept this. With KGB backing, he savaged Brusov's efforts and findings, destroying the professor's career, and launched his own investigations in Königsberg, uncovering evidence that the Nazis had scouted locations in the Prussian countryside, and also in more distant parts of Germany, as possible safehouses for the storage of looted art.

Kuchumov followed the trail of the Amber Room to Berlin, but without success, and later he and other Russian investigators, led by the KGB, returned yet again to Königsberg. Over four decades the formerly German city, now a Russian enclave and naval base called Kaliningrad, was thoroughly explored, tunnelled and excavated, but no trace of the room has ever been found.

EAST AND WEST

Meanwhile Germans from both sides of the Iron Curtain had joined the hunt, inspired by articles which insisted that the Amber Room had survived the war and awaited rediscovery, carefully placed in the international press by communist intelligence agencies. After reading the articles, and encouraged by his bosses (who knew that repatriating the Amber Room would curry favour with their masters in Russia), Stasi agent Paul Enke became an expert on all things to do with the Amber Room, eventually publishing 1986's *Bernsteinzimmer Report*, the best-known book on the subject. Enke chased the room to various castle art depositories across East Germany, but found the Soviets peculiarly uncooperative when it came to accessing

important documents. He ended up empty-handed, though convinced that the answer lay within reach.

In West Germany strawberry farmer and amateur historian George Stein took up the hunt for the Amber Room after previously helping to repatriate other art treasures to Russia. A suspect letter purporting to be from an SS officer led him to believe that the room had been shipped out of Königsberg to an old mining complex in Lower Saxony, although searches here proved fruitless. Over the next 25 years the hunt for the Amber Room would destroy Stein's family and eventually his sanity. He disembowelled himself with a scalpel in mysterious circumstances in 1987, after having become convinced that the Amber Room had been shipped off to America following the war.

Other clues and rumours have led to the Amber Room being sought in lakes and mines all over Europe, but the only traces that have ever been found are the fourth mosaic, stolen from Leningrad by a Wehrmacht soldier in 1941 and kept secret by his son until the late 1990s, and a chest of drawers also stolen before the Amber Room left Russia.

A MASSIVE HOAX?

In 1999 the British investigative reporters Catherine Scott-Clark and Adrian Levy started to research the fate of the Amber Room, publishing the results in their 2004 book *The Amber Room*. After diligently tracing all the false leads and wrong turns taken by everyone from Kuchumov to Stein, they came to a startling conclusion. The evidence clearly suggested that the Amber Room had indeed been destroyed by fire in the cellars of Königsberg Castle in 1945, just as Brusov had feared, but this conclusion had been suppressed by Kuchumov, who did not want to believe it – possibly for fear that he would be blamed for not taking down the panels and saving the Amber Room when the Nazis invaded. The Soviet state had gladly seized upon Kuchumov's version because it served to cover up an unpalatable truth: the fire that destroyed the room had been set by Soviet troops, engaged in an orgy of looting and destruction. The articles written about the Amber Room were deliberate disinformation and all the many investigations by the KGB and Stasi were smokescreens.

Even today the Russians have too much invested in the myth of the Amber Room to admit the likely truth. It remains officially the greatest of the art treasures looted by the Nazis that are still tragically missing, a symbol of the terrible wrongs inflicted on Mother Russia in the Great Patriotic War. Proving that something was completely destroyed is difficult, but if there is any proof, then it remains locked away in impenetrable Russian archives, hidden from unwelcome eyes.

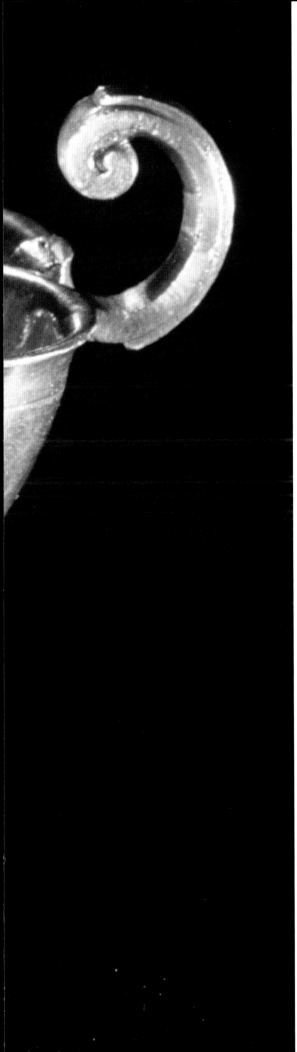

PART 4

SUNKEN TREASURES

UNESCO estimates that there are more than three million shipwrecks in the world. Many of these ships carried valuable cargoes, including gold, silver and gems, which offer tremendous rewards to those with the resources and determination to find them – when the historical value of coins and artefacts is factored in, some individual wrecks may be worth more than $1 billion. To archeologists, however, the true value of the wrecks usually lies less in their cargo of bullion and coins and more in the context of the find, the remains of the ship and the commonplace and everyday objects it carried, and these can only be usefully investigated if careful and non-invasive procedures are followed. This necessarily puts treasure hunters and guardians of heritage on a collision course, and it should be borne in mind when reading accounts of recovered sunken treasure that not everyone celebrates such finds or shares the excitement and romance of successful salvage.

The Brunei shipwreck

The discovery of a sunken cargo ship off the coast of Brunei prompted the launch of an expedition to recover the drowned loot against all the odds. Battling storms, mud and even pirates, an international team rescued a unique treasure trove of priceless medieval ceramics to shed new light on international trade in the 15th century.

On 24 May 1997 a vessel belonging to the oil company Elf (now Total Fina Elf) was prospecting off the coast of Borneo in the South China Sea, about six hours from the Sultanate of Brunei, when its sonar revealed the presence of an anomalous mass on the sea floor 61 m (200 ft) down. It was the spilled cargo of a shipwreck, potentially of enormous material and archeological value. Working with the Sultanate and other international partners, the oil company put together a team to attempt the difficult task of excavating the site and retrieving the lost treasure. Ranged against them were the depth of the wreck; the terrible conditions on the sea floor, where thick mud quickly obscured all visibility; searing heat and intermittent storms at the surface; and the ever-present threat of pirates and looters. With the cost of the project running at $65,000 a day, the team had just a few weeks to complete the project and pull off the largest undersea excavation ever managed in the South China Sea.

BLUE-AND-WHITE GOLD

Eventually more than 15,000 objects were retrieved, including thousands of pieces of Chinese porcelain with its distinctive blue-and-white glaze, and thousands of stoneware jars from other parts of South-East Asia. The story that these finds revealed was complex and surprising; a story of the birth of global trade and of how, even in the 15th century, commerce was more powerful than government.

By the 15th century China was the greatest industrial nation on Earth, its massive porcelain factories churning out vast quantities of precious ceramics to feed the world's insatiable hunger for this 'blue-and-white gold'. Only the Chinese possessed the secret of porcelain manufacture, and customers from Indonesia to Europe coveted its beauty and functionality, many even ascribing religious and magical properties to it.

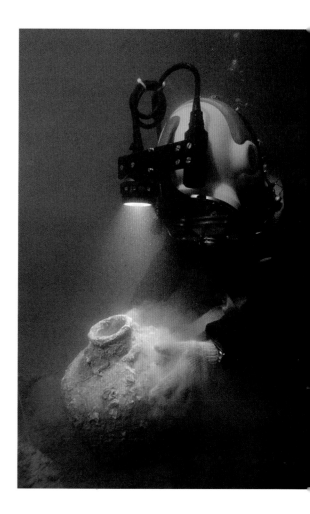

Right *The team excavating the Brunei shipwreck were hampered by difficult conditions, including thick mud that obscured visibility. Here a diver examines a stoneware jar through a haze of silt.*

At the start of the century Chinese merchants controlled trade in South-East Asia and ventured as far as Africa, Arabia and maybe even Australia in their search for profit. This mercantile hegemony peaked in 1405 with the launch of a massive expeditionary trading fleet under the eunuch-admiral Zheng He, who commanded the largest ships the world had ever seen.

But over the succeeding decades power struggles between the imperial court and the merchants triggered an extraordinary suppression of Chinese trade, as the emperors ordered all Chinese merchant ships to be scrapped and forbade their subjects to engage in international maritime trade of any kind. The Chinese authorities had decided there was nothing they wanted from the rest of the world, but this sentiment was not returned. There was still a desperate clamour for porcelain, and those willing to risk capture and death could make fortunes from smuggling.

TRADING PLACES

The Brunei shipwreck provides a vivid record of this, for in addition to its porcelain cargo, which enabled archeologists to date the wreck to the late 15th century (about the same time that Columbus was setting off in search of a westerly passage to the riches of the Orient), it also carried huge quantities of stoneware jars from Thailand and Vietnam. With the date provided by the porcelain, this suggested to the archeologists that the sunken cargo ship was not actually Chinese, or at least had not loaded up in China. Instead it was more likely that it had started its journey in Vietnam or Thailand, at a port where South-East Asian stoneware had also been gathered and to which Chinese goods had been smuggled. The profit motive was simply too strong for Chinese merchants to ignore and, despite the edicts of the emperors, the engine of international trade could not be derailed.

The precise records kept by the excavating team enabled them to reconstruct the exact distribution of the cargo in the ship when it sank, revealing that it had been carefully packed at one time, rather than picking up

loads at several different ports. Unfortunately the ship's masters had been greedy and the vessel was probably dangerously overloaded, which might explain why it came to grief not far from its likely destination – the Sultanate of Brunei.

At the time Brunei was one of the greatest trading centres in the world, with a highly ritualized exchange of goods like these ceramics for locally produced commodities such as rare woods. The porcelain might have graced the tables and temples of the Sultanate, while the stoneware jars were valued to the point of reverence by the inland tribes. A single stoneware jar might be worth dozens of buffalo, and they could even be

Above *Valuable blue-and-white porcelain from 15th century China and stoneware jars probably from South-East Asia.*

taken 'hostage' to help guarantee the obeisance of the tribe that owned them.

Not long after the ceramic-laden ship went down with its precious cargo, the Portuguese arrived in Brunei and changed the shape of trade – and global history – for ever. The Brunei shipwreck represents the end of one era, but heralds the dawn of the modern age of commerce.

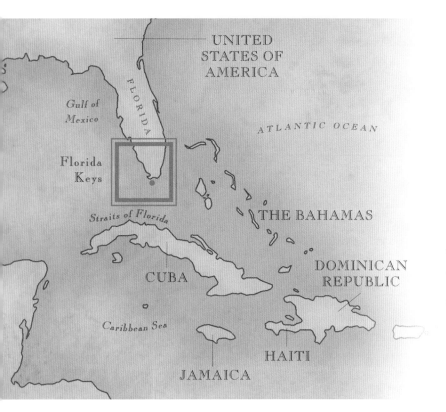

Nuestra Señora de Atocha

One of the richest and most famous shipwrecks of all time, the Atocha *is most people's mental model of a lost treasure galleon. Part of a great fleet of treasure ships that was overloaded and fatally postponed, it ran afoul of a hurricane off Florida and was wrecked on the Florida Keys.*

After more than a century of exploitation of its New World empire, Spain was the richest and most pre-eminent power in Europe, grown fat from the river of gold, silver, precious stones and rich cargo delivered each year by the *flota* system (the system of controlled and restricted trade between Spain and the New World, which revolved around an annual fleet or *flota*, see page 136). But not all was smooth sailing for the Spanish monarchy. It was embroiled in the Thirty Years War (1618–48) and relied heavily on its share of colonial booty to prop up its increasingly indebted treasury, while the conflict threatened its trade routes to the New World as English and Dutch privateers and fleets waited to pounce on fat merchant ships and treasure galleons.

TREASURES OF THE NEW WORLD
The 1622 fleet had assembled as normal from all across Spain's New World possessions. The Manila galleon (see page 134) had delivered rich pickings from the East Indies for overland transport to Veracruz in Mexico, to be picked up by the New Spain fleet, along with Mexican silver and gold. Meanwhile the

Tierra Firme (Spanish Main) fleet was loaded with silver, gold and emeralds from South America, and when the two fleets rendezvoused at Havana in Cuba they were joined by valuable loads of copper and indigo (a dye) from other ports. They were also greeted with the disturbing news that a Dutch fleet was prowling the Caribbean.

Nuestra Señora de Atocha was a powerful modern galleon with the Tierra Firme fleet, named after one of the most popular sacred sites in Spain. It was the second-strongest ship in the combined fleet, assigned the task of bringing up the rear of the convoy of merchant ships, smaller support vessels and other galleons. It was these galleons – the biggest and most heavily armed ships – that were to carry the most valuable elements of the year's booty. Chests of bullion and coins were placed at the bottom of the *Atocha*'s hold to act as ballast. The official cargo manifest included 24.5 tonnes (24 tons) of silver bullion, more than 100,000 silver coins, 125 gold ingots, 545 kg (1,200 lb) of silverware, 582 copper ingots, 350 chests of indigo and 525 bales of tobacco. The wealthy and noble passengers on board loaded their cabins with personal treasures,

including a fortune in emeralds from Muzo in Colombia. On top of all this was the undeclared cargo smuggled aboard to avoid the official register and the hefty taxes imposed by the government.

RACE AGAINST TIME
The transatlantic fleet system had only a narrow window of operations for its journey to and from the Americas. Winter storms in the North Atlantic ruled out a large portion of the year, while the deadly tropical hurricane season threatened from June/July until October. But like the 1622 fleet it was dramatically delayed by late delivery from the colonies and by adverse winds in the Caribbean. By the time the Tierra Firme fleet reached Havana it was 22 August, and the combined fleets finally set off on 4 September, six weeks behind schedule, only to sail directly into the first hurricane of the season.

On 5 September massive gales scattered the fleet, swamping some of the smaller vessels. Overnight the wind shifted into the east, driving the ships towards the deadly reefs of the Florida coast. Many of the lead vessels were fortunate, finding themselves far

enough south to pass safely by the outlying rocks and islands of the Dry Tortugas and the Straits of Florida, finding haven in the Gulf of Mexico. But the *Atocha*, its companion galleon the *Santa Margarita* and some of the smaller ships of the convoy were driven towards the Florida Keys.

The *Margarita* was grounded on the reef with relatively little loss of life, but a little way further to the east the *Atocha* was heaved up by a massive wave and smashed directly onto the coral, shearing off its masts and smashing a great hole in the hull. More waves forced the wreck off the reef into deep water on the other side and it sank like a stone. Most of the passengers and crew had taken refuge from the storm below decks, with the hatches securely fastened. They had no chance to escape; 260 people drowned and only five who had lashed themselves to the broken mizzenmast survived. The ship settled on the bottom 17 m (55 ft) down, and with it, a massive fortune in treasure.

'Chests of bullion and coins were placed at the bottom of the Nuestra Señora de Atocha*'s hold to act as ballast.'*

Above *The* Santa Margarita *was the companion ship to the Atocha. Most of its cargo was salvaged by the Spanish soon after it sank, but in 1980 treasure hunter Mel Fisher recovered coins, jewellery and gold ingots, like those pictured here.*

The *Atocha*: the Mother Lode

The Atocha *is possibly the richest and most famous treasure galleon ever salvaged, and the hunt for its drowned wealth is a tale of tragedy, perseverance, controversy and triumph, featuring one of the world's best-known treasure hunters.*

THE MEL FISHER STORY

Mel Fisher, who died in 1998, is probably the most famous name in treasure hunting. Born in Indiana, hundreds of kilometres from the sea, Fisher moved to California after the Second World War to take up poultry farming, but soon decided to pursue his hobby – scuba diving – as a business, opening a dive shop in Redondo Beach. He and his wife took to wreck diving, and after meeting Kip Wagner in Florida and learning of the potential booty on offer (see page 139), they relocated to Florida to start treasure hunting in earnest. Fisher was renowned for his dogged optimism, epitomized by his catchphrase 'Today's the day!' But he also courted controversy, being accused by both archeologists and campaigners of looting and despoiling maritime heritage, and being found guilty of selling fake gold coins just months before his death at the age of 76.

Several years of Spanish salvage operations recovered much of the loot from the *Margarita*, but the *Atocha* lay in water that was too deep for 17th-century divers to handle. After another storm scattered the remains of the ship, the wreck was lost. The Spanish spent another 60 years searching in vain for its millions, and for nearly 300 years it lay beyond the reach of treasure hunters.

HUNTING FOR THE MOTHER LODE

In 1969 treasure hunter Mel Fisher (see box) turned his sights on tracking down the *Atocha*. Although he had experienced some success with salvage from the Plate Fleet of 1715 (see page 136), Fisher and his wife and partner Deo had grown frustrated with difficult conditions and adverse press and decided to move to sunnier and potentially richer waters. They were tipped off about the existence of the *Atocha* when someone at a party produced a copy of *The Treasure Diver's Guide*, which identified the 1622 wreck as one of the richest ever lost.

So began a 16-year hunt for what Fisher and his team, who formed a company called Treasure Salvors, would come to refer to as the 'Mother Lode'. Employing specialist equipment, adapted and sometimes invented specially for them, including side-scan sonar, sand-clearing propwash deflectors known as 'mailboxes' and proton-magnetometers, the team searched the seabed off Matacumbe Key, halfway up the Florida Keys, until research in the Spanish Archives of the Indies showed them they were miles off course.

Relocating to a site near the Marquesas Keys, 32 km (20 miles) west of Key West, Fisher started to find clues. In 1973 three silver bars were found on the seabed and their markings matched up with the tally numbers recorded in the manifest of the *Atocha*. They were on the right track. Two years later Fisher's son Dirk located five of the *Atocha*'s bronze cannons, but days later tragedy struck. A small salvage vessel was capsized by heavy seas and Dirk, his wife and another diver were killed.

Fisher ploughed on, despite financial problems and restive creditors. In 1980 the

Right This stunning emerald-inlaid cross was found inside a silver box recovered from the wreck of the Atocha.

team located the wreck of the *Santa Margarita* and recovered a haul of gold ingots, silver coins and jewellery that the original Spanish salvors had missed. Finally, on 20 June 1985, Treasure Salvors HQ received a message from Fisher's other son Kane, captain of the salvage vessel *Dauntless*. 'Put away the charts; we've found the main pile!' Investigating a substantial magnetometer reading, two of Kane's divers discovered what they later described as a reef of silver bars.

THE BANK OF SPAIN

Over the next two years Fisher and his team salvaged 127,000 silver coins, 900 silver bars weighing nearly 30 kg (70 lb) each, 700 high-grade emeralds and thousands of smaller stones, more than 113 kg (250 lb) of gold, lengths of gold chain, hundreds of pieces of sometimes exquisite jewellery and a wealth of archeological material including navigation instruments and artefacts of shipboard life, not to mention a good portion of the hull. So much treasure was pulled from the wreck that team members called it 'the Bank of Spain'. Estimates of the amount recovered amount to $450 million or more, and even today salvage of the site continues.

But Fisher's treasure hunting was not without controversy. Since the early days he and other treasure hunters had been accused of pillaging archeological sites and turning heritage into personal profit. Protests had encouraged the government to pass a law requiring treasure hunters to buy a licence to salvage, and to agree to give 25 per cent of the loot to the State of Florida, who were allowed to pick the cream of the finds for the state. Further changes to the law threatened to confiscate all of Fisher's windfall and he engaged in a seven-year-long legal battle with the government, which he eventually won, although the amended laws have mostly put an end to treasure hunting Fisher-style. Today much of the *Atocha*'s treasure is displayed at the museum Fisher created, although some of it has been sold off.

Manila treasure galleons

Northern Mariana Islands, on 20 September 1638. The remains of the ship were located in 1987 and thousands of pieces of gold jewellery have since been recovered, along with many other treasures. The *Nuestra Señora del Pilar* was wrecked off the southern coast of Guam in 1690, on its way from Acapulco to Manila with a shipload of silver swords and

The greatest treasure ships of the Age of Sail were the massive Manila galleons that plied the trans-Pacific route from Manila in the Philippines to Acapulco in Mexico, laden to the gunwales with precious fabrics, porcelain, woods and spices and groaning with millions in gold and jewels.

Spanish possessions in the New World were the key to extraordinary wealth, particularly since they provided the precious silver that was among the few commodities the Chinese were willing to accept in return for their valuable porcelain, silk and gold. Portuguese control of the 'eastern hemisphere' and later Dutch control of the Cape of Good Hope at the southern tip of Africa meant that the Spanish were restricted to a trans-Pacific trade route, where silver from the New World was shipped from Acapulco to Manila, where it could be traded for the bounty of the Orient, which then had to be shipped back to Europe via Mexico.

In addition, the Spanish Crown and the Seville merchants who held the monopoly on trade with the New World were determined to maintain strict control of the trade, with the result that it was organized into a highly restrictive system. After 1593 only one or two ships a year were allowed to make the trans-Pacific crossing but these were the largest ships of the age, weighing up to 2,040 tonnes (2,000 tons) and carrying more than a thousand men.

IN PERIL ON THE SEA

The 11,100 km (6,900 mile) westward route was relatively straightforward: favourable currents and winds meant that it took on average around 100 days; but the 13,000 km (8,100 mile) return journey (longer because the ships had to sail in a northerly arc to catch

the trade winds) took twice as long. The galleons, which although massive and sturdy were often difficult to sail and unwieldy in bad weather, had to negotiate narrow straits, avoid lethal reefs, dodge pirates and hostile natives, cross vast expanses of uncharted ocean with limited supplies, cope with scurvy, disease and mutiny, and pray that they were not caught in a storm. The crossing was so dangerous that more than 40 Manila galleons were lost, each of them laden with enough wealth to entice a legion of treasure hunters.

PRICELESS WRECKS

Many (if not most) of the wrecks locations are unknown, but a few have been tracked down. Some came to grief in the final stage of their journey, when after successfully crossing the Pacific they had to make their way down the treacherous California coast to Mexico: several wrecks have been located, or are thought to be located, off Santa Catalina Island. But the most dangerous part of the journey was probably the initial passage through the narrow straits and shallow waters of the Indies, and many ships were lost in and near the Philippines – 30 of them in the straits leading into Manila alone.

Three of the most notable wrecks are of galleons wrecked on islands further to the east. The *Nuestra Señora de la Concepción*, possibly the largest ship in the world at the time, foundered on a reef in Saipan, in the

vast quantities of silver coins. More than 1,500 artefacts have been recovered by divers since 1991, but it is believed that more than $1 billion worth (in modern terms) of coins were aboard as ballast and these have yet to be recovered.

The *Santa Margarita* left Manila in July 1600, but overloading, poor ballasting, adverse winds and storms meant that six months later it was hopelessly off course. With scurvy and dissent rife among the crew, it was decided to put in at Rota, one of the Mariana Islands, but the ship was driven onto a reef and smashed to pieces, while the crew was captured, left to drown or horribly butchered by the islanders. In 1993 a salvage company called IOTA Partners entered into an agreement with the local government to locate and excavate the wreck, and attempt to recover the tens (possibly hundreds) of millions of dollars of gold, silver and other valuables that might remain. The search for its bounty, and that of many other priceless Manila galleon wrecks, continues.

① FLOATING CASTLES

Manila galleons were derived from earlier Spanish models with high fore and aft castles, but were enlarged and had more streamlined profiles. Most were built in the Philippines, where there was a plentiful supply of hardwoods. Some sources claim that the woods used in their construction were of such high quality that they could not be pierced by cannonballs, although other sources argue that this was part of a myth put about to denigrate Spanish naval valour. Manila galleons could have up to 100 cannons, helping to protect their valuable cargoes and transforming them into virtual floating castles.

② CREW'S QUARTERS

The majority of the crew of a galleon would be made up of native Filipinos, commanded by Spaniards, although dozens of other nationalities were probably also represented. Crews of 700–1,000 were common, although many of them could expect to die before reaching Acapulco. The voyage took around 200 days, stretching provisions to the limit and exposing everyone to scurvy. In one notorious case in 1657 the galleon *San Jose* was found drifting off Acapulco without a single living crew member, all having succumbed to the fatal deficiency.

③ CARGO HOLD

Official Spanish inventories of the Manila galleons were not kept, partly because merchants objected to the Crown keeping close tabs on their cargoes, which in turn might restrict their opportunities for smuggling. But reports – particularly detailed inventories kept by English privateers who managed to capture galleons – provide a vivid picture of the wealth stored below decks. This included Chinese silks and porcelain, cotton from India, ivory from Cambodia, camphor from Borneo, woods, cinnamon, pepper and cloves from the Spice Islands and precious jewels from Burma, Ceylon and Siam (Thailand), together with gold and golden jewellery stored among the other goods. There would also be huge quantities of gold and jewels smuggled aboard the ship – sometimes worth more than the official cargo.

The 1715 Plate Fleet

While the Pacific trade relied on single ships, entire fleets of treasure ships plied the seaways between Spain and the New World, bearing vast quantities of silver and gold in addition to the loot of the Indies. Known as the Plate Fleets, they were immune to most threats except the weather – as, for instance, when a huge hurricane wrecked the Plate Fleet of 1715 on the shores of Florida.

As with the Manila galleons, trade between the New World and Spain was rigidly controlled, thus ensuring that other European powers did not get a look-in, and that the Crown could extract its slice of the booty in the form of the *quinto*, the 20 per cent tithe that went to the monarchy. All trade from the Americas was restricted to an annual fleet, which would carry manufactured goods from Europe out to the New World, then bring back both the silver and gems of the Spanish colonies in Central and South America and the cargo transported overland from Acapulco, where the Manila galleons disgorged their loot. These fleets, known as the Plate Fleets because of the Chinese porcelain they carried, were worth millions at the time (and hundreds of millions today). They were generally safe from pirates and privateers because they travelled en masse; their worst foe was the weather.

BACKED-UP TREASURE
In 1715 events in Europe meant that the fleet gathering in the Caribbean for the trip back to Spain was loaded with a particularly immense treasure. The War of the Spanish Succession (1701–14) had pitted Spain against other European nations, and for the previous two years the threat from enemy navies had been deemed too serious for the fleet to travel. As a result, the treasure and trade of three years was backed up in Cartagena and Veracruz, and in Havana where the different parts of the fleet were scheduled to rendezvous before heading across the Atlantic. Normally the fleet would leave in good time to avoid the onset of the hurricane season, but its captain general was delayed in Veracruz waiting for tardy mule trains from Acapulco. When he finally made it to Havana in mid-May, the press of merchants and potentates vying for space on his ships led to further delays.

On top of all this, Captain General Don Juan Esteban de Ubilla had been given strict instructions not to set sail until he had stowed within his personal cabin the eight chests containing the Queen of Spain's dowry. Philip V (ruled 1700–46), the sex-crazed King of Spain, had recently married Isabella Farnese, Duchess of Parma, but she refused to consummate their marriage until she received the magnificent bride-price she had been promised, which was to include the finest jewellery that the Spanish colonies could muster. The king had given strict instructions that Ubilla was not to set sail without it.

IN THE EYE OF THE HURRICANE
At last, on 24 July 1715, more than three months late, the fleet set sail from Havana. There were 11 Spanish galleons, a French frigate that had been added at the last minute on the insistence of the Governor of Havana and a smaller cargo ship expressly hired by Ubilla to help carry even more treasure. This small armada was to follow a well-worn route, shadowing the coastline north past Florida, riding the Gulf Current until they could pick up the trade winds that would carry them across the Atlantic. But this was also one of the most dangerous parts of the journey, for with the reefs and rocks of Florida under their lee, the heavy Spanish galleons were vulnerable to poor weather.

For four days they enjoyed fair weather and good sailing, but on the 29th they were becalmed and on the 30th ominous signs

gathered around them – the sea and sky took on a strange cast, the swell picked up despite the absence of wind, and the flocks of seabirds that usually attended their progress vanished. What the hapless sailors did not know was that a huge storm had been shadowing their northern passage, sucking in air and growing into a full-blown hurricane. Their fate was sealed when, during the night, it changed course and drove westwards towards them.

WRECKED ON THE FLORIDA COAST

In the early hours of 31 July the fleet met a horrible end. Ubilla's flagship, the *Nuestra Señora de la Regla*, was the first to go. Survivors told how it was lifted by an immense wave and smashed against the reef with such force that the entire top half of the deck sheared off. Ubilla and 223 of his crew were killed. Eleven other ships followed, with more than 700 men drowned or battered and huge quantities of cargo scattered on the reef or dragged out into deeper waters by sinking wreckage. Only the French ship, the *Grifon*, survived, its canny captain having sailed a more easterly course and left himself enough sea room to ride out the storm without being driven against reef or shoreline. More than 48 km (30 miles) of the Florida coast, between modern-day Fort Pierce and Sebastian Inlet, was scattered with wreckage and bodies. The bedraggled survivors huddled onshore, waiting for daybreak.

Left *One of four anchors raised from the wreck of the* Urca de Lima *after it was rediscovered off Fort Pierce in 1928 by a diver wearing an air-tethered helmet. Fifteen of the wreck's cannons were also salvaged.*

The search for the 1715 Plate Fleet

When the 1715 Plate Fleet went down, a vast fortune in silver and gold went with it. For nearly 300 years treasure hunters have battled the elements, sharks and each other in their quest to retrieve it. How did one man hit the jackpot and how much treasure still lies beneath the waves, awaiting discovery?

Above *The reef where the* Urca de Lima *stuck fast, and where its remains were rediscovered in 1928, was declared the first Florida Underwater Archaeological Preserve in 1987.*

The coast of Florida may seem like an idyllic spot for treasure hunting, with clear blue waters, sandy bottoms, sunshine and kilometres of beach, but in reality conditions along east Florida's Treasure Coast (named for the many wrecks that litter it, especially the 1715 Plate Fleet) are far from ideal for salvage.

SALVORS AND FREEBOOTERS

Salvage was the first priority of the surviving Spanish. The ranking officer split the survivors into two camps and set them to work, while word was sent to the nearest colonies to ask for help. It was essential to work as quickly as possible, for the authorities knew that once word got out, a plague of scavengers would descend.

One of the ships, the *Urca de Lima*, had survived the storm relatively unscathed thanks to its thick hull and was wedged against the reef with most of its superstructure intact, and its holds were quickly cleared. Three hundred natives were pressed into service as divers and worked relentlessly, forced to perform dangerous tasks despite sharks, strong currents, heavy surf beating against the jagged reef and poor visibility from the sediment stirred up by the storm. A small fort was constructed to hold the salvage and protect it against the hordes of freebooters, criminals and pirates who quickly turned up to try their own luck at salvage, but mostly to prey on the efforts of others.

After three years the Spanish gave up, having recovered an estimated 25–30 per cent of the lost treasure (see below). They burned the surviving wrecks to the water line and left the area to the freebooters. Hostile natives, poor salvage conditions and constant violence soon discouraged them too, and within decades the locations of the wrecks were forgotten.

BEACHCOMBER STRIKES GOLD

Coins and debris would wash ashore after storms, and the lost fleet passed into vague local folklore. In 1928 divers discovered the remains of the *Urca de Lima* just offshore from Fort Pierce and its cannons and anchors were

Right *A Spanish colonial gold coin from the 1715 Plate Fleet. Note the circle of dots around the outside, probably intended to discourage clipping, where small chunks of coins were clipped off and melted down to make fake coins.*

'Coins and debris would wash ashore after storms and the lost fleet passed into local folklore.'

salvaged, but there were no serious attempts to search for treasure. Then in 1948 local builder Kip Wagner discovered seven silver coins at Sebastian Inlet, sparking a lifelong obsession with the 1715 Plate Fleet. His first attempts at treasure hunting were not successful, but in the late 1950s he struck up a friendship with a local history buff and together they decided to get serious. Hunting through old maps and accounts, and accessing the records of the Spanish Archive of the Indies, Wagner was able to piece together the tale of the lost fleet.

His real breakthrough came, however, when he was out walking his dog. The pooch started to dig at something in a depression on the beach and Wagner realized it was a freshwater well, corresponding to the site of one of the original Spanish salvage camps – a camp he knew was directly onshore from the wreck of the flagship. Recruiting a team of helpers, Wagner bought a licence to explore the reef and over the next few years

recovered a wonderful haul of treasure, ranging from intact Chinese porcelain to gold coins and necklaces, elaborate pendants, gem-encrusted rings and thousands upon thousands of silver doubloons, on one occasion even finding a 1 m (3¼ ft)-long chest stuffed full of 3,000 silver coins.

TREASURE FLEET

The amount of loot that had gone down with the fleet was staggering. The official manifests declared more 14 million *pesos* in gold and silver – more than $400 million in modern terms, by weight alone. In addition there were many other valuable commodities such as porcelain and ivory (although few of these are likely to have survived). More tellingly, it was common for the Spanish treasure fleets and galleons to be stuffed with treasure that was smuggled, in sometimes ingenious fashion, by sailors and merchants desperate to avoid the heavy tax burden.

Gems might be smuggled in hollow cheeses, while one enterprising captain cast an anchor in solid gold and painted it black. It was quite possible for a ship to be carrying as much undeclared loot as official treasure, suggesting that the fleet may have been worth in excess of $1 billion in mineral value alone (historical importance adds value).

In addition to the initial Spanish salvage effort, latter-day salvors are believed to have located and picked over at least six and possibly seven of the 12 ships that sank, including the richest wrecks. Searching for the others is difficult, with weather conditions restricting the number of diveable days a year and much of the remaining loot probably in deep water. But large numbers of coins, and possibly many of the priceless pieces of jewellery from the Queen of Spain's dowry, remain to be found, and there is always the chance that a storm will wash them ashore for a lucky metal detector to discover.

The SS *Republic*

One of the richest wrecks of all time, the SS Republic *was a pioneering steamship with a colourful past that went down bearing a huge load of gold and silver coins intended to help with post-Civil War reconstruction efforts in New Orleans.*

The US Civil War was massively destructive for the South, as Union armies left a trail of destruction, hundreds of thousands of young men perished and the economy collapsed. Reconstruction was the name given to the effort to re-establish the Union, resolve the political issues of the Civil War and rebuild the shattered economy. New Orleans was at the centre of these efforts – captured intact by Union forces, it had escaped the worst effects of the war and was a major centre for trade and commerce. But it was short of money, in the literal sense: actual currency was in short supply, and it was necessary to supply real (rather than paper) money, in order to lubricate the wheels of the southern economy. A shipment of millions of dollars of gold and silver coins was dispatched from New York; the vessel chosen to carry it was a veteran of the route, a steamship that had seen its share of action.

ACTION SHIP

The SS *Republic* was a paddle-wheel steamship that had enjoyed a varied and exciting career. Launched in Baltimore in 1853 as the *Tennessee*, it had initially served as a short-haul cargo carrier, before becoming the first transatlantic steamer to operate out of Baltimore. In 1856 it became the first steamship to ply the route from the United States to South America on a regular basis. For two years it carried a colourful collection of characters to southern ports, including prospectors desperate to make the fastest passage from the US east coast to its west coast to participate in the 1848–9 California Gold Rush, and willing to risk the fever-infested jungles of Central America to cross the isthmus by land (the Panama Canal did not yet exist). After the '49ers, the *Tennessee* transported mercenaries to Nicaragua to serve under William Walker, an American engaged in an ill-fated attempt to carve out a white-supremacist empire in Central

America. In 1857 the ship started to serve the New York to New Orleans route.

When the Civil War started, the *Tennessee* was in New Orleans and was requisitioned by the Confederates to serve as a blockade runner, although it never actually managed to break out of the harbour. Later the ship fell into Union hands, was renamed and served as a blockade and gun ship. After the war it was sold off at auction, refitted and renamed once again, as the SS *Republic*, and put back on the New York to New Orleans route. It was on its fifth voyage to the South that it met its doom.

'A PERFECT HELL'

On 18 October 1865, the *Republic* sailed out of New York, with gold and silver coins worth $400,000 in its hold alongside a variety of other trade goods that carpetbagger merchants thought would fetch a profit in New Orleans. Five days later, as it passed the Georgia coast, a hurricane blew up and the ship began to labour in the heavy seas. The passengers were set to bailing it out, and much of the cargo was ditched to lighten it, but the seas got higher and disaster threatened. Survivor William T. Nichols wrote an account of the final journey to his wife. He described the scene on the night of the 24th:

The wind was howling through the rigging like the demons of the sea, and to make it a perfect hell, the men, excited and yelling to each other, begrimed with black smut and engine grease, and their eyes glaring through the dim light of the ranging lamps, made it a scene fit for a painter. I cannot describe in words the impression which it made upon my mind. It was desperation intensified.

Left The SS Republic *in its full glory. It was a single-piston steam-engine powered ship and could carry up to 100 passengers and more than a thousand tons of cargo.*

Above A chest from the wreck of the SS Republic *– the chest itself has rotted away to reveal the mass of silver coins within, accreted together after their long immersion.*

By the next day the boilers had failed and it was decided to abandon ship. As the last of the crew and passengers climbed into the boats and a hastily constructed raft, the *Republic* went down beneath them. One man drowned at the time and 16 others were lost from the raft before they were rescued.

HUNT FOR THE *REPUBLIC*

As one of the richest wrecks ever known, the *Republic* was an obvious target for treasure-hunting salvors. But little was known about the exact location of its loss, beyond the fact that it probably lay in deep water, far beyond the reach of divers and casual prospectors.

Specialist wreck-hunting and salvage company Odyssey Marine Exploration combined historical research with modelling of currents and winds to determine the best area to search, but still had to explore 3,900 sq km (1,500 sq miles) of seabed over the course of 12 years until it located a promising target with side-scan sonar in 2003. It then used an advanced, remotely operated vehicle to survey the wreck site (including the ship's bell, which confirmed the identity of the wreck) and salvage much of the cargo.

The main prize was the *Republic*'s cargo of coins, which because of their historical as well as mineral value were estimated to be worth more than $300 million today. In the event, only about a quarter of the coins have so far been recovered, along with a fascinating variety of trade goods, including jars of preserved pickles among 6,300 bottles and 7,000 other artefacts.

Treasures of
the *Titanic*

*The most famous shipwreck – if not the most famous ship – of all time,
RMS* Titanic *carried the cream of society in palatial splendour, together
with hundreds of the less well-off. Most of them were going to their doom
aboard an 'unsinkable ship' that was all too vulnerable.*

The tale of the *Titanic* is well known around the world, not least thanks to the record-breaking 1997 movie of the same name. The biggest ship ever built, it left Southampton in England on 10 April 1912 and stopped at Cherbourg in France and at Queenstown in Ireland, before setting off across the Atlantic for New York. It was its maiden voyage, and its huge new engines and sleek lines gave it a real chance of making the crossing in record time. Its course took it through the dangerous waters of the North Atlantic, where icebergs were a real threat to shipping. A combination of factors – warm weather leading to more icebergs; a moonless night and sea conditions that made it hard to spot an approaching iceberg; and fatal over-confidence in the ship's ability to handle a collision – led to the ship colliding with an iceberg on the night of Sunday 14 April. Less than three hours later, in the early hours of Monday, the great ship sank with the loss of around 1,500 people (official US and UK estimates varied) out of an original complement of 2,208 on board.

It was one of the worst peacetime disasters of all time and caused a media frenzy, which seems hardly to have abated almost a century on. From the treasure hunter's point of view, the most interesting questions relate to what it might have been carrying and where it went down.

MILLIONAIRE'S CLUB

The *Titanic* was built in an era before aeroplanes, when sea travel was the only way to cross the Atlantic. It was intended to represent the cutting edge of maritime technology on the one hand, while providing unprecedented luxury on the other. There were opulent restaurants and ballrooms, magnificent staircases, a Turkish bath, a glass dome and even four elevators. For the richest passengers, deluxe suites were available – the most expensive, nicknamed the Millionaire's Suite, cost £900 or $4,500, at a time when an average home in America cost less than a $1,000.

The list of first-class passengers read like a *Who's Who* of Edwardian society and included some of the world's richest people. Among them were financial magnates, railroad tycoons, retail kings, Broadway producers, socialites, artists, actresses and many more, including such famous names as John Jacob Astor IV, Molly Brown, Isidor Straus and the Countess of Rothe.

Although the cargo manifest for the ship records no special consignments of valuables, this roster of the rich and famous would have guaranteed that a serious quantity of loot was aboard. In the film *Titanic*, a major plot element is a necklace featuring a priceless sapphire called the Heart of the Ocean. While this piece is fictional, it is highly likely that many of these tycoons, heiresses

***Above** The reading room on the upper promenade of the* Titanic. *Part of the appeal of the crossing was the theatre of display among the first-class passengers, to which end many would have brought along expensive jewellery.*

THE JEWELLED BOOK AND OTHER GEMS

At least one treasure is known to have been aboard. A copy of the book *The Rubáiyát of Omar Khayyám* had been purchased at auction in London and was being carried back to New York. It was specially bound, with a cover design of a peacock, made from gold and studded with more than a thousand rubies and emeralds.

There are also rumours about much greater wealth. According to Michael Harris, founder of the company that holds the salvage rights to the *Titanic* (see page 144), 'Two brothers were coming out of Switzerland. They had a shipment of diamonds they were bringing back to New York with them that they lost on *Titanic* which today would be valued at over $300 million.'

and assorted millionaires carried ornate jewellery with them (part of the theatre of the crossing would have been dressing for grand dinners).

This was also an era when hard assets were still important, and where today's wealthy people might use bank transfers or credit cards, in Edwardian times they would have relied upon portable wealth like gold and diamonds. Indeed, one telling anecdote about the rescue of survivors relates how a man picked up from the lifeboats had his pockets searched, with the result that 'seventeen diamonds rolled out in every direction upon the littered deck'.

LOST AT SEA

Four days into its journey, the *Titanic* had nearly crossed the Atlantic and was off the coast of Newfoundland when disaster struck. Its final reported position was 41° 46´ N, 50° 14´ W. Almost as soon as the ship sank, there was talk of plans to find and even attempt to raise it, but as those attempting to track it down were to discover, the reported location was incorrect. With thousands of square kilometres of uncharted seabed lying nearly 4,000 m (13,000 ft) below the waves, discovering the *Titanic* would test the limits of technology and determination.

Rescue or robbery?

Advanced submarine technology helped oceanographers to pull off an amazing coup in locating and photographing the Titanic. *But some of those same pioneering scientists are now at war with salvors over the struggle to recover the sunken titan's treasures.*

Finding the *Titanic* was one of the great prizes of ocean exploration, and it was a goal that inspired numerous efforts. Soon after the disaster a group of wealthy survivors attempted to hire a leading salvage company to undertake the unprecedented task of locating and raising a 47,000 tonne (46,000 ton)-wreck from 4 km (2½ miles) down in the ocean, but it was clearly beyond the capabilities of the day. In 1953 a crude attempt to locate the wreck with sonar, by setting off a huge explosive charge and measuring the echoes, proved unsuccessful, and in the years that followed a range of ambitious and implausible schemes were floated. The most tenacious *Titanic*-hunter was probably the eccentric Texan millionaire Jack Grimm, who launched three fruitless searches and concluded that perhaps the wreck had been irretrievably lost under a mudslide.

THE PROFESSIONALS TRIUMPH

Pioneering oceanographer Robert Ballard was undaunted. Searching for funding to develop submarine technology such as remotely operated submersibles, Ballard initially saw the search for the *Titanic* as a good way to attract backers, but after an abortive attempt in 1977 he got serious. Based at Woods Hole Oceanographic Institution in Massachusetts, he developed a high-tech submersible sled, which could be dragged behind a ship hovering just above the seabed to scan and film wide swathes of the bottom, in the hope of locating the debris field left by the sinking ship.

In 1985, with help from the French, Ballard and his team finally succeeded. On 1 September pictures being transmitted from the ocean floor showed that the bottom was disturbed and chunks of debris came into

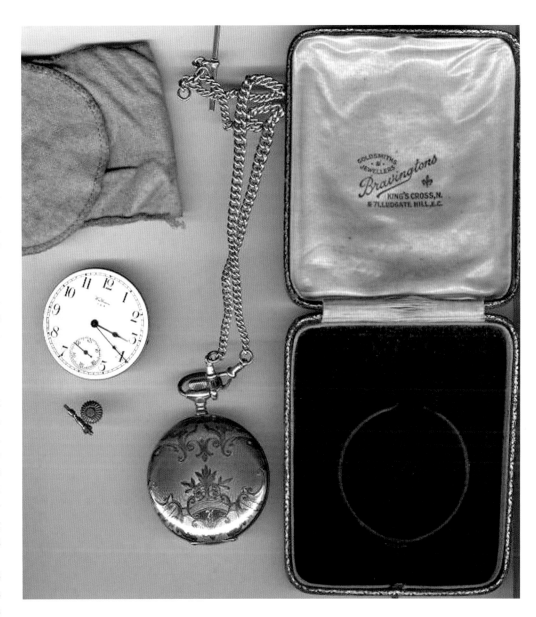

Right A gold-plated watch, rescued from the body of John Gill. The hands have stopped at 3.21 a.m., the moment witnesses reported that the vessel disappeared under the ocean.

view, including a boiler. A year later, a return visit in a manned submersible enabled Ballard to visit the wreck in person. The *Titanic* had been found and now its mysteries could be revealed. For instance, it is now known that, contrary to the official account, the ship broke in two as it sank, with the bow section going down first and the stern section plummeting to the depths a short while afterwards, coming to rest about 180 m (600 ft) apart, facing in opposite directions.

TREASURE TROVE OR TOMB?

Ballard himself views the wreck as an almost sacred site – a tomb for the hundreds who had perished, which should not be disturbed, let alone looted. In particular, he has become increasingly concerned that the wreck is disintegrating, partly because of natural processes and partly because of the number of submersibles visiting it and even landing on it. Detractors point out that he was the first to do either of these.

On the other side of the argument is RMS Titanic Inc. (RMST), the company that holds the salvage rights to the wreck and which has mounted a number of expeditions to bring up artefacts. Ostensibly these are used solely for staging travelling exhibitions, but recent court battles have seen the company accused of plotting to sell off this heritage for profit.

It is RMST that has spoken of the desire to recover diamonds and other treasure from the wreck. It reasons that it was customary in such emergencies for the ship's pursers to

Left A photograph taken by a submersible that has ventured inside the wreck of the Titanic, *showing the interior of one of the first-class staterooms.*

gather valuables from the ship's safes and the passengers and place them in special leather bags, which were intended to be stowed on the lifeboats and rescued. But the bags never made it and it is thought they might lie within the forward hold of the wreck. An expedition in 2000 to salvage this loot was hamstrung by a court order forbidding RMST from cutting into the wreck, and the expedition was a relative failure.

Some valuables *have* been recovered. A number of rings, including one studded with 60 diamonds and another set with exquisite sapphires and diamonds, have been found, together with a bracelet spelling out the name 'Amy' in gemstones. Meanwhile one of the survivors took away with her a sapphire

pendant that is now on display at a *Titanic*-related museum in Belfast, which claims that it was the inspiration for the Heart of the Ocean jewel in the film *Titanic*, and indeed for the entire plot of the movie.

The salvors insist that there is an urgent need to retrieve the 95 per cent of artefacts yet to be recovered from the wreck. RMST founder Michael Harris says, 'The ocean is basically eating the *Titanic* alive. Our fear is that we are racing against time to be able to rescue these artefacts and bring them back to the surface before they are lost for ever.' But archeologists, and even one of the remaining survivors, insist that these efforts are tantamount to grave-robbing, and that the wreck should be left to rest in peace.

GERMANY
POLAND
CZECH REPUBLIC
SLOVAKIA
Lake Toplitz
AUSTRIA
SWITZERLAND
HUNGARY
SLOVENIA
CROATIA
ITALY
Adriatic Sea

The Nazi loot of Lake Toplitz

One of the most notorious suspected Nazi stashes of ill-gotten loot is the murky and menacing Lake Toplitz, high in the Austrian Alps. Legend has it that everything from gold bullion to the Amber Room (see page 122) are hidden beneath the surface of this former secret weapons-testing site.

The Amber Room is only the most celebrated of the Nazi treasures sought since the war. Huge quantities of gold, gems, art and historical treasures were looted from occupied countries and stolen from the victims of the Holocaust. The Third Reich also had a penchant for keeping extensive records, together with a belief that surviving Nazis might foment a Fourth Reich, if they retained sufficient funds.

These facts combine to give treasure hunters good reason to hope that spectacular caches of Nazi treasure, which might include anything from gold bullion to top-secret documents, may yet be recovered. Records and prisoner statements confirm that as the war drew to a close, Nazi officials cast about for suitable hiding places. Much was stored in mines and old tunnels (see 'The Stechovice Treasure' on page 54). Lakes were also considered. Of particular interest were lakes (*see* in German) in Bavaria and across the border in Austria, regions protected from the worst of the fighting, and where the Nazis

Left A diver helps to guide a pallet bearing boxes of counterfeit British bank notes from the Nazi Operation Bernhard, recovered from Lake Toplitz in 1959 during an expedition sponsored by German magazine Stern.

believed their roots ran deep. Here was situated Hitler's Eagle's Nest headquarters and other important Nazi sites. Treasure hunters believe that the Walchensee in Bavaria and the Seetalsee across the border hold £200 million and £500 million in gold bullion respectively, while in 2002 a 10 kg (22 lb) golden urn dumped by the SS was pulled from Chiemsee near Munich.

THE SECRET LAKE

But the most celebrated of these Nazi loot lakes is Toplitz, in Austria, where some treasure hunters believe up to £1 billion in gold is secreted. Lake Toplitz is hidden away in dense forest, and during the war it was remote and hard to reach. The German Navy built a research station there for testing explosives and submarine missile-launching technology, which the Americans would later develop into the Polaris system. The station could only be reached by foot or horse and cart.

Just days before the fall of Berlin, a convoy of trucks slipped out of the city and made its way to Lake Toplitz. A local farmgirl, Ida Weisenbacher, recalled being awoken by SS officers and forced to hitch up her horse and cart to help them carry their load of crates the final distance along the lake shore. She also saw them unload the crates onto small boats, row them out onto the lake and throw them overboard. As the boxes plunged 103 m (340 ft) to the bottom they passed through a layer of fresh water and then into the dead

zone of oxygen-less salt water that lies beneath it. Here nothing beyond a few hardy bacteria and a strange species of worm can survive, and the logs and tree trunks that have fallen in over the millennia degrade extremely slowly, forming a tangled and dangerous jumble on the lake floor – a deadly net that can have, and has had, fatal consequences for divers.

OPERATION BERNHARD

The first systematic exploration of the lake was in 1959, when the German magazine *Stern* funded an expedition that recovered boxes of British banknotes. They had stumbled upon evidence of Operation Bernhard: a Nazi plan to destabilize the British economy through forgery on a massive scale. Based at Sachsenhausen concentration camp near Berlin, and using slave labour, the scheme had run out of t ime as the Russians approached and the evidence was bundled off to Lake Toplitz to be hidden. But treasure hunters were convinced there was more than just fake banknotes in Lake Toplitz, and they were not alone.

In 1963 some former SS officers employed a young local called Alfred Egner to dive to the bottom of Toplitz. It is speculated that they were after waterproof tubes containing codes to secret Swiss bank accounts. But they came away empty-handed when Egner died, possibly tangled in the lethal web of tree

trunks at the bottom. Other treasure hunters believe the lake contains hundreds of millions in gold and other treasures; documentary evidence of transfers of loot to the Vatican and to Swiss banks; lists of treasures stolen from Jews; and details of secret research programmes.

So far, however, a number of major searches have revealed only more of the remains of Operation Bernhard, including more banknotes and the printing presses used in the scheme, together with the debris left by the naval testing programme. No gold or other treasure has been discovered. A contract to execute the most comprehensive and high-tech search yet has been signed with an American outfit called Global Explorations, the boss of which, treasure hunter Norman Scott, claims to have evidence that the Amber Room may be among the unrecovered treasures.

As of 2007, Scott is still resolving contractual issues with the organization that effectively owns the lake, but claims that the mapping phase of the operation will begin soon. Experts who have already explored the lake, such as German biologist Professor Hans Fricke, who has spent 20 years researching Toplitz and its ecology, are sceptical that Scott will find anything. In 2003 Fricke commented, 'The consensus is that there is no gold there. For me, this chapter is closed. It was not an enjoyable experience ... I would never attempt to do it again.'

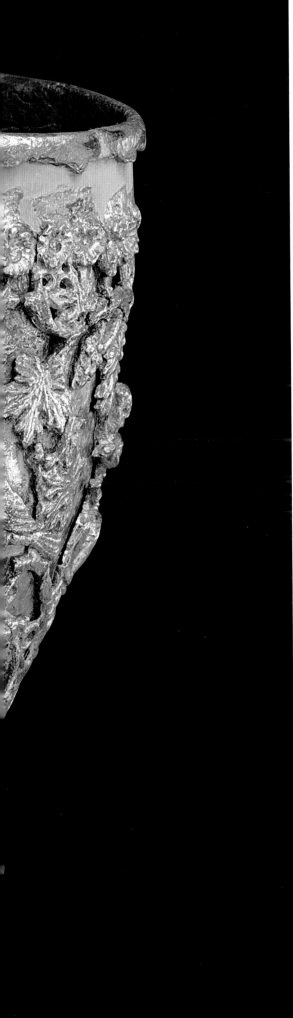

PART 5

MYSTERY TREASURES

Some of history's most famous treasures are mired in paradox, because for all the legions of treasure hunters who have picked over them, sought them out, dug, tunnelled, excavated, blasted, bored, dived, delved, quested and adventured for them, no one really knows what they are. Sometimes, as in the case of the Holy Grail, this is because the myth or legend of the treasure has changed over time, and the nature of the treasure has evolved with it. But sometimes it is because the treasure probably never existed in the first place. Sadly, this is likely to be the case with the secret treasure at the heart of the extended Grail mystery, which encompasses many of the most popular themes of fringe history today, from the Cathars to the Oak Island Money Pit. Nonetheless these legends have all the ingredients of classic treasure yarns, from secret codes to buried treasure.

The Holy Grail: history of a legend

Below A tapestry by Edward Burne-Jones. In this scene the perfect knight Sir Galahad, accompanied by Sir Bors and Sir Perceval, finally 'achieves' the Grail, after which he ascends to heaven.

The epitome of the priceless and sacred relic is the Holy Grail, which has become a byword for an ultimate and unattainable treasure. Today the Grail is popularly understood as a great secret linked to the bloodline of Christ, but its meaning has changed as its legend has developed.

The massive success of Dan Brown's *The Da Vinci Code* has introduced millions of readers and movie-goers to the notion that the Holy Grail, or *San Graal* as it was known in early versions of the legend, is really a metaphor for an explosive secret: the knowledge that Jesus survived the cross and had children, starting a bloodline that would later give rise to the Merovingian line of European kings in the Dark Ages. In fact this version of the Grail legend goes further and states that *San Graal* should be read as *Sang Real*, or Royal Blood ('royal' because Jesus was King of the Jews), and that the surviving descendants of Christ are in effect the real Holy Grail, because they carry his royal bloodline.

But this is an entirely modern conceit, developed by writers such as Michael Baigent, Richard Leigh and Henry Lincoln in their book *The Holy Blood and the Holy Grail*, which in turn is partly based on the self-promoting fantasies of a convicted fraudster called Pierre Plantard (see page 164). It bears little relation to the original versions of the Grail, which evolved during the Middle Ages.

THE HOLY CHALICE

Leaving Brown's version aside, the Grail as it is popularly understood is the cup that was used by Christ at the Last Supper for the Eucharist and which was also used to collect drops of his blood when he was on the cross.

It has magical powers, such as the ability to heal, to provide endless food and drink and even to confer immortality. In practice, however, this version is the blending of several different concepts. The cup used by Christ for the Eucharist is technically known as the Holy Chalice, while the Grail was said to be the dish that was used to serve the Paschal lamb at the Last Supper. The notion that one of these vessels was then also used to catch Christ's blood is a post-biblical invention.

In fact in its earliest known incarnation the Grail was not really any of these things. The legend of the Grail comes down to us from a series of medieval romances written in the 12th and 13th centuries, and the oldest of these is Chrétien de Troyes' *Perceval, le Conte du Graal* (or *Perceval, the Story of the Grail*), written between 1180 and 1191. In this story Chrétien describes how the knight Perceval comes to a mysterious castle and sees a procession of wondrous artefacts, including a *graal* (a dish; see the box on page 153), a bleeding lance and a silver plate. But the *graal* has no specific religious character and only in later versions does it become a sacred vessel.

After Chrétien de Troyes, the next major versions of the Grail legend include romances by Robert de Boron, whose version has Joseph of Arimathea using the Grail (which is identified as the Holy Chalice) to gather some of Christ's blood and later

bringing it to Britain and setting up shop at Glastonbury; and by Wolfram von Eschenbach, in whose *Parzival* the Grail is not a cup, but a stone that fell from heaven, which was the refuge of the Neutral Angels during Lucifer's rebellion against God. De Boron's version is what Grail scholars refer to as an Early History romance, because it deals primarily with the origins and early history of the Grail, while von Eschenbach's is a Quest romance, because it deals primarily with the quest to obtain the Grail and with the hero who attempts this.

THE MEANING OF THE WORD *GRAAL*

What is a 'grail'? The main source for the etymology of the word is the 13th-century chronicler Helinandus, a Cistercian monk, who claims that the term dates back to 717 CE when a hermit had a vision of a dish used by Jesus at the Last Supper and called it a *gradale* (from which the word *graal* later derived). Helinandus goes on to explain that the word *gradale* derives from the word for a dish used to serve meat in morsels, or 'by degrees' (*gradatim* in Latin), and partly also because

such titbits were pleasant (*grata*). An alternative but similar etymology links *gradale* to the medieval Latin *cratalis*, which in turn derives from the Latin *crater*, meaning a mixing bowl. The upshot is that a grail is really a dish, rather than the cup of popular legend.

SOURCES OF THE GRAIL LEGEND

These medieval romances probably derived from earlier, largely oral story-telling traditions. They display many motifs familiar from early Christian, Celtic and even Oriental folklore. For instance, Persian

folklore features the *Jam-e Jam*, the magical cup of the hero Jamshid, which dispenses an elixir of immortality. Celtic mythology is full of cauldrons that heal and/or dispense food and drink, and many characters in the wider Grail legend appear to be derived from Celtic sources, including Arthur and Merlin. But the core of the Grail story appears to be Christian, and one suggestion is that it became popular at a time when the Church was trying to popularize the sacrament of Holy Communion, to which the Holy Chalice is central.

Searching for the Holy Grail

For a purely mythical artefact, the Holy Grail has proved remarkably popular with treasure hunters. Like their counterparts in the Grail romances, real-life questers have travelled far and wide in the search for the Grail. Numerous locations have been linked to it, and several real-life candidates exist.

The religiously inclined may believe that the Grail, in the form of a sacred cup, really exists. The growing fringe historical movement identifies the Grail with the Knights Templar (see page 158), the Cathars (see page 156) and related places, such as Rennes-le-Château (see page 162) and the Oak Island Money Pit (see page 166). Latter-day Grail enthusiasts look to such places to find some sort of document, book, secret code or even (as outlined on page 150) someone who represents the bloodline of Christ. Others may search for the real-life object that might have inspired the legends of the Holy Grail, and there are several contenders for this crown.

THE GRAIL IN BRITAIN

Because of the prominence of the Grail in the Arthurian legends, and specifically because of Robert de Boron's romance *Joseph d'Arimathie*, written between 1192 and 1202, the Grail has long been associated with Britain. In the de Boron tale, Joseph of Arimathea is a rich Hebrew merchant with links to Britain because of the tin trade (in fact one story about Joseph is that he was the uncle of Jesus and brought him to Britain in his youth, a visit alluded to in William Blake's famous poem 'Jerusalem'). Imprisoned in Jerusalem because of his association with Jesus, Joseph is rescued by a vision of the Grail and makes his way to Britain bearing the wondrous cup, making landfall near Glastonbury Tor (a hill). Here he plants his staff, which miraculously flowers into a tree, and founds the first church in Britain. De Boron's tale goes on to explain how the Grail passes to a Grail King who lives in a Grail Castle, also a feature of some other versions of the tale, such as Wolfram von Eschenbach's (see page 154). But local tradition in Glastonbury claims that the Grail was actually buried deep within the Tor, causing a spring to come forth. Today this is known as the Chalice Well, and its characteristic red waters are said to be the result of the water flowing over the Grail and of the divine blood it contains (in reality the spring passes through iron-rich rock and picks up iron oxides).

Right *The Nanteos Cup, or rather what is left of it. It is much diminished by voracious pilgrims, who believed that mouthfuls of a sacred relic could cure their ailments.*

A legend thought to date from Victorian times tells of how the monks of Glastonbury Abbey removed the Grail during the turmoil of the Dissolution of the Monasteries (1538–41, during the reign of Henry VIII). They took it with them when they moved to south Wales and later gave it to the lord of Nanteos Manor. A small wooden bowl, said to be a 1st-century CE olive-wood vessel from the Holy Land (which would make it a viable candidate for the Holy Grail), was indeed on show at Nanteos Manor for many years and was the object of veneration by pilgrims, some of whom even went so far as to bite chunks out of the rim (presumably hoping to be cured of their illnesses).

Today it is kept in a bank vault for safekeeping. Experts think it is probably a type of medieval dish called a mazer bowl, made from witch hazel and not olive wood, and definitively does not date back to New Testament times.

Right The ornate silver gilt shell and base of the Antioch Chalice enclose a simple silver bowl, and it is this which was claimed to be the Holy Chalice.

OTHER HOLY CHALICE CONTENDERS

There are at least four other vessels that have been claimed to be the Holy Chalice:
• The first record of such an artefact even existing dates from the late 7th century, with the account of Arculf, a French monk who visited the Holy Land and reported his adventures to the monks of Iona. Arculf describes a large silver chalice with two handles that he saw in a chapel in Jerusalem, which was said to be the Holy Chalice. It is not known what became of it.
• A small silver bowl was found near

Antioch in 1908, and has since been identified as one of the earliest-known Eucharist chalices, dating back to the 6th century. Its age and location led to claims that it was the Holy Chalice. It now resides at the Metropolitan Museum in New York, which describes this attribution as 'ambitious'.
• Valencia Cathedral is home to the *Santo Caliz* – Spanish for the Holy Chalice. It is a small cup of red agate with an elaborate mount. The earliest definite records of the cup only date back to 1134, but it has a back-story

involving St Peter, who brought it to Rome, after which it was supposedly removed to Spain to save it from the Valerian persecutions of 258 CE.
• At Genoa Cathedral there is a small green bowl known as the *Sacro Catino* (Holy Basin), which was thought to be emerald until it was broken during transport back from Paris (having been looted by Napoleon) and revealed to be Egyptian glass. The earliest definite records of it date back to 1170, and it was only associated with the Holy Chalice in the late 13th century.

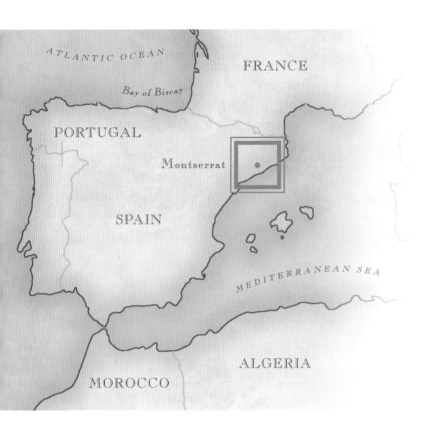

The Grail Castle

In the first literary version of the legend, the resting place of the holy vessel is identified as a magical Grail Castle, where a bloodline of guardians protect the Grail until a sufficiently pure-hearted knight shall achieve it and heal the wasted land ruled over by the Castle's king. Several places lay claim to the title of the Grail Castle – perhaps the most dramatic is the monastery at Montserrat in Spain.

Chrétien de Troyes' *Perceval*, the first literary version of the Grail story, sets out many of the elements that would later become firmly established as core aspects of Grail mythology. The Grail is kept in a strange and otherworldly castle, home of the Fisher King, a ruler whose wounds mean that he is restricted to fishing in the lake near his home, and whose ill health is reflected in the sickness of his land. Robert de Boron's *Joseph d'Arimathie* explains that the Grail Castle was first established by the son-in-law of Joseph of Arimathea, after which the sacred relic was passed on from father to son. The Grail Castle thus becomes the target of those questing for the Grail, and only a knight who is sufficiently pure may first enter the Castle and then ask the right question that will allow him to attain the Grail and fulfil his quest, in the process healing the Fisher King and his blighted land.

WHERE WAS THE GRAIL CASTLE?

According to the Grail romances, the Grail Castle was called Corbenic, the name deriving from *Caer* (castle) *Benic* (a form of Brons, the first Grail King of the romances, a figure possibly derived from the legendary Celtic hero Bran). It is possible that Corbenic was based on a real place – a hill fort in north Wales, today known as Castell Dinas Bran, where a medieval castle occupies the site where an Iron Age fort once stood. In the version of the legend by Wolfram von Eschenbach, *Parzival*, dating from c.1210–15, the Grail Castle is called Munsalvaesche, a version of *Mons Salvationis* or Mountain of Salvation. Munsalvaesche is traditionally and lexically linked to Montserrat in Spain, an impressive peak that is home to a monastery (although the true derivation of the Spanish name is probably 'toothed mountain', referring to its serrated profile). In the Middle Ages the monks of Montserrat claimed that von Eschenbach was right, and that their monastery, Santa María de Montserrat, was indeed the home of the Grail.

THE TEMPLAR CONNECTION

In von Eschenbach's *Parzival*, the Grail at Munsalvaesche is guarded by the Templiesin, thought to be a thinly veiled reference to the Templars. At the time von Eschenbach was writing, the Knights Templar were at the height of their powers, with great estates, vast wealth and tremendous influence across the Christian world. The Black Madonna provides an indirect link between Montserrat and the Templars – perhaps von Eschenbach was drawing on hidden knowledge of Montserrat and the Templars when he penned his tale.

① MOUNTAINSIDE DWELLINGS

Montserrat is a dramatic peak near Barcelona, in Spain. Its peak, Santi Jeroni, is 1,236 m (4,055 ft) high, and the limestone rock has been eroded into striking spires and towers. Caves in the mountainside housed the earliest chapels on the site and before that were inhabited by hermits. About halfway up the mountain the Benedictine monastery of Santa María is home to a community of monks and hosts thousands of tourists, who arrive by road, cable car or mountain railway. The peak is at the heart of a national park.

② THE BLACK MADONNA

One of the most notable features of the monastery is its Black Madonna. This is one of a series of statues of the Virgin Mary found across Europe, which are remarkable for being black-skinned. In the Christian era they have been the objects of intense, almost cult-like veneration in

a Christian context, but they are widely held to be holdovers from an older, pagan tradition of goddess worship, with ancient fertility symbols combining with Christian ones to produce a syncretic form of popular religion. The Black Madonna also provides another link with the Templars, who were often associated with cult sites where Black Madonnas were the focus of devotion, and with the *Da Vinci Code* nexus of legends about the Holy Grail as the bloodline of Christ. According to this school of thought, Black Madonnas relate to the story of how Mary Magdalene, bearing the child of Jesus, came to the south of France, where her bloodline was

subsequently based. Veneration of Mary Magdalene melded with local fertility-goddess worship, so that the cult of the Black Madonna became a way of maintaining the secret tradition of the bloodline of Christ in the teeth of the official Church version of history.

③ 1,000-YEAR-OLD MONASTERY

The monastery was officially founded in 1025 by Oliba, Abbot of Ripoli and Bishop of Vic, but it marked the site of an older chapel, while traditions of worship at Montserrat probably date back centuries. According to legend, the Black Madonna first appeared at Montserrat

during a visitation in a cave on the mountain in 880 CE. After bright lights and angels had been seen, searchers found the statue in a grotto. When the local bishop ordered it moved, it became supernaturally heavy, so it was decided to build a chapel to the Virgin on the site.

④ THE BASILICA

The monastery is split into two main blocks of buildings. One set caters to tourists and other visitors, while the other includes the monastery proper and the Basilica, a great cathedral-like space with a single, giant central nave and smaller chapels around the perimeter.

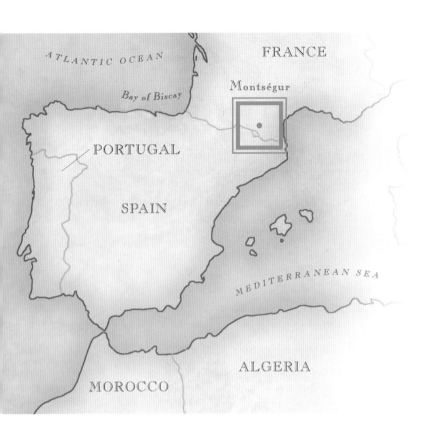

Secret treasure of the Cathars

Adherents of the most popular heresy of the Middle Ages, the Cathars were brutally suppressed by the Catholic Church and many aspects of their faith remain mysterious. Legend links them to great material and spiritual treasures, including the Holy Grail.

Differing interpretations of Christianity have been a constant feature of Church history. The dominant interpretation – in Western Europe this was Catholicism – labelled them heresies. In the Middle Ages the most successful of these was Catharism, a version of Christianity that developed from movements such as the Bogomils and Paulicians in Eastern Europe and Armenia, but which took root in southern France, particularly in the Languedoc region, from the 11th century.

The Cathars believed that the material world was corrupt, and that true salvation lay in freeing the divine spark within each person from its material bonds and returning it to the purity and sanctity of the godhead – the realm of pure spirit. In practical terms this meant that Cathar initiates, called Perfecti, followed strict vegetarian codes and were celibate, even to the point of renouncing their husbands or wives. The majority of Cathars were not this strict, however. The movement won converts and influence among the common people of Languedoc and the protection of the powerful lords who ruled the region.

Right As part of the surrender of Montségur, 200 Cathar Perfecti gave themselves up. A stockade was built and all of the prisoners were condemned without a trial and burned alive.

THE ALBINGENSIAN CRUSADE

This state of affairs upset both the secular and spiritual authorities, to whom the Cathars and their creed were a serious challenge. The Church made a series of efforts to win over the Cathars and put them back on the 'correct path' through debate and discussion, but eventually it resorted to force. Pope Innocent III launched the Albigensian Crusade (named after Albi, a town in the Cathar region) in 1208, and this was followed in 1229 by the establishment of the Inquisition. French nobles from the north joined in, encouraged by the decree that the lands of Cathar supporters were forfeit, and a bloody war raged through the Cathar lands. The last Cathari leader was finally executed in 1321, but the heresy had been broken long before this, effectively suffering a death-blow with the fall of the castle fortress of Montségur in 1244.

THE TREASURE OF MONTSÉGUR

It is here that the Cathar treasure enters the tale, at least according to latter-day legends. It is claimed that the Cathars amassed considerable material treasure through their power and influence in the region, but also that they possessed some great secret, possibly an artefact of magical power. Since all the books and scriptures of the movement were destroyed during the suppression, the only sources on Cathar beliefs and practices come from their enemies, but these supposedly speak of a 'rich cup', used in a ritual feast. Fringe historians link this to the Holy Grail, and some claim that Montségur, where the Cathars gathered for their last stand (presumably along with their treasures), is the Munsalvaesche of von Eschenbach's Grail romance *Parzival* (see page 154).

Fewer than 200 fighting men in the besieged fortress faced many thousands of attackers, but they held out for nearly a year until the enemy began erecting catapults atop a nearby height. At the beginning of March 1244 the Cathars negotiated peculiar terms of surrender. They would be allowed to remain in the fortress for 15 days, after which the Cathar Perfecti would give themselves up

Left *A distant view of Montségur Castle, perched atop its lofty peak, some 900 m(3,000 ft) high. The current fortress postdates the Cathars, of whose castle no trace remains.*

and the garrison would go free. On 16 March they duly surrendered and 200 Perfecti were burned alive.

The legend of the Cathar treasure surrounds what happened during those 15 days. Supposedly the material treasures of the movement had already been spirited out of Montségur during the siege, possibly to be hidden somewhere in the region (see 'Rennes-le-Château' on page 162), while the secret treasure was retained so that it could be used in the celebration of a final ceremonial feast on 14 March. Then, on the 16th, four of the Perfecti hid in the garrison and later escaped the fortress by lowering themselves on ropes, carrying with them the Holy Grail.

THE BLOODLINE OF CHRIST

The legend of the Cathar treasure is an integral part of the larger narrative that equates the Holy Grail with the secret bloodline of Christ. This narrative has Joseph of Arimathea, Mary Magdalene and the Holy Grail (possibly an actual cup, possibly one or more of Jesus' children) coming to the south of France and passing on their secrets – and responsibility for protecting the lineage of Jesus – to the Cathars. The Grail and other treasures are passed on in turn to the Templars, who effectively inherit the Cathar mantle of secret knowledge and covert opposition to the Church.

The problem is that there is no evidence to back up this narrative. While the truce at Montségur does seem odd, there is no evidence for the secret flit by the four Cathars, which is suspiciously similar to the tales concerning the end of the Templars (see page 158). Treasure hunters seeking the lost loot of the Cathars are probably on a wild goose chase.

The treasure of the Knights Templar

The Knights Templar were an order of warrior monks who rose from humble beginnings in the Holy Land to dizzying heights of power and influence across Europe, only to be crushed amid claims of devil worship and esoteric practices. What became of their vast wealth and their secrets?

In 1118 French knight Hughes de Payens and eight companions decided to form an order that would protect pilgrims visiting Jerusalem. The king of the Crusader kingdom of Jerusalem, Baldwin II, assigned them quarters in the Temple Mount compound, leading them to adopt the title The Poor Fellow-Soldiers of Christ and of the Temple of Solomon, or the Knights Templar. At first they lived on alms and were restricted to escorting pilgrims from Jerusalem to the banks of the Jordan, but with remarkable speed they gained favour with the Pope and with many of the princes and nobles of Europe.

The order swelled in number and was awarded gifts of vast tracts of land, lucrative estates and great wealth. By special papal dispensation it was exempted from taxation and local Church authority. The Knights Templars built massive castles in the Levant, founded commanderies (fortified garrison/ monastery complexes) all over Europe (especially in France, their main power base) and used fleets of ships to transport men and supplies to the Holy Land. They also gained expertise in banking through their experience of money transfer, and their commanderies became favoured places to deposit money (see page 160).

SUPPRESSION OF THE TEMPLARS

Their wealth and power drew envious regard from those whose authority they began to overshadow, in particular the French king Philip the Fair (ruled 1285–1314), who was said to covet their great wealth. In 1307 Philip convinced Pope Clement V to conspire with him to suppress the order. Instructions were given for the simultaneous arrest of every Templar throughout France on 13 October. Over the next five years many Templars were tortured, accused of strange and occult practices and executed, and the order was crushed in most of Europe. Only in England and particularly in Scotland was it able to survive relatively unmolested, but by 1312 it was a spent force. Philip, however, was left empty-handed, for the order proved to have empty coffers. What had happened to the great Templar treasure?

For adherents to the *Da Vinci Code* school of history, the Templar treasure was the key to their meteoric rise, rather than vice versa. Supposedly the Templars came into possession of a secret of huge significance (possibly during excavations in Solomon's Temple, see page 160), and this secret gave them the leverage to win their huge estates and papal privileges, along the way amassing a genuine material fortune. According to this narrative, a select cadre of Templar knights, forewarned of the imminent arrests, slipped out of the Paris commandery the night before the suppression of the order and spirited the treasure to La Rochelle, from where ships of the Templar fleet carried it to

(see page 160).

ROSSLYN CHAPEL

An ornate chapel near Edinburgh, built between 1440 and 1480 by William Sinclair, Earl of Orkney, Rosslyn features heavily in accounts of the Templars and the Holy Grail. It is claimed that it is modelled after Solomon's Temple and is riddled with esoteric imagery – particularly symbols of the Freemasons, which Sinclair is said to have founded in order to continue the Templar traditions and safeguard their secret knowledge. In particular, the ornately carved Apprentice Pillar within the chapel is suggested as a hiding place for the Templar loot, as are several large chests said to be buried in secret crypts beneath the church.

Like much else connected with the Templars, this seems to be mostly myth and legend. The design of Rosslyn Chapel was actually based on Glasgow Cathedral; it was built a hundred years after the suppression of the Templars; and there is no evidence that William Sinclair was some sort of secret Templar, or that he founded the Freemasons.

'The Templars' wealth and power drew envious regard from those whose authority they began to overshadow.'

England or Scotland. After this it was secreted in one of their commanderies (such as Temple Church in London, see page 160), hidden in Rosslyn Chapel near Edinburgh or even spirited off to America (see 'The Oak Island Money Pit' on page 166).

THE TRUTH ABOUT THE TEMPLARS

Alas for treasure hunters, most of this is based on false pretences. There is no evidence that the Templars ever found anything special at the Temple. Rumours about the occult practices of the Templars, which have lent credence to theories about magical artefacts they may have possessed, were mostly slander put about by their persecutors. The fleet that supposedly transported their treasures from La Rochelle did not exist, because the Templars simply hired ships when they needed them and only ever owned a handful of ships. Philip the Fair ended up empty-handed because at the time of their suppression the Templars were far from rich. Most of their assets were in the form of estates, and with the expulsion of the Crusaders from the Holy Land at the end of the 13th century, the order had lost prestige and spent too much money fighting losing battles. By 1307 the Templars were struggling to stay afloat – their mythical treasure did not exist.

In a recent post-script to the Templar story, in 2007 the Vatican published all the documentation associated with the Trial of the Templars, including the Parchment of Chinon, a document from 1308 that was only rediscovered in 2001. It shows that Pope Clement initially absolved the Templars of heresy. However, as a virtual prisoner of Philip of France, Clement succumbed to pressure and in 1312 reversed his decision, sealing the order's fate.

Left *The interior of Rosslyn Chapel, displaying the ornate carving for which it is famous. The chapel is probably based on the choir of nearby Glasgow Cathedral.*

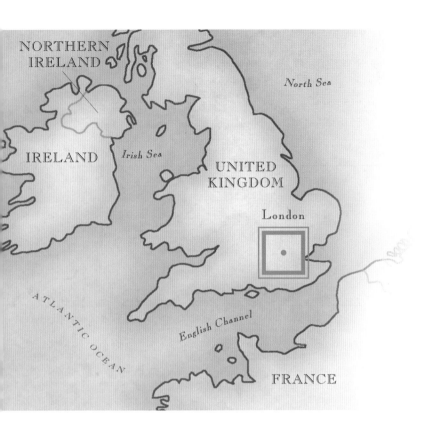

The Knights Templar: Temple Church

One of the most unusual churches in Britain and among the few surviving structures of the Templar empire, Temple Church in London dates back to the 12th century. In its time it has been the repository of great wealth and the final resting place of princes and kingmakers. But could it also guard a secret history as the hiding place of the fabulous lost treasure of the Templars?

WHAT *WAS* THE TREASURE?

Enormous speculation surrounds the legendary secret treasure of the Templars. Via their connections with the Priory of Sion or the Cathars, or their own excavations in the bowels of Solomon's Temple, they are supposed to have acquired any number of strange objects. Candidates for the Templars' treasure include the Holy Grail – as in the actual sacred cup; and the true secret of the Holy Grail – that is, that the bloodline of Christ survived in Europe. In this latter version the Templars are said to have been in possession either of the actual heirs of Jesus or simply of proof that he had children, possibly in the form of unknown or suppressed Gospels similar to the Dead Sea Scrolls (see page 50).

Another candidate for the treasure of the Templars is the head of Baphomet: the accusers of the Templars claimed that they worshipped a demon called Baphomet (probably a deliberate misconstruing of 'Mohammedans', with whom the Templars would have had many dealings in the Holy Land), and they were also associated with the worship of heads (probably as a result of their

possession of the relics of two decapitated female martyrs). These two legends became conflated so that it was said the secret Templar treasure was the head of Baphomet – possibly itself the severed head of John the Baptist or of Jesus himself, able to speak and prophesy through some dark art.

Other religious relics – including the Ark of the Covenant (see page 90), the Spear of Destiny (see page 108), the Turin Shroud (the face on which is claimed by some to be that of Jacques de Molay, last Grand Master of the order) and shards of the True Cross – are also claimed to be the Templars' treasure. More prosaically, the Templars are held to have accumulated vast material wealth that their enemies never recovered, so their great secret may be locked in a chest with a fortune in gold and jewels.

WHERE IS THE TREASURE?

After the Templars smuggled their treasure out of the port of La Rochelle, where did they take it? One of the most popular candidate destinations is Scotland, where the Templars were safe from persecution, and in recent years, particularly thanks to *The Da Vinci Code*,

attention has focused on Rosslyn Chapel (see page 158). Supposed links between the Scottish Templars and the exploration of North America have also pointed the finger at Oak Island off Nova Scotia (see page 166). But the Templars also had many commanderies in England, another country where they escaped the harsh persecution of the Continent. Could their supposed treasure have been spirited away to one of these? One of the few surviving Templar structures is the Temple Church in London.

Temple Church was consecrated in 1185 by the Patriarch of Jerusalem at a ceremony attended by King Henry II (ruled 1154–89), reflecting the power and prestige of the Templars at the time. It was the central element of a complex of buildings that included residences, offices and training facilities, which formed the order's headquarters in England. After the order was suppressed, ownership of the Temple precinct passed to the Knights Hospitaller, and eventually to the Crown, but from the 14th century it was let to colleges of lawyers, who still reside there today. Of the original structures, only the Round Church survives.

① THE ROUND CHURCH

The most notable part of Temple Church is the circular Round Church, actually the nave. Its Templar design is almost unique in church architecture and was probably based on the Church of the Holy Sepulchre in Jerusalem. This is the original building from the 12th century. Inside it features a ring of freestanding marble columns, the originals of which were the first of their kind, along with a number of effigies of knights on the floor and grotesque heads decorating the interior (normally these are found only on the exterior of churches, but here they echo the grotesque carvings inside Rosslyn Chapel). This was where new recruits into the order underwent their initiation rites.

② SEAT OF POWER

Temple Church lay at the heart of the headquarters of one of the most powerful organizations in medieval England, rivalled only by the Church and the Crown. The Master of the Temple sat in Parliament as the first baron of the realm, and in 1215 the then Master, William Marshal, brokered a meeting between King John (ruled 1199–1216) and his barons that led to the Magna Carta. Marshal was later regent of the realm during the minority of John's successor Henry III. He was buried in the Chancel, which adjoins the Round Church, and a royal prince was later interred beside him.

③ EMPTY EFFIGIES

The most striking features of the interior are the ten effigies on the floor (although one is actually in the form of a coffin lid rather than a figure), which include William Marshal and his descendants. Until restoration work to repair bomb damage after the Second World War, it was believed that the effigies covered actual tombs, but this is not the case.

④ TREASURE HOUSE

One of the prime functions of the Temple was to act as a financial repository. In the Middle Ages security was at a premium, and rich lords and merchants would store their gold and silver in the safest place possible – and few places were as safe as Templar HQ. Fortunes were stored here, sometimes in direct opposition to the will of the Crown. So if the Templars fleeing persecution in France had been looking for somewhere to stash their loot, they might have looked to their own stronghold. In other parts of England, Templar commanderies are associated with tunnels and cellars. If this association extends to Temple Church, perhaps secrets still lurk beneath the streets of central London.

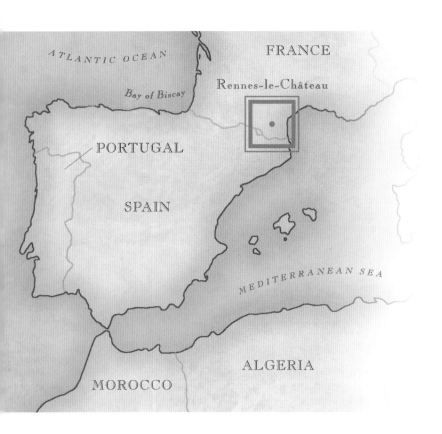

Rennes-le-Château: the legend

A tiny village in the deep south of France has become the epicentre of the massive, sprawling conspiracy theory that gave rise to **The Da Vinci Code.** *Tens of thousands converge on Rennes-le-Château every year, drawn by a lurid tale of hidden treasure, the occult demi-monde and a secret that could bring down the Church.*

Deep in Cathar country, the tiny village of Rennes-le-Château (henceforth Rennes) is one of the great mystery sites of the world. Rumours of treasure bring 100,000 tourists a year to a community of just over 100 people, and the ground beneath it is said to be honeycombed with tunnels and passages – some natural, some dug by treasure hunters.

ABBÉ SAUNIÈRE

The reason for the extraordinary popularity of Rennes is the legend of Bérenger Saunière. He was a lowly priest appointed to the poor backwater parish of Rennes in 1885, who in 1896 began to spend money hand over fist, and in very peculiar ways. He paid for expensive renovations and redecorations of the parish church, including the installation of Stations of the Cross featuring incongruous elements, such as a boy wearing a kilt; an inscription above the entrance that read '*Terribilis est locus iste*' ('This is a terrible place'); and a grotesque statue of a devil, crouching in the porch.

Saunière also bought up tracts of land around the village and had an imposing house called the Villa Bethania built for him,

together with a library housed in a folly known as the Magdala Tower. He spent lavishly on hobbies such as stamp and book collecting, gathered a menagerie of exotic animals and hosted decadent parties. He travelled to Paris and gained entrée to the salons of the demi-monde, mingling with people of influence and figures from the occult world. He was even rumoured to be having an affair with the famous opera singer Emma Calvé, known as the queen of the occult salons. His profligate spending got him into trouble with the Church authorities and Saunière was suspended from his duties. However, he refused to leave the village and was still making grand plans when he died in 1917.

HIDDEN TREASURE

The mystery of Saunière's sudden and inexplicable wealth lingered unsolved until the 1950s, when the story behind it began to circulate. It was said that the Abbé had stumbled upon mysterious documents hidden within a 'Visigoth' pillar in the Church (Rennes had been an important site during the Visigoth era of the 6th and 7th centuries BC) – tourists can see the pillar

Above *Bérenger Saunière, the man at the heart of the mystery of Rennes-le-Château. Saunière rose from lowly village priest to high society figure with inexplicably deep pockets.*

The Nazis in Languedoc

Adding to the mystery are rumours about Nazi activity in the region. Much of the ideological basis of Nazism can be traced back to a lurid mix of pseudo-history and mysticism linking ancient Aryan utopias to hidden currents of esoteric knowledge. Leading Nazis such as Himmler were fascinated by topics like the Holy Grail (see 'The Spear of Destiny' on page 108) and saw themselves and the SS as modern-day Grail knights. Himmler set up an organization called the *Ahnenerbe* (the German Ancestry Research and Teaching Society), which investigated Grail lore. One of its recruits was a Cathar-obsessive named Otto Rahn, who led expeditions to Montségur and the Languedoc, allegedly in search of the Grail. Rahn died in mysterious circumstances on a mountaintop in 1939, but it has been rumoured that during the Second World War Nazi interest in the region continued. Could teams of SS treasure hunters have been among those delving beneath Rennes-le-Château?

Left The carvings and the many inscriptions above the main door of the Mary Magdalene Church in Rennes, including the famous and strange legend 'Terribilis est locus iste' – 'This is a terrible place'.

today, on show in the village's Saunière Museum. The hidden parchments were written in Latin, and in code.

In 1969 British writer Henry Lincoln investigated these mysterious parchments, eventually coming to co-write *The Holy Blood and the Holy Grail*, the book that inspired *The Da Vinci Code*. This and other books purported to reveal the whole incredible tale of Rennes. The documents that Saunière had discovered pointed to the secret knowledge that Christ's bloodline had come to France, ruled as the Merovingian dynasty, but later had been suppressed by the Catholic Church,

which was based on a false version of history. To protect the holy bloodline a secretive, but immensely influential secret society known as the Priory of Sion had been set up. As well as counting luminaries from Leonardo da Vinci to Isaac Newton and Voltaire among its Grand Masters, the Priory had also operated via the Cathars and the Templars – both in on the explosive secret – and later through Masonic groups to contend with the Church for hegemony of Europe. Saunière had stumbled upon this web of secrets, and had bartered them into power and popularity. Possibly he had also recovered hidden Cathar

or Templar gold, which had been stashed in caves or tunnels under or near Rennes (much of which may yet linger there).

Subsequent books have claimed that Rennes and the surrounding area are home to everything from the tomb of Christ and/or Mary Magdalene to the Ark of the Covenant and the Holy Grail. The hills and valleys of the region are said to have been chosen or even shaped – possibly using ancient lore dating back to the Temple builders, the Egyptians and even the Atlanteans – into a sacred landscape with meaning and symbolism carved into every contour.

Rennes-le-Château: the truth

Could the extraordinary tale of Rennes and the mysterious Abbé Saunière be true? And if not, where did this lurid concoction of hidden scrolls, sacred treasures and shadowy secret societies engaged in an epic battle for the overlordship of Europe come from?

The Da Vinci Code claims to be based on historical fact – namely, the incredible narrative related by *The Holy Blood and the Holy Grail* and the related corpus of writings on Rennes and the Grail as the bloodline of Jesus. The story of Saunière and the revelatory documents he uncovered are central to this myth, but the evidence is that these are insecure foundations for a house of cards.

THE REAL SAUNIÈRE

There is no doubt that Saunière was an eccentric character who made some strange alterations to his adopted village and kept eclectic company on occasion. But there is no evidence that he found any scrolls or dug up any treasures or secrets. The purported 'Visigoth' pillar displayed to tourists is probably a fake and there is no evidence it was ever in the church in Rennes. His 'inexplicable' wealth has probably been wildly overstated, and towards the end of his life he was so poor he was reduced to asking for loans.

The true source of the money he did spend was almost certainly that he engaged in the illegal practice of selling masses – which is why he was suspended by the Church. The strange decorations he added to the church at Rennes probably relate to his political views, which were radically pro-royalist and in favour of recombining Church and State, and the symbolism of the devil and other changes reflect this. Even the peculiar inscription over the entrance to the church might have an innocuous explanation – it could be a reference to a mass said when dedicating a church, with *terribilis* being read in the sense of 'awesome' rather than 'terrible'. Despite the reams of text written on the matter, no treasure or relics have ever been discovered in or around Rennes.

FAKES AND FRAUDSTERS

If Saunière was simply a corrupt priest, where did these extraordinary legends spring from? Most of them can be traced back to hoaxes and fraudsters. The first of these was Noël Corbu, a restaurateur who had opened an eatery in the Villa Bethania – Saunière's old home – and who hoped to drum up custom by peddling a juicy treasure mystery. In 1956 French newspapers caught on to Corbu's yarn and the hoax began to snowball. Rennes became established as a focus for mystery-seekers and treasure hunters.

From here the hoax was taken up by Pierre Plantard. He held reactionary pro-royalist, anti-Semitic views and developed an elaborate fantasy in which he became a key figure in French history. In this alternate version of history, Plantard himself was the last scion of a royal house that traced its antecedents back to the Merovingian kings, and which awaited its chance to regain the throne, institute a sort of neo-fascist utopia and restore France to greatness. Included in this fiction was the shadowy Priory of Sion, supposedly founded a thousand years ago. Documents in the French national archives at the Bibliothèque Nationale appeared to support this tale, but in fact these were forgeries planted by Plantard's cronies. The Priory did exist, but only because it had been founded in 1956 by Plantard himself as a vehicle for his religious-nationalist preoccupations.

PLANTARD'S FICTION

Plantard collaborated with a friend to produce a book called *The Gold of Rennes* (published in 1967 and later retitled *The Cursed Treasure of Rennes-le-Château*), placing Rennes at the centre of the fantasy. Included in the book were alleged copies of the actual documents that Saunière had recovered from his hollow pillar, complete with coded references to the Priory. The book was a best-seller, but Plantard's fiction really went global with the tremendous success of 1982's *Holy Blood*, which expanded the story to connect Rennes and the Priory to the Holy Grail and the bloodline of Christ, including the startling revelation that Plantard was a descendant of Jesus and Mary Magdalene. This house of cards could not stand up to scrutiny and it was soon demolished by researchers, and by confessions by many of those involved in the hoax. Plantard was exposed as a con-artist and charlatan, and was banned from any activities relating to the Priory when he was caught up in a 1993 fraud trial.

THE LEGACY OF RENNES

This thorough debunking has done little to dent fascination with Rennes and its supposed secrets, and the village gets more tourists than ever, thanks to its tangential association with the Dan Brown book and film. Today it plays host to an engaging cast of eccentrics and seekers known as 'Rennies', including a 'Mole of Rennes', who has dug a labyrinth of tunnels that threatens the village's foundations. For these and many others, the allure of Rennes no longer relies upon the discredited Priory myth, but on the 'vibe' it generates in its role as a sort of French Glastonbury.

Left *The Magdala Tower on Saunière's former estate in Rennes, constructed between 1901 and 1906 to his strict specifications. The ground floor is covered with highly decorative tiles. Enthusiasts read great significance into the siting, proportions and design of the Tower and the tiles.*

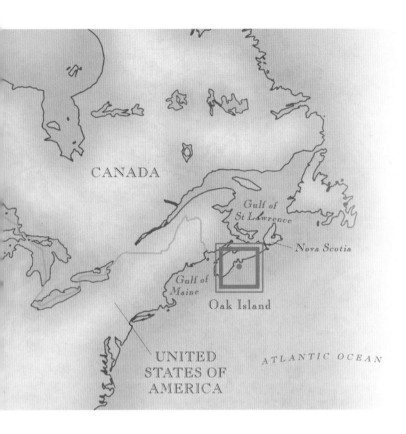

CANADA

Gulf of
St Lawrence

Nova Scotia

Gulf of
Maine

Oak Island

UNITED
STATES OF
AMERICA

ATLANTIC OCEAN

The Oak Island Money Pit

The Oak Island Money Pit is a shaft supposedly containing buried treasure, located on a small wooded island off the coast of Nova Scotia in Canada. Occupying a starring role in the pantheon of American treasure legends, the tale of the Oak Island Money Pit is a classic yarn of adventure, intrigue and mystery, attracting figures as diverse as Franklin D. Roosevelt and John Wayne to join a difficult and sometimes dangerous treasure hunt.

One of the most sustained and intensive treasure hunts in history has seen a bewildering range of excavations and investigations played out, at tremendous financial and human cost, generating a plethora of theories and counter-theories about who constructed the Pit and what might lie within.

THE ORIGINAL TALE

The Oak Island story has become a well-worn folk yarn, but the oldest sources of the tale are newspaper accounts dating from the mid-19th century, which relate events said to have begun much earlier. Different versions give slightly differing details, but the basic narrative is that in 1795 young Daniel McGinnis (or McInnis, or McInnies) was exploring the 1.3 sq km (½ sq mile) island, possibly drawn there by reports of strange lights. While roaming he came upon a suspicious-looking hollow or shallow depression in the ground beneath an overhanging branch – in some versions the telltale detail is that an old pulley was hanging from a tree branch directly above the hollow.

Right A pit on Oak Island, said to be the original Money Pit. Whether this is truly accurate, or it is one of the many subsequent shafts and pits dug by prospectors, is unclear, since the exact location of the original Pit has been lost.

Left An aerial view of Oak Island off the coast of Nova Scotia. At the bottom left is the causeway to the mainland, while the alleged location of the Money Pit is at the top right of the island, where a small collection of buildings is visible.

His curiosity aroused, McGinnis recruited two friends to help him dig, and the hollow proved to be a pit filled with loose soil. A little way below the surface the men found a layer of flagstones, and further down a layer of beams or logs. Digging any further was beyond the three friends, but they were now convinced that this was a manmade pit, presumably dug with a purpose. The coast abounded with rumours of hidden pirate gold, particularly in connection to the notorious Captain Kidd (see page 46); could McGinnis have stumbled upon the long-dead brigand's main stash?

Recruiting backers, the three men returned a few years later and began a full excavation. As they dug deeper they encountered successive layers – more platforms of oak logs or beams, layers of clay and charcoal, and matting similar to coconut fibre. In some versions strange markings were found in the shaft. But when the dig reached a climax, with the apparent discovery of a chest, the shaft suddenly flooded and could not be drained.

CELEBRITY INVESTORS

These initial efforts were followed by a series of increasingly involved excavations, featuring heavy machinery and mining gear (in the 1960s, for instance, a causeway to the island was built so that a mechanical digger could be brought across). The legend of the Money Pit attracted investors and adventurers, including such luminaries as Franklin D. Roosevelt (who actually spent some time on the island helping with the excavations) and John Wayne. Further levels of oak beams were discovered. Exploratory drilling brought up a core of material that supposedly included links from a gold chain. Some accounts speak of old tools and fragments of parchment, while a stone tablet inscribed with a coded message was allegedly found in the early 19th century, only to disappear and then reappear in 1919. The only evidence of the stone is a 1970 'record' of the markings, which were decoded and proved to spell out the message: 'Forty Feet Below Two Million Pounds Are Buried'. A video camera lowered down a borehole in 1971 obtained indistinct footage that was claimed to show a wooden chest and a severed hand.

BOOBY-TRAPPED CHAMBER

But all the excavations ended in the same result. Just as a promising level or chamber was reached, the shaft would collapse or the bottom would give way and water would rush in and flood the pit. This even happened to the many parallel shafts that were bored. The work proved dangerous as well: in the 19th century one man died when a boiler blew up and another when a hoist broke, while in 1965 four miners were asphyxiated by gas.

The failure of even the most professional attempts has led to speculation about the seemingly impressive engineering skills of the Money Pit's constructors. Somehow, using pre-19th-century technology, they had dug a shaft over 30 m (100 ft) deep and rigged it to include a series of elaborate water traps, where any 'unauthorized' breach of the main treasure chamber would result in its collapse, so that the chests of loot would drop out of reach and sea water from the nearby ocean would flood in and frustrate the miners.

OAK ISLAND TODAY

Today excavations on Oak Island are, at least temporarily, suspended, but two centuries of digging have taken their toll. The island is riddled with so many parallel and subsidiary shafts and boreholes that the location of the original Money Pit has been lost, while any information that a serious archeological survey might have gleaned has been hopelessly contaminated by the dozens of digs. Treasure hunters, however, are undaunted, and further explorations are planned for the future. What might they find, and is there really anything there to discover?

Oak Island: the Templar connection

Could a puzzling shaft on a remote island hold the solutions to some of the world's great historical mysteries, from the secret knowledge of the Knights Templar to the pirate gold of Captain Kidd? Or is the solution to the Money Pit mystery something rather more prosaic?

Since the story of the Money Pit first surfaced, people have been speculating about what it might contain. Initially it was thought likely to be linked to pirate treasure, and in addition to the legendary loot of Captain Kidd, a variety of other pirates were proposed as the Pit's originators, including Blackbeard (Edward Teach) and Henry Morgan. Other theories included Spanish survivors of a treasure galleon blown off course, or British sailors who had captured such a galleon and did not want to pay tax on their haul. Lending credence to these suggestions was the fact that both pirates and the British Navy had been known to frequent Mahone Bay where Oak Island is located. Also, the apparent structure of the Pit was said to resemble British military engineering techniques used in the 17th century.

COMING TO AMERICA

Later the pirate treasure theory was supplanted by more fantastic speculation. Today the Oak Island Money Pit is most commonly linked to theories about the Knights Templar. In the involved narrative concerning the fate of the Templar treasures, the Money Pit is the final destination for the treasure smuggled out of France and taken to Scotland under the protection of the Sinclair family (see page 160). The Sinclair family's Norse heritage supposedly gave them access to the secrets of transatlantic travel before

Columbus, enabling Henry Sinclair to navigate the Templar fleet to Nova Scotia, pitching up on Oak Island where the Templars employed the secrets of monumental masonry (handed down to them from the Atlanteans via the Temple builders, and later passed on to the Freemasons) to construct the Money Pit. The upshot of this fantastic tale is that the Money Pit might conceal anything from stacks of Templar bullion to the Holy Grail itself. But this theory should also be seen in the light of the racist agenda that attempts to prove pre-Columbian title to the Americas for whites (see page 119).

Other outlandish candidates for creators of the Money Pit include space aliens, Incas

or Aztecs hiding gold from the conquistadors, and ancient Atlanteans. Dr Orville Ward Owen claims to have decoded ciphers that prove that leading Elizabethan philosopher and statesman Sir Francis Bacon was the true author of Shakespeare's works and that he hid documents proving this in the Money Pit.

NATURAL HISTORY

But perhaps no one is responsible for digging the Money Pit. A survey of Oak Island by the Woods Hole Oceanographic Institution in 1995 concluded that the Pit was most likely the result of natural processes. The geology of the island lends itself to the formation of underground caverns, and these sometimes collapse, causing a sinkhole or pit to open up. These pits may then be filled in with soil and other debris over time, with layers of fallen logs and branches washed in during floods or storms. The end result could appear to an excavator like an artificially constructed and filled-in pit. The constant flooding of the excavated shaft can be explained by the presence of fissures and cracks that enable sea water to penetrate deep into the island.

TALL TALES

If the Pit is just a natural feature, how did it acquire such a body of legend? There are no accounts of the Money Pit contemporary with the date of its alleged discovery: the earliest come from newspaper reports of the 1850s and 1860s, a period when papers were well known for inventing stories and even running 'tall tale-telling' competitions. The Money Pit yarn has all the ingredients of such a tale, and it may not be a coincidence that it resembles the popular Edgar Allan Poe short story *The Gold Bug*, which had come out a few years earlier (in 1843). Poe's tale concerns a

Left *Captain Edward Teach, shown with his characteristic bandoliers of pistols and burning fuse cords twisted into his hair. Loot buried by Teach is among the treasures thought to lie at the bottom of the Pit.*

'The Money Pit might conceal anything from stacks of Templar bullion to the Holy Grail itself.'

buried treasure – possibly Captain Kidd's – discovered by dangling a rope from an overhanging branch to reveal the location of a pit.

Subsequent details of the Money Pit legend, such as the gold links and old tools recovered by excavators, or the cipher stone pulled from the pit, are equally suspect. The former may simply be inventions or, if real, they could have been 'salted' by prospectors looking to drum up investment. As for the stone, there is no proof that it ever existed, and the 'transcription' from 1970 is almost certainly an invention. So the Money Pit may be nothing more than a newspaper prank that got out of hand, accumulating spurious details as its legend grew, but also costing money and lives that were all too real.

Researcher Joe Nickell has developed a more involved theory about why such a

Above *A replica of the cipher stone allegedly found in the Money Pit, but which mysteriously vanished sometime after 1919 (though not before a transcription was taken, which itself surfaced in 1970).*

fiction might have been brewed up in the first place. He argues that many elements of the original tale mirror the symbolism and lore of the Freemasons: for example, the three companions who first investigate; the layers of stone, charcoal and clay found in the Pit – in particular an initiation rite for the Royal Arch degree. The story may originally have been an elaborate Masonic allegory, but outgrew its intended audience and became a popular mystery.

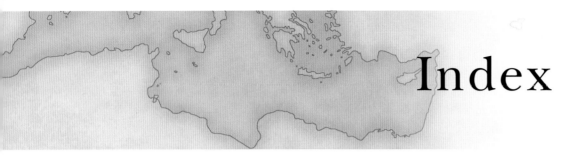

Index

Acknowledgements

PICTURE ACKNOWLEGEMENTS

akg-images 27, 66, 68, 81, 125, 156, Peter Connolly 98, Erich Lessing 71, 97, Nimatallah 102, Ruhrgas AG 11. **Alamy** Jon Arnold Images Ltd 99, Juliet Butler 123, 124, Rod Edwards 78, Israel Images 51, Miguel A Muñoz Pellicer 163, North Wind Picture Archives 47, 168, Jochem Wijnands/Picture Contact 157. **Ancient Art & Architecture Collection** Ronald Sheridan 103. **The Art Archive** Anagni Cathedral, Italy/Dagli Orti 90, Heraklion Museum/Dagli Orti 105, Museo Ciudad, Mexico/Dagli Orti 82, 85, Museo del Oro, Bogota, Dagli Orti 33, National Anthropological Museum, Mexico/Dagli Orti 84. **Art Directors & Trip** Allen Brookes 165, Tom Mackie 57, Jane Sweeney 8–9, 96, Rita Zampese 116. **Bridgeman Art Library** Birmingham Museums and Art Gallery 150–151, Boltin Picture Library 76, British Museum, London, UK 37, Brooklyn Museum of Art, New York, USA 38, Chetham's Library, Manchester, UK 79, Egyptian National Museum, Cairo, Egypt, Giraudon 61, The Hermitage, St Petersburg, Russia 31, Library of Congress, Washington D.C., USA 46, Noortman, Maastricht, Netherlands 42, St Peter's, Vatican, Rome, Italy 109. **British Library Images** 35. **The Trustees of the British Museum, London** 12–13, 16, 17, 21, 23, 25, 58, 65, 77, 88, 113, 121. **Corbis** Dave Bartruff 95, Jonathan Blair 131, 133, Henry Aldridge and Son/epa 145, Hulton Deutsch Collection 7, 69, Kevin Fleming 41, Hanan Isachar 94, Liu Liqun 80, Pictures Unlimited/Corbis Sygma 146, 147, © Underwood & Underwood 143, Sandro Vannini 159, West Semitic Research, Dead Sea Scrolls Foundation 50. **Czech Republic Tourist Office** 54-55. **Le Département des recherches archéologiques subaquatiques et sous-marines** Frederic Osada 128, 129. **George Edmunds** 48, 49 left & right. **Florida Bureau of Archaeological Research** John Loupinot 138, St Lucie Historical Museum 137. **The State Hermitage Museum, St Petersburg** 73. **Collection of Tom Jonas** 40. **Jorge Kuljis** for John Villegas of Zingara Travel, La Paz by arrangement with DINAR, with thanks to Jim Allen/www.atlantisbolivia.org 119. **Kunsthistorisches Museum, Vienna** 108. **Peter Langer/Associated Media Group** 43, 64, 117. **Lansmuseet Gotland** 111. **Musée Guimet** 15. **Nanteos Mansion** Janet Joel 152. **National Geographic** Victor R Boswell Junior 126, 132, Emory Kristof 144. **National Trust Photographic Library** Joe Cornish 74. **Oak Island Treasure.co.uk** 166, 167, 169. **Odyssey Marine Exploration** 10, 140, 141. **PA Photos** Bureau of Immigration and Custom/AP 139, Empics 29. **www.renneslechateau.com** 162. **Scala** The Metropolitan Museum of Art, Cloisters Collection/Art Resource 148–149, 153. **South American Pictures** 34, Jason P Howe 32, Tony Morrison 39. **Stan Sherer** with thanks to Dr Marjorie Senechal/Smith College History of Science Museum of Ancient Inventions 107. **Topfoto.co.uk** 75, The British Museum/HIP 20.

Executive Editor Sandra Rigby
Managing Editor Clare Churly
Executive Art Editor Sally Bond
Designer Nicola Liddiard
Illustrator Lee Gibbons
Picture Researcher Sarah Hopper
Senior Production Controller Simone Nauerth